Television Technology Demystified

Television Technology Demystified

A Non-technical Guide

Aleksandar Louis Todorović

AMSTERDAM • BOSTON • HEIDELBERG • LONDON
NEW YORK • OXFORD • PARIS • SAN DIEGO
SAN FRANCISCO • SINGAPORE • SYDNEY • TOKYO

Focal Press is an imprint of Elsevier

Acquisitions Editor:	Elinor Actipis
Project Manager:	Andrew Therriault
Associate Editor:	Becky Golden-Harrell
Assistant Editor:	Robin Weston
Marketing Manager:	Christine Degon Veroulis
Cover Design:	Hannus Design

Focal Press is an imprint of Elsevier
30 Corporate Drive, Suite 400, Burlington, MA 01803, USA
Linacre House, Jordan Hill, Oxford OX2 8DP, UK

∞ Recognizing the importance of preserving what has been written, Elsevier prints its
books on acid-free paper whenever possible.

Library of Congress Cataloging-in-Publication Data
Application Submitted.

British Library Cataloguing-in-Publication Data
A catalogue record for this book is available from the British Library.

ISBN 13: 978-0-240-80684-6
ISBN 10: 0-240-80684-0

For information on all Focal Press publications
visit our website at www.books.elsevier.com

06 07 08 09 10   10 9 8 7 6 5 4 3 2 1

Printed in the United States of America

Contents

4
Color Television 33

5
Digital Television 55

6
Digital Compression as the Key to Success 73

7
Digital Audio Compression Methods   97

8
Exchanging Program Material as Bitstreams   111

9
Television Cameras   131

10
Video Recording   155

Introduction

We experience the world around us by seizing its sights and sounds. Science has proven that sight is possible because our eyes are able to capture and our brains to decipher the electromagnetic radiation that is light, at certain frequencies. In the same way, we hear sounds, which are the vibrations of air particles whose frequencies are within the sensing abilities of our ear-brain combination. Since the dawn of civilization, humanity has desired to fix, transport, and recreate these sights and sounds. However, for millennia the only way to pass along this information was to transform it into spoken or written words. These had the power to ignite our imaginations but could not offer the benefit of direct experience that a virtual replica of the sounds and sights witnessed by a narrator or author could provide.

By the end of the nineteenth and the beginning of the twentieth century we had discovered how to transmit sounds over long distances, then how to record sound and then visual information, and eventually, with television, how to transport sights and sounds instantly over great distances. A television system can be simply described as a complex device that transforms light and sounds into electrical signals, transports those signals over very long distances, and transforms them back into light and sounds. Over the last 60 years, televised moving images have grown into the most powerful system of transmission of ideas, concepts, and thoughts, but also into the most powerful entertainment medium the world has ever known. Just as the nineteenth could be defined as the century of steam power, the omnipresence and influence of television makes it legitimate to define the twentieth century as the century of television.

Digital technology facilitates the creation of new production tools that are more reliable and simpler to operate than analog tools. Gone are the long and tedious daily alignments of myriad parameters. Present-day equipment can be safely used without the permanent presence and devoted care of skilled engineers. At the same time, those digital and computer-based tools offer considerably more creative possibilities than their analog predecessors. But all these capabilities can only be fully exploited if users know the basic operating principles of how the equipment works, which should then help them understand its power as well as its limitations.

The aim of this book is to help all current and future nontechnical members of a production team become familiar with the technical fundamentals of analog and digital television, the operation of essential elements of a television production chain, and the possibilities and limitations of these production tools. All descriptions and explanations in this book will be nonmathematical, and essential concepts and parameters will be easy to understand without the need to call upon previous scientific or engineering knowledge. The author hopes that this book will prove to be particularly useful for all students in communications, film, and television departments, for all those future program creators and media professionals who should acquire during their education process a good insight into the modus operandi of modern television production tools.

The reader will notice that this book covers mainly the video aspect of television production. Such a focus was purposefully selected not only because covering all aspects of audio production would require many additional chapters but also because that subject is already very well described in a number of excellent and easily understandable books. However, since compressed audio signals determine a number of important aspects of digital recording, file-transfer mechanisms, and media asset-management systems, it proved necessary to dedicate one chapter to digital audio and digital audio compression.

The development of television production technology is moving at an increasingly rapid pace. Not only new pieces of equipment but also new concepts and technologies appear daily on the market. Therefore, the reader should note that all references to "modern" or "current" solutions or systems correspond to the state of the art in the year 2005.

1

Development of Television Technology—A Sweep through History

Today, in the first years of the twenty-first century, we take for granted a number of technological marvels that are irreplaceable components of our everyday life. Having lived in the century that witnessed the development of marvels such as aviation, telecommunications, cars, and television, we tend to forget that almost all the core discoveries and breakthroughs that were essential for the development of these technologies were made during that fascinatingly entrepreneurial nineteenth century. Television is undoubtedly one of these marvels.

The simplest definition of *television* is that it is the transmission of moving images at a distance and that its workings can be compared to that of the human visual system. The eye captures the light reflected from an object in the surrounding world and transforms that *photo energy* into *neural impulses*. These impulses travel to the brain where they are deciphered and, through processes still only partially understood, transformed into a mental reproduction of the original object. In television, as in human vision, the first step in the process of achieving transmission is to transform the light reflected from the world around us into another form of energy. In this case it is transformed into electric energy, which is then handled, memorized, or transmitted by means of specific methods and techniques.

1.1 Optoelectric Transformation

The first of the series of nineteenth-century discoveries that would eventually become the basis of television was the essential discovery of *optoelectric conversion*. Interestingly, this important discovery was made by chance rather than as a result of serious scientific research. In 1873 an Irish telegraph operator named

Leonard May observed that his telegraph behaved differently depending on the time of day. Upon further investigation he realized that a selenium bar, which was part of the apparatus, changed its resistance in relation to the amount of sunlight falling on it. In full sunlight there was less resistance, but resistance increased as the sun moved toward the horizon. This photoelectric (or optoelectric) phenomenon was not to be used in television technology for another 80 years or so, but it should be recognized as one of the most important milestones—the first registered transformation of the energy of light into electric energy. The phenomenon discovered by May (who, incidentally, never profited from it) would later be named *photoconductivity*.

Photoelectric phenomena, that is, changes in the behavior of electrons due to variations in amount of light illuminating a given material, were at that time being scrutinized by a number of scientists. In 1888 a German physicist, Wilhelm Hallwachs, discovered another very important photoelectric phenomenon—photoemission. *Photoemission* is the act of releasing free electrons in the surrounding space. Namely some materials have a greater or more modest capacity to release, or as it is usually said, emit free electrons under the impact of light. The number of emitted electrons is directly proportional to the intensity of the incoming light. In other words, the brighter the light illuminating the piece of material, the more free electrons will appear. This physical property would be used to develop the first television experiments some 30 years later.

The first theoretical descriptions of a hypothetical television system, proposed by George Carey in the United States as early as 1875, advocated the use of a mosaic structure similar to the structure of the human eye. He proposed to assemble two mosaics—one of photosensitive cells possessing the capacity to produce at each point an electric charge proportional to the amount of light falling on that particular element, and the other of cells that would display a reverse effect, that is, would produce a certain quantity of light proportional to the received electric impulse. According to Carey, if all cells belonging to these two panels were mutually connected with pairs of wires, one to one, it would be possible to transmit an optical moving picture at a given distance.

Theoretically, such a parallel channel system could allow the transmission of moving images but only theoretically as the obstacles to its realization were numerous. First, in 1875 the necessary technology for its materialization was not available. Second, and even more important, there were so many elements that had to be connected at the same time; a simultaneous system of transmission was and still is very cumbersome and very difficult to achieve in practice. Using a large number of parallel channels for the transmission of one single piece of information was not a viable solution, either economically or technically. One of the basic economic principles in communications is to use always the *minimum channel capacity*, i.e. the narrowest channel possible, or in some instances the minimum number of channels for the transmission of maximum information. From the technical point of view, it is always preferable to use one single channel instead of a number of parallel ones since all parallel channels should behave identically under all circumstances, and, practically speaking, that is almost impossible to achieve.

The only viable alternative to a *simultaneous* capturing and transmission system is to analyze, or *scan*, the picture to be transmitted by dissecting it into a series of tightly spaced *consecutive* pieces of information and sending them through one single channel. Since these discrete elements will be displayed at the receiving end in very quick succession, the human visual system will not see them as a series of separate pieces of information but will integrate them into a single picture. Experiments have shown that the most appropriate method of scanning is *linear scanning*, that is, the analysis of individual picture elements, one by one, disposed on consecutive parallel horizontal lines. The number of picture elements analyzed and the number of scanning lines used will determine the *resolution* of the system, that is, its capacity to reproduce fine details.

1.2 The Nipkow Disk

The first scanning device was developed in 1884 by Paul Nipkow, a German physicist of Polish origin. He made a special perforated disk designed for a point-by-point analysis, that is, for scanning of optical pictures. This mechanical scanning device disassembled simultaneous optical pictures into a number of discrete partial elements. It consisted of a flat circular plate that rotated around an axis located at its center. It was perforated with a number of holes following a spiral path from the center to the outside of the disk (see Figure 1.1.).

If the light reflected from a picture to be transmitted is projected with an optical lens to a certain area of the rotating disk, only discrete values of points of illumination will pass through the perforations to the other side of the disk, there to fall on a photosensitive element. That element will consequently generate a quick succession of electric charges proportional to the quantity of light falling on it at a given moment. The holes on the rotating disk will, in fact, scan the projected optical picture line by line, and the photosensitive element will generate a continuous electric stream of variable intensity. The net result of that operation is that the simultaneous optical picture is transformed into a continuous stream of discrete, sequentially transmitted information whose transmission requires just one channel. One full rotation of the disk scans one full optical picture. The number of holes in the disk will determine the number of lines used to scan or analyze one picture and the number of sequentially analyzed pictures will therefore depend on the rotational speed of the disk—a faster rotational speed will mean more

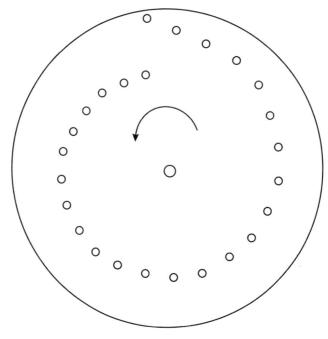

Figure 1.1   Nipkow disk: The first television scanning device.

full rotations in a unit of time and consequently more scanned/analyzed pictures during that same unit of time. At the same time it is well known that a quick succession of static pictures is integrated by the human visual system as a continuous reproduction of movement.

The electric signal thus generated can be transmitted over a distance by any standard wire or wireless transmission method. However, at the end of the chain it has to be transformed again into a light picture so that the human eye can perceive it. The first experimental television installations used two Nipkow disks—one to scan the optical picture and the other to perform the role of a display device. The latter rotated between the eyes of the viewer and the light source as it changed its radiated light power in relation to the intensity of the incoming electric signal. If both rotating disks were fully synchronous (meaning that they start and stop rotating at the same time and that their rotational speeds are identical) and in phase (meaning that the positions of the holes on both disks compared to the scanned object are always identical, i.e. when the hole number one of the first disk is at the upper left corner of the projected picture the hole number one of the second disk should be at the corresponding position of the reproduced picture), the holes of the display disk would reconstruct, line by line, the transmitted picture. Such a system was acceptable for the early experiments in which the picture was reduced to black shadows on a white background and the resolution was limited to about 60 lines. But the systems based on a Nipkow disk were hobbled by the limitations of the disks: they were crude mechanical devices, burdened by inertia and synchronization problems as well as by the inability of early artificial light sources to react adequately to the extremely fast changes of the incoming signal. In order to reproduce all the tones from black to white passing by different shades of gray (the gray scale), the light source would have to have been capable of changing its intensity several hundred times in the course of one television line, that is, during one 60th of the duration of one picture, which means during one fraction of a second. However, there was practically no incandescent light source capable of such performance.

1.3 The Cathode-Ray Tube

Further research in the development of television shows that even by the standards of the period, the Nipkow disk was not a viable solution for the display of transmitted moving images. Fortunately, by the end of the nineteenth century another German physicist, Ferdinand Braun, developed the cathode-ray tube (CRT), the essential and basic television display device. This device, shown in Figure 1.2, is equipped with two electrodes connected through an electric circuit. The first of these electrodes is the *cathode*—an element capable of emitting free electrons under the effect of thermal heating. The other electrode, called the *anode*, is installed at the opposite side of the glass tube and is at a positive electric potential and therefore attracts these negatively charged electrons. In the neck of the glass tube, past the cathode, there are several plates connected to sources of electricity.

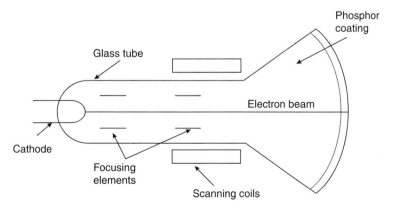

Figure 1.2 Simplified representation of the cross section of a Braun CRT.

Thanks to the electrical power supplied here, a field (called an *electrostatic field*) is created between the plates and acts as a sort of electrical lens focusing the liberated electrons into a concentrated beam flowing toward the anode that attracts the electrons. Outside the tube, around its neck, two coils are mounted. These coils are connected to another electric source. The current flowing through the windings of the coils creates a magnetic field in the glass tube that has the ability to move the electron beam. The magnetic fields created by these two coils are in fact responsible for the scanning movement of the beam over the front surface of the tube. The anode part of the tube is covered with a *phosphor* coating—a special material that emits visible light at the point of impact of the electron beam. The intensity of that light is directly proportional to the intensity of the beam at the moment of impact. Adequately created electromagnetic fields can control the movement of the electron beam, making it scan the front end of the tube at a selected scanning speed.

By the beginning of the twentieth century, the three essential elements of a television chain—the optoelectric conversion, the scanning of the optical picture, and the electro-optic transformation—were in place. However, several elements were still missing: a better understanding of the behavior and propagation of electromagnetic waves; the mastering of the amplification of electrical signals; and the expertise, discoveries, and developments that would be achieved by great scientists like Marconi, Tesla, Lee de Forest, and Branly. Also missing at the time was the person who would seize the moment when relevant discoveries reached critical mass and who would have the courage and ability to envision bringing together these discoveries in order to transform a science-fiction toy into a physical reality. More than 20 years would elapse before the first crude moving images would be transmitted between two adjacent rooms on Frith Street in London.

1.4 The Birth of Television

By the early 1920s two visionaries began almost simultaneously but independently to develop a chain capable of transmitting moving images. In 1923 Charles Francis Jenkins in the United States and John Logie Baird in United Kingdom (see Figure 1.3) presented the results of their experiments. The images they showed were just black shadows, cruder than children's shadow puppets against a white wall, and the distance of transmission was limited to several meters between the transmitter and the receiver that were located in adjacent rooms, but it was the first time that moving images were transmitted. Encouraged by these first results, both men continued with their work and by 1925 were able to demonstrate pictures with *halftones*, that is, pictures with different shades of gray corresponding to different grades of illumination from the black level to the brightest white.

Figure 1.3 John Logie Baird.

The resolution and the quality of the transmitted gray scale was certainly very limited, but nevertheless these were "real" pictures, and, consequently, 1925 is considered the year when television was born.

Even after that auspicious beginning, 10 additional years of research and development elapsed before the first television service was introduced. The efforts of pioneers like Baird and Jenkins were not enough. The creation of television would demand the efforts of a number of other researchers and the endeavors of powerful companies such as RCA, EMI, and Telefunken, along with a gradually developing general awareness of the importance and the potential of that new medium.

Both Jenkins and Baird based their television systems on mechanical scanning of optical images with Nipkow disks. Presumably they were aware of the limitations of mechanical systems and even knew the theoretical arguments of Boris Rosing from Russia and Alan Archibald Campbell-Swinton from the United Kingdom, published in 1911, that proved that television would be viable only if all elements of its chain were electric. But in the 1920s, the only available scanning device was mechanical.

Baird's activities—his public appearances, his public demonstrations of improved pictures and devices, and his advocacy of the importance of television—eventually changed public opinion, and in the early 1930s, British official authorities began discussions on a possible introduction of a limited television service. By that time Baird's company was no longer the sole developer of television. It had to face a formidable competitor—the EMI Company under the dynamic leadership of Isaac Shoenberg.

When they started their research, scientists at the EMI labs had read about the work of Philo Farnsworth and Vladimir Zworykine who worked on the development of electronic scanning, or *pick-up*, devices and they took these achievements as their starting point. Consequently, the concept of the EMI television system was fully based on Campbell-Swinton and Rosing's postulates—it was an all-electric system, from the pick-up through transmission to the display, based on an improved version of Braun's CRT.

Faced with two contenders, the post office (which was at the state level in charge of the whole field of telecommunications) and the BBC (who already ran a nationwide radio service) decided to organize a parallel public testing of both systems—the mechanical/electrical system proposed by Baird, operating at 240 lines, and the all-electric EMI system that offered (as it was advertised at that time) "high definition" at 405 lines.

Two studios were set up in Alexandra Palace in London (see Figure 1.4), one equipped by Baird and the other by EMI. On alternate days, programs were aired

Figure 1.4   Alexandra Palace today. (Courtesy J. Todorovic, Belgrade)

from one or the other studio and received on several receivers scattered around the city. At the end of the test period, the result was clear cut: the EMI system was unequivocally superior and was therefore officially selected as a standard for the planned television service. And so the beginning of the first public television service in 1936 was, paradoxically, a victory for Baird, who had toiled for 15 years advocating the cause of television, but also a defeat of the system that he had developed.

Light and the Human Eye 2

It might perhaps be expected that this discussion should begin by saying what light really is; but this is not possible, since light is more primitive that any of the terms that might be used in an effort to explain it. The nature of light is describable only by enumerating its properties and founding them on the simplest possible principles. As these principles transcend ordinary experience they must be cast in a purely logical (mathematical) form … .

—Encyclopedia Britannica

Acknowledging the statement above, we can say that light is a physical phenomenon that we perceive through our sense of sight. We see the world around us thanks to the light reflected by the objects in it. Such a definition leads us immediately to the next statement—any discussion related to light has to take into account both its physical properties and the human psychological reaction to those properties. We know that the most essential element in a television system is the conversion of light to electricity (optoelectric conversion) at the beginning of the chain and the conversion of electricity back into light (electro-optic conversion) at its end. Consequently, light, its characteristics, and its usage are of a paramount importance for the technology of television as everything starts and ends with light.

2.1 Light in Television Production

In any visual production—film, television, or theater—light is one of the most important creative tools. In film and television it is also the prerequisite for normal camera operation because, after all, what we are looking at is merely a reflection of light into the lens. It could be said that lighting in theater, film, and television is a mixture of creativity and technology. Good lighting requires a lot of imagination and creativity but also an excellent knowledge of the technology used as well as precise planning and an understanding of the features and limitations of the whole video chain.

Lighting in television has to fulfill a certain number of functions, which, according to Alan Wurtzel (Wurtzel&Rosenbaum 1995), can be summarized in the following way:

1. **To satisfy the requirements of the technical system.** In other words, there must be a general light level that will ensure normal operation of television cameras. The absolute level depends on the type of cameras used, but in general terms, the light level should be such that it ensures an optimum photographic quality of the output video signal when the iris aperture is set at a middle value.
2. **To create a three-dimensional (3D) effect.** Television pictures are two-dimensional (2D) and so are defined by their height and width. The third dimension, the depth, is the result of the angle of shooting, set design, and creative lighting. Good lighting will considerably enhance the desired 3D effect.
3. **To give prominence to some parts of the picture.** Light and shadow can be very well used to attract the viewer's attention to different areas of the scene or of the shot.
4. **To define the atmosphere.** Light can be used to define the atmosphere of the scene. Dark, shadowy shots will indicate tension, drama, or mystery while brightly lit scenes will suggest happiness, joy, or cheerfulness.
5. **To define the time of action.** Light can be used to define the time of day when the action takes place.
6. **To enhance the overall aesthetic impact of the picture.** The camera work, staging, and light are three inseparable factors defining the aesthetic quality of any shot.

It is clear that all television productions do not require all the aforementioned functions, although three duties will always have to be fulfilled: ensure normal operating conditions for television cameras, achieve the three-dimensional (3D) effect, and always keep in mind the overall aesthetic quality of the picture.

2.2 The Nature of Light and Human Vision

As soon as we decide to define the basic physical properties of light, we are confronted with a serious obstacle: over the years of research, two theories defining the nature of light have evolved. The first one, called the *electromagnetic theory*, states that light is electromagnetic radiation, which can be perceived by our eyes at wavelengths between 380 and 700 nanometers (nm). The other theory, called *corpuscular theory*, states that light has a corpuscular character and that it is made up of a number of elementary particles called photons. The ultimate complexity of the quest to define light becomes apparent with the present-day approach, which says that light is both an electromagnetic wave and a stream of particles and that it behaves sometimes like a wave and sometimes like a stream of particles.

Fortunately for our purposes in discussing television, we can consider light only as an electromagnetic wave. As mentioned, we perceive electromagnetic radiation at wavelengths between 380 and 700 nm. That part of the electromagnetic spectrum is known as the *visible spectrum* since our visual system is capable of creating responses in the brain to wavelengths inside these boundaries.

We perceive our environment by receiving the light reflected from the surfaces of all objects that surround us. The reflected light penetrates our eye through the pupil, passes through the lens, and is projected onto the retina, which is the basic receptor. The retina is composed of two types of sensors named by their shapes—cones and rods. The rods are more numerous than cones and are primarily sensitive to the brightness of the light source. The cones are less sensitive to the brightness of the incoming light, but they react to different wavelengths, and so they are more responsible for seeing color.

At low light levels, seeing is mostly done by the rods; differences in brightness are the only ones perceived. At higher light levels, the cones are active and they sense the differences in color of the perceived light. According to the Young–Helmholz theory, the human vision is *trichromatic*. This means that not all cones are identical; they can be differentiated by their respective spectral sensitivity. One group of cones, according to this theory, is more sensitive to the red colors, another to the green ones, and the third group, to the blue part of the spectrum. Consequently, it seems that the human eye splits the incoming light into three components and transforms them into three streams of neural pulses, which are then conducted to the brain where they are recomposed into a mental multicolored picture.

The human eye is more sensitive to the differences in brightness than to the differences in color, and it is not equally sensitive to all parts of the visible spectrum. You can see that for yourself by conducting a very simple experiment with a test chart as shown in Figure 2.1.

The chart is divided into two flat areas, one white and the other black, separated by a sharp, straight transition until, at three-quarters height, the line becomes saw-toothed. At a relatively short distance away, the eye will easily recognize both the straight and the saw-toothed boundary between the two surfaces. But, if the distance between the eyes and the test chart is increased, at a certain point the eye will no longer be able to distinguish the saw-toothed part; rather, it will only see a smooth and straight transition between the white and the black surfaces. If we use that distance as the baseline reference and then change the color of the two flat surfaces, we will discover that the distances at which the eye ceases to distinguish

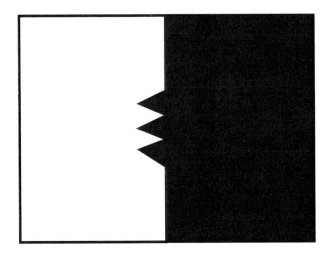

Figure 2.1   Chart for testing the acuteness of human vision.

the saw-toothed part of the transition will vary depending on the colors used. For example, with a green/red combination the saw-toothed part will "disappear" at 40% of the original reference distance; with a blue/red combination that distance will fall to 23%; in the case of a blue/green combination it will be only 19% of the reference distance. This shows that the human eye is much more sensitive to differences in brightness (black and white combinations) than to differences in color and also that it is less sensitive to hues in the area of blue than to those in the area of red.

2.3   White Light and Color Temperature

What we perceive as a *white light* is in fact the mixture of radiations of all wavelengths of the visible spectrum. The spectrum of a given white light could be *continuous*, which means it continuously contains all wavelengths (as with normal daylight), or it could be *discrete*, which means it encompasses a sufficient number of components to create the perception of white light even though some components are missing (see Figure 2.2). In real life, different light sources can have different spectral distributions, or characteristics. Differences in spectral distribution will cause differences in the character of white light and consequently more or less important subjective changes in the hue of the lighted objects and in the overall texture of the view.

It is easy to observe such a change in our everyday environment. If we carefully follow the changes of daylight from dawn to dusk, we can see that early

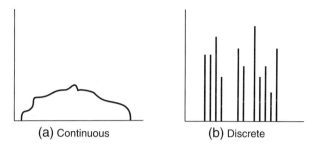

Figure 2.2   Continuous and discrete spectrum of white light.

in the morning (the time cinematographers call the "golden hour"), the overall impression is of a warm, almost reddish-orange light, and all objects around us have a sort of golden appearance. At noon, the light is blue-white, and our entire environment has a different appearance than it had several hours earlier. By sunset, the second "golden hour" of the day, we experience again a sort of yellow-red light, and all the colors have much warmer tones. Although our visual adaptation makes us accept different lightings as "white," we know well that, for example, some fabrics or paint colors look different in daylight than under an artificial light source.

In order to define precisely that changing character of white light or, in other words, to have a single definition for a given spectral characteristic, we use the notion of *color temperature* as an unequivocal description of the character of a given white light. The notion of color temperature, like all other photometric elements (elements that are measured in order to permit the definition of a given light), is based on a comparison or an analogy. The official definition of that parameter is the temperature of a given light expressed in degrees Kelvin (K), which has to reach a theoretical black body in order to radiate light identical to the observed one.

This definition may seem somewhat cryptic, but I will try to make it more understandable. The degrees Kelvin relate to a temperature scale whose zero point corresponds to the point at which precious gasses reach their liquid state and all materials become superconductors (that is, do not offer any resistance to the passage of electric current). That zero point is equivalent to −273.15°C. The "theoretical black body" referred to in the definition is a solid object that behaves with an absolute regularity, radiating light the character of which depends exclusively on the temperature of the object (which is not the case with real-life physical objects, whose behavior depends very much on their composition, which can never be "ideal").

In order to explain the above definition, let us set aside the "theoretical black body" and imagine instead an iron block that is gradually heated under controlled conditions. At a certain point, the block will start to radiate a reddish light. With a further increase in temperature, that light will become yellow, then blue, and finally blue-white. Controlling these different points and expressing the temperature reached by the iron block in degrees Kelvin, we will find that the temperature of the block radiating red light is about 2800 K, yellow at about 3200 K, and the blue-white is seen at over 5500 K. Therefore, we can say, by analogy, that the color temperature of bright daylight at noon is about 6000 K, that incandescent lamps deliver light at a temperature of about 3200 K, and so on. In short, we can define the color temperature of a given light source by comparing it with the light radiated from a heated block, and when the two lights are identical, we note the temperature of the block as the value. Today there are special instruments for measuring light temperature, and there is no need to have a furnace at hand.

Since white light can have different spectral compositions and still be considered subjectively "white," it is necessary, for the sake of *colorimetry* (definition of specific colors), to determine a commonly agreed-upon standard white. Consequently, a set of standards has been set by the International Electrotechnical Commission (IEC), determining three standard white lights or three *illuminants*:

- Illuminant A corresponds to 2856 K.
- Illuminant C represents an average daylight corresponding to a color temperature of 6774 K.
- Illuminant D_{65} represents another type of daylight corresponding to a color temperature of 6504 K.

Color temperature is a very important factor in television production. It is obvious that the quality of the white light used during production will influence the color rendition of objects in front of the camera. All color cameras can be balanced to ensure a correct reproduction of all colors of the scene. However, when the color temperature of the light used is changed, the camera has to be readjusted and rebalanced. Consequently and obviously, a constant color temperature must be maintained over the whole televised scene. Lights, or light sources, whose color temperatures are different from one another must not be mixed.

2.4 Monochromatic Light

As already mentioned, if the radiated light energy contains components of all wavelengths of the visible spectrum, such light is perceived by our visual system as a white light. On the other hand, if the light is radiated on a single wavelength inside the visible spectrum, it is perceived by our visual system as one of the colors of the spectrum and is called *monochromatic light*. The natural light that surrounds us is never monochromatic. It is always a white light, or a combination of a number of components scattered along the visible spectrum. Since the artificial light sources developed by humans were usually intended to reproduce natural light, they also radiate white light.

Every monochromatic light has three essential characteristics:

1. *Brightness,* which corresponds to the amount of radiated energy
2. *Saturation,* which represents the ratio of the monochromatic and the white light
3. *Hue,* which is the color as perceived by our visual system

A change in wavelength is perceived by the human eye as a change in hue or color. However, the human eye is not a particularly discriminative device; it does not discern small variations in wavelength as variations of hue. Radiations with wavelengths relatively close to each other are perceived as the same color, roughly in accordance with the following list:

400–440	purple
440–490	blue
490–565	green
565–595	yellow
595–620	orange
620–750	red

2.5 Color Matching

We know from experience that it is possible to mix different colors and obtain new hues as a result. However, colors can be combined in two different ways, by using either subtractive or additive matching.

The *subtractive* method consists of the application of different sorts of filters to subtract some components from the white light. We perceive the flat surface in front of our eyes as green, for example, simply because that surface absorbs all of the components of the visible spectrum from incoming white light except for a range of wavelengths from the area of green colors, which are reflected toward our eyes. And when a painter mixes colors to achieve a desired hue, a new filter is created that will absorb a given part of the spectrum and reflect only selected wavelengths toward our eyes, thus creating the desired perception in the visual system of the viewer.

On the other hand, the *additive* method consists of a direct addition of different monochromatic lights. If two monochromatic light sources (e.g., two projectors) are projected onto the same white surface, the hue of the light spot created by the superposition of the two light beams will be different from the color of the two original light sources; it will be a new color—the result of a direct addition of two monochromatic lights.

By definition, white light represents the mixture of all components of the visible spectrum. However, following the experiments of Isaac Newton, James Clerk Maxwell developed a theory that posits that white light can be produced through additive mixing of three monochromatic lights only, with the stipulation that none of these three monochromatic lights is the product of the mixing of the other two. The colors of these three monochromatic lights are known as primary colors, or *primaries*. In order to avoid possible misunderstandings it is important to stress once more the difference between two color mixing methods:

- in the case of subtractive mixing we mix pigments thus creating a sort of filter that will reflect one hue and absorb all the others; the three primaries for such a sort of mixing are red, blue and yellow;
- in the case of additive mixing we mix directly monochromatic lights so that the illuminated surface will reflect towards our eyes a new colored light that is the product of the mixing; the three primaries in this instance are red, green and blue.

Additive mixing can easily be demonstrated by using a simple instrument known as a *colorimeter*. That instrument (see Figure 2.3) consists of two separate but adjacent flat surfaces that can be simultaneously observed. One of the surfaces is illuminated by a light source radiating standard white light (a white light with characteristics precisely defined by IEC standards) and the other by three different monochromatic light sources (red, green and blue), all projecting light that falls

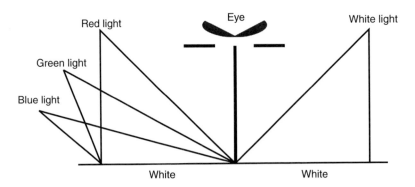

Figure 2.3 Colorimeter.

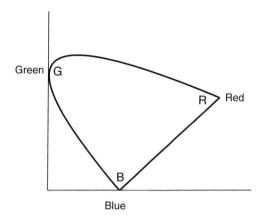

Figure 2.4 Plank's chromaticity diagram.

on the same spot. By changing the intensity of these monochromatic sources, we can produce a wide variety of different colors on the illuminated spot, but at one moment a point will be reached when the spot will reflect toward the eye of the viewer the same white as the white of the reference spot on the other side of the colorimeter. That experiment shows that all colors of the visible spectrum can be obtained by mixing additively in different proportions the three primaries (R,G,B) and that a given mixture of these three colors will produce the standard white.

It is possible, by using appropriate mathematical transformations, to represent all visible colors on one two-dimensional (2D) diagram known as a *chromaticity diagram*, or *Plank diagram* (see Figure 2.4), of a quasi-triangular shape. The extreme ends of that diagram, or "corners of the triangle," are the locations at which different shades of red, green, and blue, respectively, can be found. Theoretically, any three colors lying inside this triangle can be used as primaries (of course, observing the condition that none of them is the product of the mixing of the other two, that is if we select purple and yellow, for example, the third color should not be the product of an additive mixing of purple and yellow). However, whatever colors are selected as primaries, their matching in different proportions will produce only those colors whose coordinates lie inside a triangle with corners corresponding to the coordinates of the three selected primaries. The selection of primaries lying closer to the corners of the chromaticity diagram, that is, the selection of given shades of red, green, and blue, which are located in these parts of the triangle, will result in a larger palette of colors.

The trichromatic character of white light and the selection of red, green, and blue primaries coincide with the Young–Helmholtz theory on human trichromatic vision, and we will see later that the basic principles of color television are quite similar to the processes of human trichromatic vision.

2.6 Measurement of Light

Light is a form of energy, and consequently we could measure it by using different spectroscopic methods, but the results of such measurements would be of no importance in the domain of television shooting. The photometric measurement methods used in film and television are essentially based on different comparisons—on comparing the situation in front of the camera with some predetermined reference values. In that respect, two values are generally routinely measured—the color temperature and the intensity of the incoming light.

We have seen already how color temperature is defined and measured. The other operational parameter, light intensity, is also measured by comparing the light on the scene to an arbitrarily selected reference light. One of the first reference values used for a comparative measurement of light intensity was *candlepower*, the light of one candle whose composition was precisely defined. As a much more precise and reproducible reference, we use today the 1/60-part of the light intensity radiated by an ideal black body (see part on color temperature) heated to the melting temperature of platinum. That reference value is still called "one candle."

Theoretically an ideal *punctual* source, that is a theoretical source shaped as a dot having no physical dimensions, radiates equally in all directions. The amount of light radiated in one second by a source of one candle is called a *lumen*. The illumination of a given surface is equal to the quantity of light falling on a surface unit in one time unit. The ensuing unit will, of course, depend on the measurement units adopted for the surface. Consequently, if we take metric measures one *meter-candle* or *lux* will correspond to the amount of light emanating from a source of one candle located in the center of a sphere with a diameter of one meter and falling on the internal surface of that sphere. Similarly, if the sphere has one foot in diameter, the corresponding light measurement unit will be a *foot-candle* .

In television we usually measure the incoming light. The light meter is placed on the spot where the performers are expected to be. Such a measurement ensures sufficient information for the adjustment of lighting, which, as already mentioned, has to fulfill the technical requirements of the system and the creative requirements of the director. For reasons of economy, comfort, and operating convenience, the overall light level is always adjusted at the lowest level acceptable for normal camera operation.

It is important to stress that the television system has a considerably lower capability for handling extreme differences in illumination values than the human eye or then cinematographic film. In fact the *contrast range*, or *contrast ratio*, accepted by the television system is only 1:20, that is, the brightest element of one picture can be only 20 times brighter than the darkest element of that same picture. Since television cameras are not very good at handling extremely bright or dark spots, it is expected that the darkest area in front of the camera would correspond to a reflectivity of 3% and the brightest to 60%. These two values are sometimes called *television black* and *television white*.

When a scene is lighted, the contrast-handling capacity of the television system should be taken into account and measurements made at both the lightest and the darkest points of the scene in order to define the contrast range on the set. Having in mind that the human face has a reflectance of some 35%–40%, all other elements have to be adjusted in such a way as to ensure a full prominence of the human face while keeping all other elements of the scene inside the limits of the acceptable television contrast range.

3

Generating a Television Picture

We have seen that the only effective way to transmit an optical image at a distance is to "dissect" or scan it, thereby transforming a simultaneous phenomenon into a sequential succession of individual pieces of optical information. On the receiving end, these individual pieces of optical information are transformed back into electric signals whose succession is sufficiently rapid to blend into one continuous signal.

3.1 Picture Scanning

The first scanning device used by television pioneers was the Nipkow disk (as shown in Figure 1.1), which undoubtedly played a crucial role in the development of television. It allowed the practical realization of the transmission of moving images and proved the feasibility of a television system. However, as a mechanical device, it was very much limited in its capacities and development potential, and it had no future in the system it helped to create.

The Nipkow disk had a number of problems inherent in its mechanical nature: inertia, instability, limited precision, and so on. For example, the quality of a reproduced television picture is considered acceptable only if the number of its analyzed elements is considerably superior to 150,000. The most advanced model of Baird's scanner had 240 holes, thus generating 240 lines, or only 57,600 picture elements, which was a far cry from a good picture. At the same time, the disk was expected to rotate precisely at 50 *revolutions per second* (rps) with no fluctuations and no vibrations, which was hard to achieve. The limitations of the mechanical system forced researchers to look for other solutions, and they found them in the domain of electronics. The necessary breakthrough was brought on by two major television pioneers, Philo Farnsworth and Vladimir Zworykin, who developed the first modern sensors: electronic vacuum pick-up tubes.

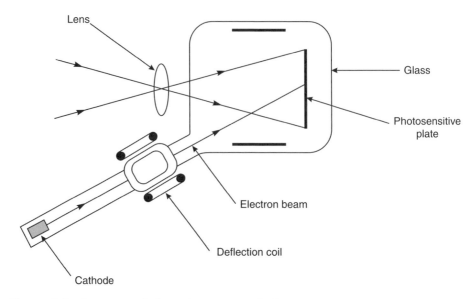

Figure 3.1   Iconoscope (schematic representation).

A pick-up tube basically consists of a photosensitive target onto which the lens projects the light reflected from an image. Under the impact of the projected light, the photosensitive target generates a series of electric charges commensurate with the brightness of each particular point. All of those charges create an *electronic image*—an electronic replica of the optical image in front of the lens. That image is then scanned and neutralized by a focused electron beam generating a continuous electric signal—the *video signal,* which is the electric representation of the optical picture projected onto the photosensitive target. Compared to the mechanical scanning devices, the electron beam has no inertia (in practical terms) and can be easily controlled. Further, its speed can be easily adjusted and held constant, and it is rather insensitive to external mechanical disturbances.

Both researchers based their discoveries on all-electronic principles, but the *iconoscope*, the pick-up tube developed by Zworykin, was more influential in the development of television technology (see Figure 3.1). It also had a more lasting influence because the scanning principle, based on a focused beam of electrons, would consequently be used in all electronic vacuum-tube pick-up devices until the early 1980s, when solid-state sensors gradually replaced pick-up tubes.

The simplest and most logical scanning system is based on parallel lines. That system is, in fact, identical to the way we read a printed text: our eyes follow the line of text at a given speed and notice all characters; then at the end of the line our eyes return quickly to the beginning of the next line, stepping down one line.

During that return, our eyes do not collect any information, and we could just as well keep our eyes closed during the *flyback*. In television systems, the scanning beam starts from the upper-left corner of the picture. Once the first line is scanned, the beam is switched off and returns with considerably greater speed back to the left side, stepping down at the same time to the starting point of the next line. There the beam is switched on again to scan the second line.

The number of lines and the overall *frequency bandwidth* (i.e. the span of frequencies from the lowest to the highest one, which a transmission channel or a piece of equipment can accept at its input and deliver at its output) determines the *resolution* of the television system, that is, its overall capacity to transmit the fine details of the picture. However, the relationship between the number of lines and the subjective assessment of the quality of a television picture is not linear. For a given screen size and viewing distance, we can determine a point at which the eye is saturated and further increases in scanning lines will not correspond to a subjectively finer or better picture.

On the other hand, the number of scanning lines and the overall frequency bandwidth determine the necessary capacity of the transmitting channel. The greater the number of scanning lines and analyzed picture elements, the greater will be the increased complexity of equipment and need for larger transmission channels. Therefore, the choice of the number of lines and the setting of the overall *channel bandwidth* (i.e. a frequency bandwidth of a given channel) has to be a compromise of sorts between the desired subjective quality of the picture and the economics of technology and channel scarcity. When the first regular television service started in the United Kingdom in 1936, the number of lines was fixed at 405. Not only was that considered "high definition," but some engineers at EMI (the British company that provided the necessary equipment for the first television service in 1936) even assessed that number of lines as unachievable. However, after some experimental broadcasts only a couple of years later, the United States set their scanning standard at 525 lines. When television services resumed after the end of World War II, countries which had regular service before the war decided to apply the same old parameters: 405 lines in the United Kingdom, 525 lines in the United States, and 415 lines in France. Other countries opted to benefit from the latest advances in technology and selected 625 lines as a good and viable compromise between the pre-war standards and some new proposals featuring over 800 lines. Compared to 625 lines, the pre-war standards offered a visibly inferior picture quality, while going over 800 lines drastically complicated the use of already determined channel widths without counterbalancing it by a sufficient difference in picture quality. Then the confusion multiplied: France abandoned its obsolete 415-line service but refused to join the others and set its standard at 819 lines. Later on, with the introduction of a second television channel and color television, the United Kingdom and France would join other European countries and also adopt a 625-line scanning standard. From then on the whole television world would remain divided into two parts: one using 625 and the other, 525 scanning lines.

3.2 Progressive and Interlaced Scanning

The electron beam in the pick-up tube or in the CRT takes some time to scan one full picture. The number of pictures, or frames, progressively scanned (line by line) in one second must be determined in such a way as to satisfy the requirements of the human visual system, which integrates a sufficiently quick succession of static pictures to create a sensation of seeing continuous movement. In the 1930s, the cinema had already adopted a new standard of 24 pictures or *frames per second* (fps) as the optimum rate for good movement reproduction. The same number of frames should therefore have been acceptable for television. However, the television electric scanning and display devices get their energy supply from the power lines, which deliver an alternate electric current at a frequency of 50 hertz (Hz) in Europe and 60 Hz in the United States. The equipment we use today for the generation and reproduction of television pictures is practically insensitive to the frequency of the power supply, but in the early 1930s, when the technology was less developed, the difference between the frequency of the supply alternate current and the frequency of 24 fps created visible and very annoying disturbances in the reproduced pictures. The only way to avoid such disturbances was to generate a number of television frames per second that would be equal either to the frequency of the power supply or to a multiple or a submultiple of that frequency. For that reason, the frame rate was fixed at 25 fps in Europe and 30 fps in the United States.

There are two basic ways that a television picture can be scanned. One possibility is to produce the necessary minimum of 25 (or 30) fps by scanning each one of them with 625 (or 525) lines. Such a system, known as *progressive scanning*, has a number of advantages, especially in the domain of special effects. However, this type of scanning will create problems on the display side. Namely, as already explained, the front plate of a CRT is coated with a phosphor-emitting light under the impact of the focused electron beam. The phosphor has a *persistence*, that is, it will not stop emitting light immediately after the passage of the electron beam but will instead fade out. The light-sensitive part of the human eye (retina) behaves in a similar manner; it has its own persistence. Once exposed to a light image, the retina retains that image for a given period of time before allowing it to fade out. The combination of these two specific properties will result in a distracting flicker if pictures are displayed with a rate of 25 or 30 pictures per second.

A similar flicker effect was noticed much earlier in cinematography, and it was discovered that the disturbance virtually disappears (or becomes barely noticeable) if the film is projected at more than 40 pictures per second. Although our visual system requires only 24 static pictures per second for acceptable movement reproduction, the elimination of flicker requires the refreshing of the eye at a much higher rate. Shooting film with such a high number of *photograms* (or frames) per second would mean a considerable increase of production costs. Therefore, the problem was circumvented by shooting at 24 fps and, during the projection, keeping each film frame in the projector gate for the time necessary to expose it twice to the projector light, in this way simulating a 48-fps projection.

The flicker problem in television could be solved either by increasing the number of progressively scanned pictures to 50 (or 60), or by developing a similar palliative system. Increasing the number of progressively scanned pictures to 50 would result in a twofold increase of the overall signal bandwidth, which would then require more complex equipment and larger transmission channels.

The solution came in the mid-1930s from the RCA laboratories,* where an alternative scanning system, interlaced scanning, was developed (see Figure 3.2). The *interlaced scanning*, used today by all television systems consists in scanning first all odd lines (first, third, fifth, etc.) and then all even lines that are located

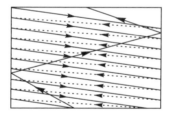 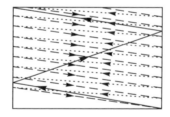

Figure 3.2 The principle of interlaced scanning.

---

*Since the flicker was an acute problem, a number of research teams were busy in the mid-1930s searching for a solution. Later on several of them claimed primacy in developing the interlaced approach.

between the previously scanned odd ones. In that way, the eye and the phosphor are refreshed at a rate of 50 (or 60) times per second, thus reducing the flicker to an acceptable level. Each of those refreshing cycles, or *fields*, consists of only 312.5 (262.5) lines. Two such fields, one odd and one even, form a picture, or a *frame*, of 625 (or 525) lines. However, mixing in one piece of frame information belonging to two fields that are in fact 1/25 (or 1/30) of a second apart leads to the appearance of motion artifacts and a loss of vertical resolution. But that conscious sacrifice in vertical resolution as well as the relatively minor motion problems, which do not seriously affect the overall quality impression, are well compensated for by the virtual elimination of the flicker and by the halving of bandwidth requirements.

Therefore we define today the existing scanning standards as 625/50 2:1 and 525/60 2:1, which means 625 (or 525) lines, 50 (or 60) fields, and interlaced scanning.* When the NTSC (National Television Standards Committee) color standard was introduced in the 1950s, the scanning parameters for the 525 system were slightly changed, and as a result, the frame rate was reduced to 59.94 *fields per second*. However, it is still customary to identify that standard as 525/60 (see Chapter 4 for the reasons behind the change of the frame rate).

Another basic television standard was fixed in the early 1930s—the aspect ratio. The *aspect ratio*—the relationship between the width and the height of the display screen—was very much debated in the 1970s at the time of the initial development of high-definition television. But in the 1930s it seemed natural to adopt the same screen aspect ratio as was used for cinema and known as the *academy format*, in which the proportions were 4:3. Not only had that format already been accepted by millions of moviegoers, it was also expected that the majority of television programs would originate on film. Finally, such a choice was quite rational since at that time the front surface of the CRTs, where the picture is displayed, had a circular form. A circular picture certainly does not look particularly natural, and a rectangular frame was much more appropriate. For the most logical use of the available, rather small surface of the Braun tube, it was necessary that the width and the height of the picture be almost identical, and the 4:3 ratio in that respect was not a bad compromise between a square (the most efficient) and an elongated rectangle (the most similar to the human panoramic view). Later, the appearance of CinemaScope and other wide-screen cinema formats and research in the domain of High-Definition Television (HDTV) that showed

---

*It should be noted that the term "scanning" is still officially and unofficially used worldwide. We will use it throughout this book, although all modern pick-up devices—sensors, and a good number of electronic displays—do not scan the picture in the literal sense. There are no electron beams that scan photosensitive surfaces, but rather a number of cells that operate on a sort of "flash" exposure principle.

that wider-screen formats more closely approximated the field of human vision, challenged the rationale for the choice of the 4:3 format.

From 1930 to 1948 (with a five-year gap due to World War II), all essential elements of television standards were set: the number of lines, the type of scanning, the number of fields, and the aspect ratio. These elements would prove to be long-lived and difficult to change even if the change promised a considerable improvement of service quality. In fact, changing any of these parameters has been difficult and costly. When a change is agreed upon, its introduction has to be very well planned, particularly in view of all the home receivers incompatible with the new standard. When the decision was made in the United Kingdom to introduce a color service and at the same time switch from the already obsolete standard of 405 lines to the generally used European standard of 625 lines, the only acceptable solution was to simulcast all programs in 625 and 405 and promote the acquisition of new receivers. In spite of all the promotion, the attractiveness of color television, and even some financial incentives, it took 20 years to reach the point when the 405 service could be phased out.

3.3 The Basic Video Signal

The electric signal resulting from the scanning process in the picture source, with the addition of synchronizing pulses, is known as the *video signal*—the basic electronic information used throughout the whole television chain.

When one television line is extracted from the signal and that video, or electric, signal is displayed on the screen of the instrument used for the visualization of such signals (known as *oscilloscope* or *waveform monitor*), its *waveform* (appearance) will look like Figure 3.3. The video signal of one television line consists of

- the picture content, that is, the part that carries information about the transmitted picture
- the horizontal blanking intervals
- the horizontal sync pulses

The part of the television line carrying information on picture content is called the *active line,* and in the 625 television system, its scanning time is 52 microseconds (μs). The *blanking interval* represents the flyback (*retrace*) phase, during which the scanning beam is switched off and returns from the end of one active line to the beginning of the next one; its duration is only 12 μs. Therefore, the total duration of one television line is 64 μs. For 525 systems, the active line period is 52.855 μs, the flyback time 10.7 μs, and the total duration of one television line is 63.555555 μs.

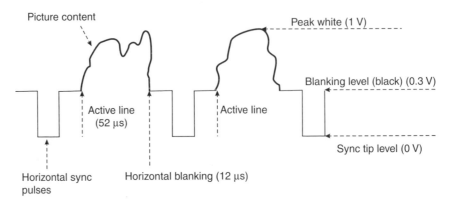

Picture content

Peak white (1 V)

Blanking level (black) (0.3 V)

Active line
(52 μs)

Active line

Sync tip level (0 V)

Horizontal sync
pulses

Horizontal blanking (12 μs)

Figure 3.3   The analog video signal of one television line as it appears on the waveform monitor screen.

A television picture is scanned (analyzed) in the pick-up device and then reconstructed (synthesized) in the receiving or displaying device—a receiver or a picture monitor. The precondition for achieving a stable picture on the receiving screen is the synchronism of the scanning processes in the camera and in the display device. When the scanning of the television picture in the television camera starts from its position at the upper-left corner, the scanning beam in the receiver's CRT has to start at the same moment from that same spot.

That synchronization is ensured by *horizontal synchronizing pulses* (commonly called *sync pulses*) inserted between every two consecutive lines in the blanking interval and by *vertical synchronizing pulses* inserted between every two consecutive fields in the vertical blanking interval. The VBI is the interval between two consecutive fields, having a duration of 20 lines plus 10.7 μs (525) or 25 lines plus 12 μs (625). During that period of time the extinguished electron beam returns from the end of scanning one field to the beginning of scanning the next one.

All parameters of a video signal are strictly standardized in order to allow a normal functioning of the television chain. The maximum allowed amplitude of the video signal, corresponding to the highest white level in the optical picture, is 700 millivolts (mV); the black level is at 0 mV; and the amplitude of all synchronizing pulses should be exactly 300 mV. It is important to stress that the amplitude, the duration, and the position of synchronizing pulses inside their respective blanking intervals are of the utmost importance for normal functioning of the television system. These pulses control not only the scanning processes in the camera and the display, but they also condition the operation of most of the equipment in the whole television chain, from the camera to the home receiver. Any problem with sync pulses will create visible disturbances in the displayed picture.

The blanking interval carries synchronization but no pictorial information. It can, therefore, be used for the transmission of additional, or ancillary, information. For example, the horizontal blanking interval, or more precisely the horizontal sync pulses, could be used to carry digitally coded sound signals, eliminating the need to use sound channels in addition to the video channel on international circuits. Such a system, known as *Sound in Syncs* (SiS), was widely used in Europe for analog point-to-point transmissions. With the rapid digitization of production plants and transmission channels, the hybrid SiS technique was gradually replaced by all-digital methods.

On the other hand, the vertical blanking interval (VBI), by its duration, offers many more possibilities. Since the electron beam in the CRT is switched off during the vertical blanking interval (vertical retrace period), inserted information is not visible nor does it disturb the correct reproduction of television pictures. However, it can be extracted and made visible by using specialized equipment or circuitry. At the same time, the operation of contemporary receivers is not affected by additional waveforms inserted in the VBI. Consequently, the VBI became a precious resource that could be used for a number of applications.

Some of those applications are reserved for the internal use of television stations and transmitting organizations, for example, the transmission of special test signals that allow the permanent control of the transmission path, the carrying of standard time and frequency signals, or the carrying of telecommands to studios and transmitters. Other applications offer an additional service to the end user, such as

- **Program delivery control (PDC).** PDC is a set of data that identifies every program in a station's schedule and enables the viewer's home VCR to correctly record the desired program even if the actual start time differs from the announced one (the video program system [VPS] is a German development offering the same features as the PDC).
- **Teletext magazines, particularly popular in Europe.** Teletext is a way to send "magazines" consisting of a relatively large number of pages displaying different sorts of information, from breaking news and sports results to service information and advertising. Each page carries 24 rows of 40 characters each; the number of pages is theoretically unlimited, but considering that the transmission of one page is spread over a number of vertical blanking intervals and that all the pages are transmitted as a sort of carousel, it is clear that a larger number of pages will mean a longer waiting time for the display of a selected page. Different forms of teletext are used in other parts of the world and some of them do not carry magazines but are used for data transmission.

- **Closed captioning.** This is the transmission in the VBI of subtitles either via teletext or other specially developed transport mechanisms. As opposed to open captioning, in which subtitles are irreversibly inserted into the visible picture, closed captioning represents subtitles "hidden" in the VBI; a viewer can select, call, and make visible such subtitles by using the commands of a decoder. Closed captioning is used either for transmitting multilingual subtitles or for providing short written descriptions of sound effects and a transcription of voice-over or dialogues for the benefit of the hard of hearing.

Color Television

4

The first mention of a color television system based on the separation of incoming light into three primary colors is found in a German patent from 1904. This was very much ahead of its time, and the technology was not yet ripe for the implementation of such a system. Even a black-and-white television transmission would require 20 additional years of research and development. As early as 1928 John Logie Baird demonstrated color television pictures using the Nipkow disk as a scanning device. Just before World War II, Peter Goldmark in the United States demonstrated a field-sequential color television system with 343 lines and 20 fps. Once the war was over, the same scientist, taking advantage of the development of electronics during the war, proposed to the Federal Communications Commission (FCC) in 1949 an improved version of his system. It was again a field-sequential system, this time based on 405 lines and 24 frames. The FCC gave him permission to implement such a system, and by 1951 Goldmark started experimental broadcasts of his noncompatible color system. However, because there were already nearly ten million black-and-white receivers in the U.S. market, a noncompatible color system was doomed.

In order to offer a compatible service to the market, the FCC created the National Television System Committee (NTSC) whose task was to investigate the technology, evaluate all submissions, and propose a compatible color television system to the FCC. In 1953 the committee submitted its proposal to the FCC. That proposal, essentially based on the RCA development work, was seriously debated and after numerous hearings, adopted as a national standard. By 1954 the first color television broadcasts compatible with the black-and-white systems went on the air using the newly adopted system named after the body that selected it—NTSC.

British television expert (and author of excellent technical books) Boris Townsend has defined color television as a "judicious combination of human imperfections and clever technical solutions." In fact, color television systems are based largely on psychophysical characteristics of human sight and on technical means developed to make use of these characteristics.

Black-and-white television signals can be generated by using photosensitive elements that react to differences in the brightness of the light that is reflected from the objects that surround us. Color television must reproduce not only different levels of brightness but also the multitude of colors existing in the real world. Creating a color television system meant finding answers to three essential questions:

1. How will we deal with the multitude of colors we can see in the surrounding world and generate electric signals that will faithfully represent these colors?
2. How will we transmit these electric signals?
3. How will we reconstruct a multicolored optical picture that the human visual system will accept as a relatively faithful reproduction of the real world?

4.1   Splitting the White Light and the Selection of Primaries

We can see around us an extremely large number of colors. To deal separately with each of them, with each shade, each hue, each saturation and brightness, would require an immensely complex and elaborate technical system. However, in Chapter 2 it was shown that white light, which surrounds us, can be obtained by an additive matching of three adequately selected monochromatic colors, the three primaries. By varying the proportions of these three primaries, it is possible to obtain all colors of the visible spectrum. Therefore, the reverse statement must be true—we can split into three primaries the light reflected from the objects and beings around us and represent that multicolored world by different proportions of these primaries.

The selection of the primaries is a delicate operation. On the one hand, it is necessary to select them in such a way as to ensure that the triangle they create is as large as possible, thus providing as wide a gamut of colors as possible. On the other hand it is necessary to ensure that it is possible to produce at a reasonable cost materials (phosphors), which would radiate with a sufficient efficiency the monochromatic lights selected as primaries. In that respect, a statistical study was conducted that showed that over 90% of colors encountered in our surroundings lie within a space that is smaller than the one occupied by the chromaticity diagram (Figure 4.1). In other words, it was possible to choose shades of red, green, and blue to define a "color triangle" that would adequately reproduce the multicolored world around us by offering most colors that we encountered every day.

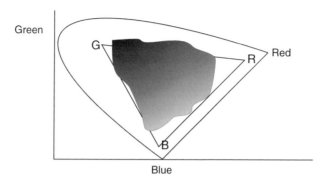

Figure 4.1 The space of real colors and the selected primaries.

The selection of the precise shades of red, green, and blue was dictated not only by the availability of phosphors with a good brightness but of those that could be manufactured at a reasonable cost.

In the early 1950s the U.S. Federal Communications Commission (FCC) defined precisely the coordinates of these three colors using the standardized white light, known as Illuminant C, as a reference white (see Chapter 2). That set of values became known as *FCC primaries*. Following that, major developments in the manufacture of phosphors offered a much wider choice and allowed the selection of a different set of primaries, which would allow the enlargement of the color triangle. The European Broadcasting Union (EBU) therefore proposed the adoption of a different set of values whose reference white was another standardized white light, the Illuminant D_{65}. Due to a lack of international standardization, or rather, due to its failure, both sets of primaries are now used in parallel in different parts of the world, causing some confusion.

In order to obtain a white color, the selected FCC primaries have to be matched in the following proportions:

$$0.30\,\text{red} + 0.59\,\text{green} + 0.11\,\text{blue} = \text{white}$$

Matching of just two of the three primaries produces complementary colors:

$$\text{red} + \text{green} = \text{yellow}$$
$$\text{green} + \text{blue} = \text{cyan}$$
$$\text{blue} + \text{red} = \text{purple}$$

It is important to stress again that this "color matching" represents the additive process of direct mixing of colored lights and not the subtractive process of mixing colored pigments.

While the primaries are at the corners of the color triangle, the complementary colors are located at the middle of each side. The matching of the three complementary colors in the following proportions will lead again to white:

$$0.70\,\text{cyan} + 04.1\,\text{purple} + 0.89\,\text{yellow} = \text{white}$$

Although we could make white in this way, if we used the complementary colors as corner points, we would define a different color triangle of smaller dimensions encompassing a white light but a smaller number of natural colors. Therefore, red, green, and blue are selected as primaries because the color triangle that has them as corner-points encompasses the largest number of natural colors.

Starting from a selected set of primaries, it is possible to base a television system on the following operations:

- separation of the incoming optical picture into three primaries
- conversion of these lights into three electric signals
- transmission of these three signals
- their reconversion, at the receiving end, into three primary light signals
- reconstruction, through additive matching, of the optical picture

This chain is in principle similar to the processes of the eye-brain system of human vision:

- The incoming light is split within the eye into three pieces of primary neural information.
- These are then relayed to the brain where the multicolored picture is reconstructed.

The hypothetical system represented in Figure 4.2 intended to show how color television pictures are generated, transmitted, and displayed. Three black-and-white cameras are pointed at the same scene. In front of each camera is a filter—red, green, or blue. By allowing the passage of only one primary color per camera, these filters split the incoming light into three primaries. Consequently each camera will receive a filtered light (red, green, or blue) and will each generate one electric signal that will represent the red, green, or blue contents of the optical picture.

Assume we convey these three signals via three separate transmission paths to three black-and-white television screens, or CRTs, having a sufficiently powerful light output to be able to project the displayed picture on a screen. If in front of each of these three CRTs we install the same type of filter that we used in front of the cameras, we shall obtain three superimposed pictures on the screen—one

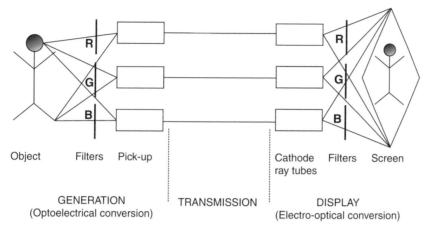

Figure 4.2 The color television system.

red, one green, and one blue. In accordance with the laws of color matching, the viewer should experience a faithful color reproduction of the real scene shot by the cameras.

A system like this would be very cumbersome and inefficient, but it is a convenient support for our explanation. This "color television system" can be divided into three parts:

1. picture generation or optoelectric conversion
2. transmission of electric signals
3. picture display or electro-optic conversion

4.2 Picture Generation or Optoelectric Conversion

A system with three cameras and three filters is undoubtedly unrealistic; in fact, it is unacceptable. It is necessary to find a more elegant and technically sound way to split the incoming light into three primaries and convert them into three electric signals. The solution, implemented in all color cameras since the beginning of color television, comprises the construction of a special optical block that can split the incoming light into three primaries and installation of such a block between the lens and three optoelectric converters or sensors.

That optical block, known as a *dichroic block*, is a set of three glued prisms (see Figure 4.3). The contact surface between two adjacent prisms is covered with *dichroic coating*—a special sort of coating that reflects certain wavelengths and allows free passage of others, thereby minimizing light-energy losses.

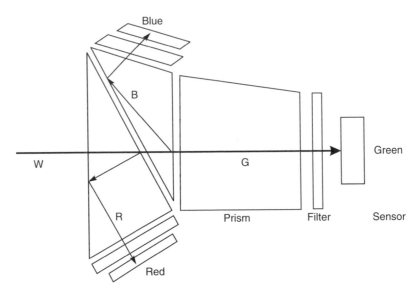

Figure 4.3   3 Dichroic block.

When the incoming white light transiting through the dichroic block encounters the first coated surface, its blue content (blue primary) is reflected while the two others (green and red) pass through. At the next coated surface, the red content of the incoming white light (red primary) will be reflected while the remaining green is transmitted. In such a way the three primaries, separated from the incoming white light by the dichroic layers, become available at the three sides of the dichroic block (see Figure 4-3). The dichroic coating can be very precisely "tuned," that is, adjusted to the desired wavelength of the monochromatic light meant to be reflected. The purity of the separated primary light is enhanced by the addition of trimming optical filters, whose task is to additionally refine the purity of the primary light. These filters are glued to the external surfaces of the splitting block, between the block and the sensors that act as optoelectric converters, and they convert the incoming light energy into electric energy. That electric energy appears as three separate analog electric signals named after the light components from which they originate—r(ed), g(reen) and b(lue), that is, the *RGB* primary electric signals.

4.3   Picture Display

Leaving aside for the moment the transmission path, let us look at the display side of the system. Again, three CRTs with three filters is not an elegant or efficient solution. It is true that the system can be improved if, instead of black-and-white standard CRTs and filters, we employ three special tubes featuring a very high brightness, each of them coated with a different phosphor—one radiating red, the other green, and the third a blue light. For a number of years video projectors were built in that way (and some projectors of this type can still be found in operation). However, at the time of the development of color television standards, such CRTs were not available, and, in any event, a video projection system was not considered the most appropriate device for home use. Home viewing required a solution that would not be different from the black-and-white set to which the viewer was already accustomed—a solution based on a single, color CRT.

Such a CRT was developed in the early 1950s by the U.S. company RCA. These first color CRTs were relatively low in brightness, rather unstable, and very delicate during manufacture. However, very soon they were much improved and became standard high-quality products, known as *shadow mask tubes*.

As explained in Chapter 1, the black-and-white CRT is equipped with one cathode, or *cathode gun*, that is, one element that is capable of radiating free electrons under the effect of thermal heating. These electrons are focused into one beam, which is attracted by the anode at the opposite side of the tube. The internal side of this part of the tube is coated with the phosphor, which has the capacity to radiate visible light under the impact of the electron beam. The intensity of the radiated light is at any moment proportional to the intensity of the electron beam that has landed on that particular spot. The incoming video signal (representing the picture) and the electron beam are coupled in such a way that the intensity of the beam changes in accordance with the changes of the amplitude of the video signal. The beam will be at highest intensity when the video signal represents the whitest spot on the picture and at lowest intensity when the darkest spot is represented (i.e., the video signal modulates the intensity of the beam). The brightness of the spot on the screen where such a beam has landed will vary accordingly. Since the beam is moved in parallel lines across the screen, it will create, line by line, a replica of the original optical picture on the front side of the CRT.

In color television there are three signals corresponding to three primary colors. Therefore, it is necessary to ensure that there are three cathode guns, installed on the same "gun base" (see Figure 4-4b) and three beams, each of them modulated by one of the RGB signals. The screen of the color CRT has to be capable of reproducing three pictures in three primary colors. The solution developed by RCA consisted of replacing the uniform coating of black-and-white tubes with triads of phosphor dots. Each *triad* consisted of red, green, and blue phosphor dots respectively. That first color CRT had a three-dot phosphor screen of about 1,200,000 dots grouped in 400,000 triads. Between the coated screen and the cathode guns, close to the screen, a metal foil perforated with 400,000 holes was installed.

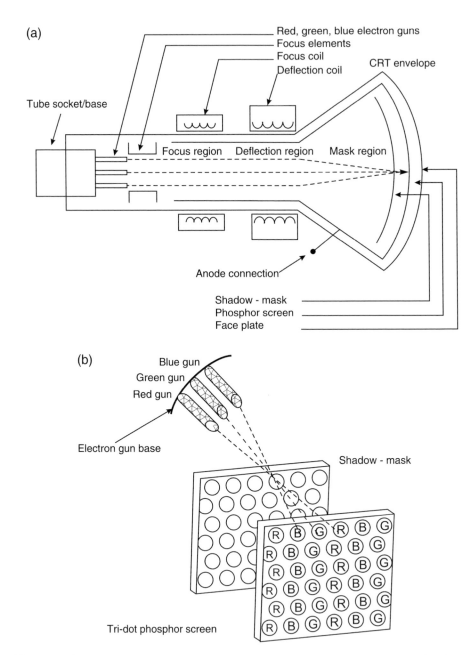

Figure 4.4 The operating principle of the shadow mask tube: (a) Longitudinal cross section and (b) Shadow mask principle.

The role of the foil, or *mask*, was to control the beams in such a way that a beam modulated by one primary signal hit only dots of the corresponding color. In that way the three beams simultaneously created three pictures of different colors. Since the individual dots are of such a small size, the eye will receive the resulting additive matching of the three colors and see a single multicolored picture. (see Figure 4-4)

These CRTs, known as shadow mask tubes, would later be supplanted by more efficient, stable, and precise ones, like the Trinitron, In-line, or Delta tubes, but all of them would just be different expressions of the basic concept developed first by RCA: three electron guns, three beams modulated by three RGB signals, a multiphosphor coating, and a device between the guns and the coating to control the impact of the beam on the phosphor (which corresponds in color to the signal that modulates that beam). However, although they worked quite well, all of these CRTs had unavoidable drawbacks:

- Since they were essentially made of glass, they were rather fragile, and the large ones in particular were very heavy.
- The concept of three beams and three different phosphors required delicate alignment systems and procedures .
- The same concept of three electron guns and three beams imposed a special, rather clumsy construction with a long neck behind the front plate.

Years ago, these and other shortcomings prompted the search for another operating principle that would allow the construction of a flat screen, that is, a display device that would:

- be less fragile and lighter
- not require delicate alignments
- have the shape of a framed picture that could be hung on the wall

These efforts were eventually successful, and we have today in operation several types of flat screens based on liquid crystals or plasma cells.

4.4 Transmission Path

As shown in Figure 4.2, the pick-up devices output three signals. As already mentioned in Chapter 1, using three transmission channels for something that in fact represents one piece of information is not a technically or economically acceptable solution. Early color television also faced a compatibility problem. At the time that color television was under development, a black-and-white service was already reasonably well developed, and a large number of black-and-white receivers were in use in the field. It would be difficult to deprive the owners of these sets of programs once they were broadcast in color, yet the plan was to progressively replace black-and-white with color programs. Furthermore, the scarcity of color receivers during the introductory stage would mean transmitting into "a void," which was commercially unacceptable. Consequently, it was stipulated that the color service should be engineered in such a way as to permit black-and-white receivers to display—with no other impairments than the absence of color information—all the programs produced in color. At the same time, color receivers should be able to display programs originally produced in black and white.

This meant that the technical solution for color television had to satisfy the following requirements:

- It had to use channels designed for black-and-white transmission.
- It had to be receivable and decodable simultaneously by both black-and-white and color television sets.

The solution to the problem of transmitting more information (color) through a channel of the same bandwidth as the one used for black-and-white broadcasts was to be found in the specificities of the human vision system. Since the human eye differentiates small and fine details of a picture by their difference in brightness rather than by their difference in color, we can achieve a compatible television service by transmitting all available brightness information (a *luminance signal*, or *Y signal*), which corresponds in practical terms to the normal black-and-white television signal and by sending some additional color information with a considerably reduced bandwidth.

As we already saw, the color camera generates three electrical signals corresponding to the three primaries R, G and B. Therefore the luminance signal is obtained by performing an additive mixing of these three signals in precisely determined proportions:

$$Y = 0.299R + 0.587G + 0.114B$$

Therefore, when for the sake of creating a compatible color television system the luminance signal is transmitted, there is no need to simultaneously transmit all three color primaries since the luminance (the black-and-white signal), as the result of the additive mixing of the primaries, already contains all these three pieces of color information. In fact it is sufficient to transmit only two additional pieces of color information, for example, the red (R) and the blue (B), with the assumption that the green (G) information can be extracted at the reception point by subtracting the R and B information from the luminance signal Y.

However, although based on that same idea of transmitting a luminance signal and two additional color information, the real color television systems are a little bit more complex. Namely, it was found that the improvement of the black-and-white-compatible reception required replacing the straight R and B signals with somewhat more complicated signals called *chrominance* or *color difference signals* whose mathematical expressions are R-Y and B-Y. The whole process so far could be summarized as follows:

- the incoming light reflected from the scene is splitted by the dichroic block into three primary lights—red, green and blue—that correspond to the red, green and blue content of that incoming light;
- these three primary lights fall on three sensors generating three electrical signals R, G and B;
- in the processing circuitry these three signals (R, G, and B) are used to generate three new signals—Y (luminance), R-Y and B-Y (color difference signals)—called *component signals*;
- bearing in mind the initially proclaimed goal to transmit color television pictures as a single signal using the same channel that was used for the transmission of the black-and-white television, the next processing step would consist in combining these three component signals, or *components* into one *composite signal.*

The different technical solutions used to integrate the three components—Y, R-Y, and B-Y—into one composite signal of the same bandwidth as the standard black-and-white television signal essentially represent the differences between the three currently coexisting color standards: NTSC, PAL, and SECAM.

4.5 The Principle of Modulation

Before discussing these specific color standards, we will look at a very important concept—*modulation*.

Modulation is the method used in the world of communications for the transmission of information, or messages, by using appropriate carriers. The *message* is the information that has to be transmitted to a selected person or simultaneously to an undefined number of persons. The *carrier* is the resource used to transmit the message. We are normally surrounded by a number of carriers, carrying different messages, aimed at the same or different recipients. When we want to receive a specific message we must have the means to select it from the surrounding multitude of messages and then, once the desired message is separated, to separate it from the carrier. Such selective reception can be achieved only if a separate carrier transports each of these messages and if every carrier can be unambiguously differentiated from the others. But it is important to stress that we need to identify the carrier only to facilitate the reception of the message it carries—our real interest is the message, not the carrier.

In the domain of electric communications we use regular high-frequency electric signals as carriers. These signals travel quite well through different media, and it is not particularly difficult to develop and build receiving circuits that select a chosen frequency and separate it from the others, circuits that can be *tuned*, that is, adjusted to accept only the selected carrier. Once a carrier is defined it is necessary to define two other frequencies—one somewhat higher and the other lower than the carrier. These two frequencies represent the boundaries inside which the carrier and the message have to fit—they define the channel and its bandwidth. Therefore, receiving equipment is set to detect the carrier and to accept all pieces of information that are contained inside of the predetermined channel bandwidth. The width of the channel determines, among other parameters, the quality of the service—the maximum obtainable amount of information that will produce the maximum quality of the decoded message at the receiving end. However, the frequency spectrum (the span of frequencies that can be used for telecommunication purposes) is a unique and limited commodity, and all technical solutions in communications tend to use the narrowest channel possible for a given quality of service, or to squeeze as many channels as is practicable in a given frequency band.

In the broadcasting industry the transmitted information comprises sounds and pictures, or, to be precise, the electric signals representing sounds and pictures. The transport of this information is ensured by the modulation process: the superimposing of low-frequency information on a high-frequency carrier. In the modulation process one can differentiate between

- **the carrier**—the high-frequency signal that is used to transmit information at a distance
- **the modulating signal**—the electrical representation of the information being transmitted (in the case of broadcasting, that information is composed of sights and sounds or video and audio signals)
- **the modulating method**—the parameter (amplitude or frequency) of the carrier that is changed in the rhythm of the modulating signal

For example, in the case of amplitude modulation (AM), the parameter to be changed during the modulation process is the amplitude of the carrier.

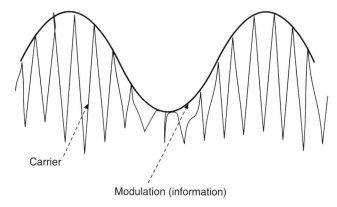

Carrier

Modulation (information)

Figure 4.5   The principle of amplitude modulation.

The carrier is generated with a constant amplitude, and in the modulation process that amplitude can be changed at any moment in accordance with the variations of the amplitude of the modulating signal, which in turn represents the content to be transmitted (see Figure 4.5).

At the receiving end, the receiver detects only the changes of the carrier amplitude as information and discards the carrier itself. The amplitude modulation process is similar to the old system of light communication between ships at sea: a strong projector on one ship is beamed toward the other ship and a sailor operating the "transmitter" periodically interrupts the beam with short and slightly longer intervals (dots and dashes), which correspond to the Morse code. In other words, the sailor changes the amplitude of the light beam from 100% to 0% in accordance with the information being transmitted. In this case the light beam is the carrier: it can be seen (detected by another ship) but does not represent any information unless it is modulated by the interruptions defined by Morse code. On the receiving end, another sailor takes note of the interruptions and interprets the message. Color, shape, and any other characteristics of the light beam are ignored. Only amplitude is important to the sailor who is demodulating the signal to extract the information. The carrier is, in effect, discarded.

In telecommunications, a number of different modulation schemes are used. However, for the purpose of this book, two of them are particularly important—frequency modulation (FM) and the previously explained amplitude modulation (AM). *Frequency modulation* consists of changing the momentary frequency of the carrier in accordance with the variations of the information represented by the modulation signal. We shall revert to the analogy of the light-beam communication between ships. The FM communication could be compared to a light communication where we would not interrupt the beam but would change its color: a monochromatic light beam, say of red color, that rapidly changes to blue for dots and to green for dashes, could be said to transmit information by the rapid change of hue, that is, by change of its momentary frequency, also described as a frequency modulation of the carrier.

Amplitude modulation has a specific characteristic that facilitates the creation of NTSC and PAL color composite signals: a single AM carrier can be simultaneously modulated by two different information signals. Such modulation schemes where one carrier can simultaneously transport two different and separately decodable pieces of information is called *modulation in quadrature*. Again referring to the light-beam communication between ships, the modulation in quadrature resembles a hypothetical system where it would be possible to change, independently and simultaneously, the width and the height of a light-beam cross section. These changes are two independent and independently decodable pieces of information superimposed on the carrier, one in the horizontal and the other in the vertical plane.

4.6 The NTSC System

Using the same channel bandwidth as the one used for 525/60 black-and-white television, the NTSC system allows the transmission of a complete luminance signal, which includes information on the brightness of any particular picture element, so it can be normally received and displayed on black-and-white receivers. At the same time, bandwidth-reduced color information is transmitted, which does not disturb the quality of the picture displayed on black-and-white screens but can be used by color receivers to display a full color picture.

The NTSC composite color signal consists of a full-bandwidth luminance signal (4.2 MHz) with additional color information inserted as a modulated carrier in the upper part of the spectrum (see Figure 4.6).

That carrier is called a *subcarrier* to differentiate it from the main carrier used for transmitting the whole television picture signal from the transmitter to the home receiver. The subcarrier is modulated in quadrature by two signals corresponding to the R-Y and B-Y chrominance components, that is, a single carrier is used to carry two independent and different pieces of information. On the receiving side, adequate decoder and demodulation circuits ensure the separate extraction of all three pieces of information: the Y (luminance signal) and the R-Y and B-Y (chrominance signals).

At the beginning of the process at the camera, three primaries (R, G, and B) are obtained by optically splitting the incoming white light. Through three optoelectric converters called *sensors, three* corresponding R, G, and B electric signals are generated. The Y, R-Y, and B-Y component signals are then generated by a special

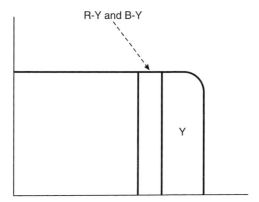

Figure 4.6 Spectrum of the composite color signal. Notice that the bandwidth needed for color information (R-Y and B-Y) is a fraction of that used for the luminance.

processing circuitry known as *the matrix*. The NTSC coder codes these three components into one single composite color signal that is forwarded to the output. Consequently, at the receiving end, that process has to be inverted—the NTSC composite signal has to be decoded into the Y, R-Y, and B-Y components and the components dematrixed in order to obtain the R, G, and B electric primaries that will control the three electron beams of the color cathode-ray tube and thus recreate on the screen the multicolored picture captured by the camera.

As explained above, the NTSC color television signal is constituted by the luminance (Y) and the two color difference signals (R-Y and B-Y) that modulate in quadrature one subcarrier. The selection of the frequency of that subcarrier is dictated by the desire to minimize the visibility of that inserted component. By putting the subcarrier in the area of higher frequencies, the visibility of interference on black-and-white receivers is minimized, but it happens that the selected value (3.579545 MHz—a multiple of the line-scanning frequency) causes an annoying interference with the sound carrier in the television emission channel. In order to minimize that effect, a slight change is introduced in the line-scanning frequency, resulting in a change of the frame rate, which becomes slightly lower than 60 Hz (or 60 fields per second) to become 59.94 Hz. Such slight change of the horizontal scanning frequency and of the frame rate do not impose a modification on the existing black-and-white receivers since the circuitry responsible for horizontal and vertical received picture synchronization have by definition sufficiently large tolerances that easily encompass these new values.

The NTSC system was undoubtedly a major step forward in the development of television technology and certainly represented a very clever engineering solution, but it had its drawbacks. One of the major ones was that distortions

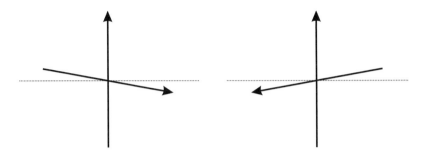

Figure 4.7 PAL phase shifting in two consecutive lines.

(known as *phase distortions*) accumulated along the transmission path and appeared at the receiving end as errors of the hue of the reproduced color. That is why some people jokingly refer to NTSC as an acronym for "Never Twice the Same Color."

4.7 The PAL System

The development and introduction of a compatible color television service in the United States was closely monitored in other parts of the world. However, the overall economic situation in Europe, and especially the fact that color receivers were at that time considerably more expensive than their black-and-white counterparts, postponed the introduction of color television in Europe. By the mid-1960s, it seemed conceivable to introduce such a service in some European countries, and two competing color television systems emerged. Developed in Europe, both of them were based on the same idea as the NTSC—to insert in the luminance bandwidth one subcarrier that would transport the chrominance information—and both systems were developed with the ambition to overcome the problem of hue errors.

One of them, known as PAL, was developed in Germany by Dr. Walter Bruch. Basically this system was very similar to the NTSC: a subcarrier was inserted in the upper part of the luminance spectrum. The subcarrier was modulated in quadrature by two chrominance or color difference signals. To overcome the problem of hue errors, the *phase* of one of the two modulating signals was shifted 180° in each consecutive line (see Figure 4.7). On that figure the slightly tilted horizontal arrow represents one of the modulating signals whose direction is reversed, that is, its phase is shifted 180°.

Let us refer again to the light-beam communication analogy. We have seen that the modulation in quadrature is similar to a hypothetical situation where the width and the height of the beam cross section are modulated by two different and independent pieces of information. If we simplify the system for the sake of explanation, we could say that the PAL approach consists in modulating all the time the height of the beam's cross section with information R-Y. The width of the beam's cross section will be modulated by the information B-Y. However, that change of width will differ from one line to another. In the first line the extreme right hand edge of the beam will remain fixed as the reference point and the change in width will be achieved by moving the extreme left hand edge of the beam closer and farther away from that reference point. During the next line the situation will be reversed – the left hand edge of the beam will be used as the fixed reference and the right hand one will be moved to achieve the desired modulation. Since the hue error in NTSC is the result of unwanted changes of the subcarrier phase, a systematic change of the phase of one of the modulating signals from line to line turns a positive error in one line to a negative one in the following line. The net result when putting these two lines together is a sort of self-canceling effect (see Figure 4.7). That system of changing the phase in each line gave the name to the PAL color system—(P)hase (A)lternation (L)ine. The PAL system also has a nickname. Because it was adopted by the large majority of countries in the world, it came to be called "Peace At Last."

4.8 The SECAM System

In developing his color television system, the French researcher Henri de France believed frequency modulation would be a more robust system for the transport of color difference signals than amplitude modulation. Unfortunately, FM does not allow the transport of two pieces of information simultaneously on the same carrier. To overcome that problem, de France turned again to the specific characteristics of human sight. Since the eye is considerably less sensitive to differences in color than to differences in brightness in small picture details, it would not be able to differentiate which color belonged to which of two consecutive television lines. Therefore, Henri de France proposed a system where a full luminance (Y) signal is transmitted in one television line with the addition, in the upper part of its spectrum, of a subcarrier frequency modulated by one of the two color difference signals (for example R-Y). The next television line consists again of the full Y signal, but this time the subcarrier is modulated with the other color difference signal (B-Y). The receiver, for its part, is equipped with one delay line so that the R-Y from the previous line can be memorized and added to the Y and B-Y contained in the currently transmitted line. Similarly, the B-Y is memorized to be added to the following line where Y and R-Y are transmitted. In that manner, each line consists of its own luminance information, the first color difference

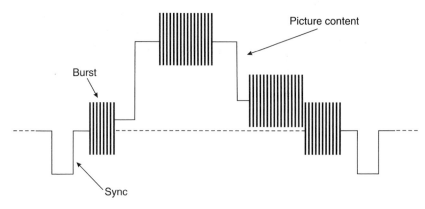

Figure 4.8   Composite color video signal.

information that belonged to that line, and the second color difference information "borrowed" from the previous line. Due to its limitations, the eye is not able to detect any inadequacy in the displayed picture.

Such a sequential way of transmitting color difference signals gave the name to this system: Séquentiel Couleur A Mémoire (Sequential Color with a Memory)—SECAM. Like its competitors, the French system could not escape being nicknamed. Being developed in the time of General de Gaulle and his refusal to unconditionally accept the American leadership in NATO, the system was called "Something Essentially Contrary to the American System."

A color video signal basically looks like a black-and-white one (see Figure 4.8), but with the color information (as a modulated subcarrier) superimposed on the luminance waveform. Furthermore, in the horizontal blanking interval between the sync pulse and the beginning of the picture information, an additional piece of synchronizing information, consisting of several cycles of the subcarrier frequency, is inserted. That synchronizing information—called the *burst*—is vital for the normal demodulation and decoding of chrominance components. The burst consists of several oscillations of the subcarrier frequency, and the appearance of that short series of oscillations that are "bursting suddenly" is the basis for the name. The decoding circuitry detects the frequency, the amplitude, and the duration of the burst because all these parameters carry pieces of information that are relevant for the operation of the circuits responsible for decoding of chrominance components.

Composite color systems offer a big advantage by squeezing all three pieces of information in one single television channel initially standardized for black-and-white transmissions. It should be stressed that in the 1950s and 1960s that was practically the only available method of "compressing" and "packaging" all necessary color information for the sake of production and transmission of television programs. However, it should be underscored that from the beginning, it was clear that all of these systems had a number of drawbacks.

We have already seen that NTSC suffers from hue errors. In the PAL system the R-Y component is shifted 180° in consecutive lines, and at the same time the phase of the color synchronization signal is changed as well. As a result of these changes introduced in alternate lines, two consecutive PAL frames differ in construction. Thus, the third and fourth frames in a sequence will differ from the first one and only the fifth frame will have a structure identical to the first one. Instead of having a video signal constituted of identically constructed frames, each of them composed by one even and one odd field , there are series of four slightly different frames (or eight slightly different fields) following each other and constituting a sequence known as the *eight-field PAL sequence*. Practically, that means that in editing it is not permitted to take just any PAL frame and attach it to any other PAL frame, or to edit frame by frame. To obtain correct edits it is always necessary to cut from the last frame in one PAL sequence to the first frame in another PAL sequence—that is, it is necessary to observe the eight-field PAL sequence rule.

Another drawback of the PAL system is its difficult decoding process. If the decoding of the PAL composite signal into three components is done once at the end of the chain in the receiver, the quality of decoding is fully satisfactory and the resulting picture is virtually identical to the original. However, if several coding-decoding processes follow each other in a cascade, the impairments will soon become visible and objectionable. Over the years, considerable progress in the construction of decoders has made this problem less critical; nevertheless it could be claimed that achieving a fully transparent* PAL decoding, free of any "PAL footprints," still represents a challenge.

The SECAM system has difficulties with mixing. Namely, it is not possible to cross-fade two composite SECAM signals, or to perform any special effect, without previous decoding of the composite signal. Once the SECAM signal is decoded, the cross-fade or the special effect will be done with the components, and the result will be coded again before the output of the mixer.

Finally all composite systems have a propensity toward a defect known as *high-frequency cross talk*. That problem stems from an interaction between the inserted color information and the upper part of the luminance signal spectrum, and it results in *moiré*, which is a distortion that looks like a flickering fine mesh

---

*In the context of electronic technology, "transparent" means that such a piece of equipment, a signal transmission chain or a processing do not introduce any sort of noticeable degradation, so that the output signal can be considered as being an identical replica of the input one.

superimposed on the reproduced picture and particularly visible on some critical patterns like fine cross-hatching or a common fabric pattern for men's suits known as the "Prince of Wales check."

It is not surprising therefore that composite systems were happily abandoned as soon as it was possible to do so. It happened first in the domain of analog component recording (see Chapter 10) and later in some other pieces of equipment based on the analog component principle. With the advent of digital technology and the adoption of international standards based on digital components, the component approach became universal and permeated the whole television production chain.

4.9 Transcoding and Standards Conversion

Back in the 1960s when Europe planned to introduce color television, a number of international meetings and formal conferences were held in an attempt to select one color system worldwide or at least to introduce in parallel with the NTSC only one additional system. Nevertheless, important national and economic interests were vested in each of the three systems, and, unavoidably, the outcome of that "war of color standards" was a stalemate in which all three color systems had to coexist. North America, Japan, and some other countries opted for NTSC. France, the former Soviet Union, Greece, and the countries of Eastern and Central Europe, together with French-speaking countries in Africa, selected SECAM. The rest of the world embraced PAL. The advent of color brought an added complexity to the world of television: from now on broadcasters had to cope not only with two scanning standards (625/50 and 525/60) but also with three different color-coding schemes.

Such situations had a number of disadvantages: television equipment had to be developed separately for different scanning and color-coding systems, which increased its price and penalized the exchange of programs between different countries since the systems had to cope with different color and scanning standards. To overcome that divide, two technical solutions were developed: transcoding and standards conversion.

Transcoding is the simpler and less critical operation when the scanning parameters are identical but the color-coding methods are different. For example, in Europe, some countries introduced PAL while others opted for SECAM, but all of them had previously adopted the same 625/50 scanning standard. Therefore, in program exchange it was sufficient to use transcoding, that is, to decode one composite color signal, for example PAL, into its Y, R-Y, and B-Y components and then to reencode these components in accordance with the rules of another color system (for example, SECAM). The major problem in transcoding was the decoding process and particularly the PAL decoding, but it was still relatively easy to achieve a fairly transparent transcoding.

Standards conversion is a much more complex operation. Conversion from NTSC to PAL, for example, necessitates changing the color-coding method, the duration, and the number of horizontal lines, as well as the number of fields. We have seen that transcoding is not a particularly complex or delicate operation, but the conversion of line and field rates certainly is. That particular problem existed even before the introduction of different color systems, in the world of black-and-white television. Over the years, a number of different solutions were attempted, but as long as they were based on analog methods and techniques, their results were barely acceptable.

The dramatic breakthrough occurred in the mid-1970s when a development team of the Independent Television Authority labs in the United Kingdom, led by John Baldwin, succeeded in building an all-digital standards converter—the DICE (Digital Intercontinental Conversion Equipment). Once the digital road was open, the standards conversion techniques advanced in giant leaps, reaching a point today where the process represents no operational problem and can be performed almost transparently. The basic principles of the digital techniques used for this purpose will be explained in Chapter 5.

Digital Television

In the 1970s, digital technology in television appeared timidly, almost through the back door, as an already mature technology widely used in different areas of telecommunications and in the computer industry. In fact, one could say that it was an old technology since it is possible to trace the first mention of something resembling a digital approach to the works of the famous English scientist and philosopher Roger Bacon, who lived in the thirteenth century. Six centuries later, English mathematician Charles Babbage developed the necessary mathematical apparatus for this technology, and in 1937 another Englishman, an engineer this time, Alec Reeves, submitted the first patent describing a possible application of PCM (pulse code modulation) in the transmission of speech. Nevertheless, several decades of development of electronic devices and circuitry would have to pass before Reeves's ideas could be implemented.

5.1 What Is a Digital Signal?

What is the meaning of *digital*? What is a digital signal? What is the difference between analog and digital signals? Perhaps the simplest way to answer these questions is to take some examples from our everyday experience. The majority of, if not all, natural phenomena around us are *continuous* phenomena: the outside temperature, the atmospheric pressure, the humidity, and so on; all these environmental conditions are permanently present, and they all change over time and in a continuous manner. There is no discontinuity between one state or level and another; there is no quantum step between two values but always a continuous—faster or slower—transition.

All electronic devices used for the measurement of these environmental conditions generate continuously variable electronic signals that represent the measured physical phenomenon. Such signals, in a way, are analogous to the

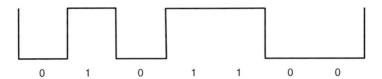

Figure 5.1   A digital signal.

physical phenomenon: the higher the temperature, the higher the amplitude of the generated signal will be; the faster the change of temperature, the steeper the curve of the electronic signal representing it will become. These electronic devices also generate signals whose shape is analogous to the shape of change of the physical phenomena—the outside temperature, audible sounds (microphones), or light reflected from some objects (camera)—and such signals are therefore called *analog*. Furthermore, all electronic devices generating or accepting such signals at their input or processing and delivering them at their output are called *analog devices*. Until recently the whole world of electronic media was analog. The totality of the broadcasting equipment, from the microphone and the camera on the scene, through the processing, recording, and transmitting devices, to the consumer's receiver—all of the chain and its links, were analog.

A *digital signal* is constituted by a series of *discrete* values, separate pulses that are, in fact, a series of two discrete statuses—the presence or absence of a pulse (see Figure 5.1). By an accepted convention, the presence of a pulse is marked by "1" and its absence by a "0." Such marking is known as a *binary* marking—a marking with only two values—two binary digits or *bits*. The amplitude and the duration of the pulses in a pulse stream are identical, but their absolute value is irrelevant for their interpretation; it is their sequence that is relevant. In other words, there is no analogy between a phenomenon and the digital signal that represents it. A digital signal can be considered a mathematical interpretation of the physical phenomenon.

In our everyday experience we express certain continuous physical values as multiples of single arbitrarily agreed-upon units or discrete values. For example, when we state that a solid object weighs "32 kilograms," we in fact state that its weight is represented by 32 agreed-upon measurement units of 1 kg each. Although it seems possible to transform continuous analog electric signals into discrete digital ones in a similar way, such transformation is much more complex than the simple process of multiplication. To be transformed into a stream of digital pulses, an analog signal must pass through the process of *analog-to-digital (A/D) conversion*.

On the other hand, our senses can accept and interpret only analog phenomena (such as sound and light) because our eyes and ears are analog sensors; so all the display (audio or video) engines are analog. Therefore, at the end of the chain, at the input of screens and loudspeakers, digital signals representing light (video) and sound (audio) have to be returned to their analog form—they have to pass through a *digital-to-analog (D/A) conversion*. All these A/D and D/A processes have to be as transparent as possible in order to ensure a faithful reproduction at the end of the chain of the sounds and sights that were really present in front of the cameras and microphones.

5.2 Analog-to-Digital Conversion

The A/D conversion process consists of three steps:

1. sampling
2. quantizing
3. coding

The *sampling* process means the taking of a number of sample values at evenly spaced intervals across a continuous signal. As shown in Figure 5.2, a higher-repetition frequency of the sample-taking process will result in better assessment and, later, representation of that signal. To sample analog electric signals that change over time means to take as many samples in a unit of time as is workable. An insufficient number of samples leads to an inadequate assessment and possible misinterpretation of the original form of the sampled signal, but too many samples can lead to an unnecessary accumulation of redundant data, thus wasting time and resources. For example, measuring the outside temperature two times a day, for example, at 8:00 a.m. and 8:00 p.m. and obtaining identical values in each sample could lead to an erroneous conclusion that the temperature was constant for 24 hours while in reality it was probably higher at noon and lower

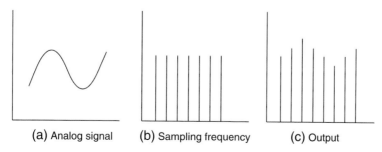

(a) Analog signal   (b) Sampling frequency   (c) Output

Figure 5.2 Sampling.

during the night. The insufficient number of sample values results in the wrong assessment of the measured phenomena. On the other hand, if measurements are taken every 10 seconds, they will provide 8,640 values for one day, of which a good deal will be redundant as it takes longer that 10 seconds for there to be a noticeable change in the outside temperature. *Subsampling* leads to an erroneous interpretation of the observed phenomena, while *oversampling* results in a waste of time and resources and a lot of largely redundant data.

Neglecting the frequency at which a sampled signal changes over time and subsampling it could result in the appearance of undesired artifacts known as *aliasing effects*. The most obvious example of an aliasing effect is the impression one has in Western movies that stagecoach wheels rotate backwards. The technique of motion reproduction in movie-making is based on a temporal sampling of the action that takes place in front of the lens. The action is sampled with a frequency of 24 pictures per second, which is far below the rotational frequency of the wheels. Consequently, such a subsampling produces a visible aliasing effect of backward rotation of the wheels. Namely, between two samples (two frames) the wheels have achieved more than one full revolution and the second sample (frame) appears to show the wheel in a position that precedes the one captured in the first frame.

It is therefore necessary to define the optimum number of samples, or the optimum value for the sampling frequency, that would permit a good assessment of the sampled signal and, at the same time, avoid the accumulation of redundant data. That optimum value is defined by the theorem of the Swedish mathematician Nyquist, which could be summarized as: "The sampling frequency should be at least two times higher than the highest frequency of the sampled signal." So, for example, if the observed phenomenon changes 10 times during a given time interval, we should sample it at least 20 times during that same time interval. That value of sampling frequency is frequently called the *Nyquist limit*, the *Nyquist criterion*, or the *Nyquist frequency*.

Figure 5.2a represents an analog signal. The sampling of that signal with a selected sampling frequency (Figure 5.2b) will result in a number of discrete samples or pulses, which have the chosen repetition rate (equal to the sampling frequency) and whose amplitudes correspond to the values of the amplitude of the sampled analog signal at the point of its intersection with the sampling frequency (Figure 5.2c). As stated previously, the precision of that first step in the digitization process depends on the selected sampling frequency. To ensure an optimum interpretation of the sampled signal, it is recommended to select a sampling frequency that is at least 20% higher than the theoretical minimum set by the Nyquist theorem. The highest frequency of a video signal is usually 5 MHz, which means that the sampling frequency for video signals must be higher than 10 MHz.

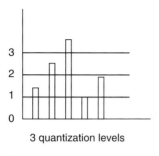 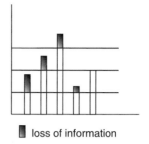

3 quantization levels   loss of information

Figure 5.3 Quantizing.

Quantizing is the next step of the digitization process. In a way, it is a similar process to sampling as it consists of interpreting the value of the amplitude of each sample with a set of predetermined equidistant steps. As can be seen in Figure 5.3, the amplitude of each sample is approximated to the nearest predetermined level, so that any value that is higher than the previous predetermined level and lower than the next one will be disregarded as nonexistent. Therefore, it could be stated that an insufficient number of selected levels (only four in the illustrated example—from 0 to 3) unavoidably results in a considerable loss of valuable information or, in other words, in a misinterpretation of the real value of the quantized amplitudes. Also as with sampling, more levels will result in more data to handle, and for each application there is a limit to how much is technically and economically viable. The number of levels is determined by the nature of the sampled signal, the acuity of our senses, and the desired or needed level of transparency of the coupled A/D and D/A conversions.

In the third step, *coding*, each of the amplitude levels that coincides with the predetermined quantizing steps or levels will be represented with a given symbol composed of a set of binary values of 1 and 0 (bits), values that correspond to the two states of the constant amplitude pulse stream—the presence or absence of a pulse. Such a set of bits used for the description of amplitude levels is called a *binary group* or *binary word*.

The example in Figure 5.3 shows four predetermined levels. These four levels can be described with different combinations (or sets) of only two bits:

Level 0   00
Level 1   01
Level 2   10
Level 3   11

This example shows that with two given binary values (0 and 1) and with two bits, it is possible to achieve four combinations, that is, to describe only four levels (or, expressed mathematically, $2^2 = 4$ combinations), which is adequate for our simplified explanation but not for coding complex signals. But from this simple case it is possible to draw a general rule that the number of levels that can be unequivocally described by different combinations of the bits constituting the selected binary could be expressed as 2 to the power of n, where n is the selected number of bits.

It is clear that the complexity of the video signal will require more than four levels for an adequate digital description of the analog signal. Theoretically there is no limit to the number of quantization levels that can be used, although more levels means more bits needed to describe them resulting in a higher overall bit rate to be handled. The higher the bit rate to be handled, the larger the necessary bandwidth of the transmission channel and the higher the complexity and cost of the equipment needed to handle such digital signals. Therefore, the exact definition of the number of quantization levels needed for an acceptable description of a video signal has to take into account the criteria of the acuity of human senses, the required transparency of the A/D and D/A processes, and the always-present need to keep the bit rate at an acceptable level. After long studies and debates, eight-bit binary words were adopted as an optimum solution for video signals, allowing thus the description of 2^8, or 256 predetermined levels.

The situation in the audio domain is slightly different. The highest sound frequency is considerably lower than the upper video frequency and is usually set at 20 or 22 kHz. On the other hand, the character of the sound signal and the psychophysical characteristics of the ear-brain combination require a considerably finer definition, thus a much larger number of quantizing levels. In view of that, it has been agreed to adopt 16 to 20 bits per sample for the definition of digital audio signals.

As mentioned above, in the digital domain the complexity of the necessary equipment and the required channel bandwidth are determined by the *bit rate*, or the quantity of bits per second that have to be transported or handled. That value can be simply obtained by multiplying the chosen sampling frequency, expressed in hertz, by the selected number of bits per sample.

Summing up, the result of an analog-to-digital conversion of a given analog signal, achieved in three steps (sampling, quantizing, and coding), is a stream of constant amplitude pulses of a given repetition rate that can be considered to be a mathematical description of the original signal. The quality and precision of that "description" will determine how faithful to the original analog signal will be the signal obtained at the end of the line through an inverse process of digital-to-analog conversion. It is clear that in broadcasting the parameters selected for the A/D conversion have to ensure a maximum transparency between the original analog signal and the analog signal at the output of the D/A converter that is at the end of the chain.

5.3 Why a Digital Signal?

The digitization process is not an easy, simple, or straightforward one. It requires complex circuitry and delicate operational methods, and it carries the danger of distortions, aliasing, and deterioration of the reconstructed analog signal. Furthermore, at the end of a digital chain it is necessary to revert to the analog form of the signal. Therefore it is legitimate to ask, "Why bother? Why digitize at all?"

The passage to digital, the *digitization*, is motivated and justified by a number of advantages. In the first place, digital signals are, by definition, considerably more robust and immune to distortions and degradations than analog signals. All analog signals, passing through a piece of equipment—a recording, processing, or distribution device—suffer from a number of unavoidable degradations. The severity and visibility of such degradations depend on the quality of the device, the precision of its alignments, the complexity of the internal processing, and so on. But even in an ideal case of a nearly perfect piece of equipment, some degradations will be introduced. These degradations take different forms—from an omnipresent increase of noise and subsequent degradation of the *signal-to-noise ratio* to different distortions of the signal waveform.

The signal-to-noise ratio is an essential parameter in both the objective and subjective evaluations of the signal quality. Namely, every electronic component generates a certain quantity of chaotic, uncontrolled and unwanted electron movements, which are not part of the useful signal and are therefore considered as noise. In the case of video signals, noise is visible in the form of small picture-unrelated points that randomly move across the screen and are commonly called "snow" due to their resemblance to snow flakes. Once generated the noise will accompany the signal throughout its path. All elements on that path will add their own noise and every time the signal is amplified the noise is amplified as well. In order to assess the potential nuisance that will be produced by the noise, we do not measure the absolute level of noise, but only the ratio between the peak-to-peak value of the signal and the mean value of the noise, expressed as a logarithmic computation. The measurement unit for that ratio is the *decibel*, or dB. Such an approach is justified by our subjective perception of the level of nuisance caused by the noise. If the noise level is low when compared to the level of the useful signal the ensuing signal-to-noise ratio will have a higher value, meaning that the noise is subjectively less perceptible.

A picture or sound signal transits from its source to the display through a number of electronic devices, and degradations accumulate. Since there are only limited ways in the analog domain to repair degradations that have already occurred, these accumulated degradations will be visible (or audible) at the output of the chain in the form of noise, distortions, loss of resolution, multiplication of the edges of reproduced objects ("ghosts"), and so on.

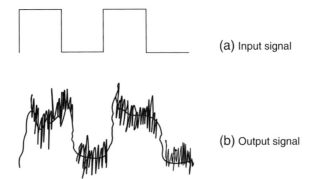

(a) Input signal

(b) Output signal

Figure 5.4   Signal degradation.

Figure 5.4 represents an exaggerated result of the transition of a pulse signal through a set of electronic devices. The waveform is distorted, and some random noise is added to the signal. All those degradations would be visible in the case of an analog signal as a noisy picture without crisp transitions, with some ghosts, and so on. But if this pulse train represents a digital signal, all these distortions will be irrelevant for the signal reconstruction. In the case of a digital signal, the exact shape of the received signal is irrelevant, as it is not the *shape* of the pulses that carries the information but the absence or presence of the pulses. Therefore, as long as the shape of the signal permits detection of whether or not a pulse is present, the reconstruction of the signal will be nearly perfect. The reception of a digital signal becomes endangered only when it becomes difficult or impossible to distinguish between a pulse and the absence of a pulse. Thus it is legitimate to claim that digital signals are considerably more robust than their analog counterparts because they can transit virtually unscathed through long and complex chains, they better support adverse conditions that can exist along these chains, and they are less sensitive to the accumulation of noise. In practical terms it means that a digital television production chain, comprising a number of cascaded (aligned one after the other) recording, reproducing, special effects, editing, and distributing processes can be virtually transparent, delivering at its output a signal that will have no visible distortions, no more noise than the input one—in short, to be its absolutely faithful replica.

Another important advantage of the digital principle lies in the digitization process itself. A digitized picture is not a whole, that is, a continuous stream of continuously changing information; it is a string of discrete values representing minute portions of the digitized picture, of picture elements called *pixels*. Each pixel is unequivocally described by its horizontal and vertical coordinates at a given moment in time, as well as with the values of its luminance and color content. In standard-definition television, one 625/50 picture is constituted by 720 × 576 pixels (720 × 486 for 525/60 pictures). The continuous stream is transformed into a set of clearly distinguishable discrete values that can be individually generated, accessed, processed, and manipulated. Such a signal representation has facilitated the development and construction of a rich panoply of processing and special effects tools that were once hardly imaginable and even more difficult to realize in the analog age and domain. Huge new vistas of artistic creativity have been opened.

5.4 Digital Standards Conversion

A good example of the capabilities of digital technologies is the standards conversion. As explained in Chapter 4, in spite of all endeavors it was not possible to achieve satisfactory analog standards conversion. The goal seemed suddenly near at hand when the first all-digital standards converter appeared on the market. And, in fact, very soon after a series of improvements, broadcasters had in their hands excellent, practical, and affordable digital standards converters.

Converting from one scanning standard to another, from 525 to 625, or from the standard definition to high definition, is a very complex operation requiring changes in the following:

- **line length** (for example the line duration in the 525 standard is 52.86 μs while in the 625 standard that duration is 52 μs only)
- **number of lines** (including their repositioning since the lines in two scanning systems have different geometrical positions on the screen)
- **number of fields** (a given number of fields means also a given temporal sampling, that is, the movement of an object in front of the camera will be portrayed with 50 pictures per second in one case and 60 pictures per second in the other)

Consequently, it is not possible to just "drop lines" and simply repeat twice some of the fields when passing from 625 to 525, or to "drop fields" and repeat some of the lines when going in the opposite direction. Such procedures would result in unacceptable picture degradations. The digital standards conversion is based on the application of a technique called *interpolation*—the computing of the position and "importance" of each pixel from a number of samples taken in its vicinity and then the re-creation of a new set of pixels whose geometrical position and number will correspond to the requirements of the selected output standard.

The simplest part of the standards conversion process is the change in line length, the *horizontal conversion*. The physical length of one line depends on the width of a screen, but in two scanning standards, the duration of that line is different, or, in digital terms, the number of active pixels in 625/50 and 525/60 standards is different. Therefore the horizontal conversion consists of taking the active pixels from a line in one standard, computing from them a new set of pixels corresponding to the other standard, and interpolating these pixels in the correct positions. For example, when converting from 625/50 to 525/60, 714 active pixels from a 625 line will be used for the computation of the 702 pixels of a 525 line.

The change of the number of lines (the *vertical conversion*) is more complex. It is not only necessary to deal with a considerably larger amount of data to be processed in order to achieve a good interpolation, but it is also necessary to take into account that all present-day standards are interlaced. Consequently the interpolation cannot involve all of the available data inside one field and change the number of lines in that field since they represent only one half of the total vertical information. Therefore, to achieve an excellent vertical conversion, it is necessary first to use sophisticated methods to deinterlace the frame and then to compute the lines on the basis of data from three consecutive fields. Such conversion does not require a large amount of memory and can be made virtually transparent.

The conversion of picture rates is the most delicate problem. Not only are the number of fields different, but this conversion is also correlated to the sampling of movement. In a 625/50 standard, each movement is sampled at the rate of 50 Hz, that is, decomposed into 50 static pictures each second, while in the 525/60 standard, the same movement is decomposed into 60 static pictures. Therefore, when converting from one standard to the other, it is necessary to take care not only of the number of fields, as such, but also of the preservation of the quality and smoothness of the movement rendition. For that reason this part of the conversion process is called *temporal conversion* since it consists of converting from one temporal movement representation to another.

The simplest and the crudest way to make such a conversion would be to simply drop every sixth field when converting from 60 to 50 fields or to repeat every fifth field when converting in the opposite direction. However, the lack of one phase or the repetition of one phase of the decomposed movement would create a defect; either would appear as repeated jumps in movement rendition. A better solution would be to generate a new field that has to be added in the 50 to 60 conversion on the basis of the data collected from several fields. This method eliminates the jumps but still does not insure a smooth movement rendering. In the case of a moving object in a shot or of a camera movement, the data collected from several fields will also register the object or the background in different positions. The resulting picture will display a lack of movement smoothness, something like a hesitation or a trembling of the edges, called *judder*.

The best results are obtained with systems that estimate the motion contained in the frame and take that parameter into account when performing temporal interpolation. Such converters offer the best judder-free and high-resolution pictures. In its simplest form, the motion estimation consists in evaluating the position of a moving object in two consecutive fields (A and B) and assessing the most probable characteristics of the movement that brings the object from position A to position B. Once these *motion vectors* showing movement characteristics are detected (direction of movement, speed, etc.), a new field is interpolated between these two analyzed fields. The position of the moving object in this new field is computed on the basis of data offered by motion vectors extracted from the previous and the following fields. Considering that in a given shot a number of objects can move in different directions, one set of motion vectors cannot describe all these movements. Therefore the picture area is subdivided in several sections, and in each section a separate set of motion vectors is detected. The larger the number of sections, the better the movement rendition but also the greater the complexity of the standards converter.

5.5 The International Digitization Standard

The first digital pieces of equipment to enter the television production market were "black boxes" with analog inputs and outputs, meant to accomplish some specific tasks requiring internal processing that could be performed only with digital signals. Since digital signals were confined inside the walls of a black box and all the interfaces were analog, manufacturers freely selected digitization parameters, setting their own proprietary standards and even introducing a new set of digitization parameters with each new model. However, it soon became obvious that the generalization of the digital principle could bring very important benefits to broadcasting production and distribution technology. Consequently, with the advancement of technology, the number and diversity of digital engines on the market increased and more digital elements were integrated into an all-analog environment. Professionals used to call them "digital islands," adding that they were surrounded by an "analog sea."

Due to the lack of digital standardization, the only way to establish a chain of interconnected digital units was to use analog interfaces. It was necessary to perform a D/A conversion at the output of each unit and reconvert to digital at the input of the next piece of equipment. Such a cascading of D/A and A/D conversions was a serious threat to the signal quality. Therefore, digital signals were not any more exclusively part of the internal processing of a relatively modest number of single pieces of equipment, became, or aimed to become, the general operating principle of the whole production chain. But the prerequisite for the design and operation of an all-digital production chain was the establishment of a single set of essential characteristics of digital interface signals—in other words, the adoption of internationally agreed-upon standards. By the end of the 1970s, the time was ripe to initiate a process of international standardization.

The digital future seemed very promising, and a number of manufacturers, research institutes, and broadcasting organizations allocated their best human resources to the task of optimizing and standardizing the digitization parameters. Two engineering bodies were particularly active in this field—the European Broadcasting Union (EBU) and the Society of Motion Picture and Television Engineers (SMPTE). Conducting parallel research and discussions on the two sides of the ocean, these two organizations soon established a permanent liaison and a joint task force.

The first step along the standardization path was to agree which video signals to digitize—the composite (PAL, SECAM or NTSC signals) or component ones (Y, R-Y and B-Y). At that time in the late 1970s, all the shortcomings and limitations of composite signals were well known. On the other hand, the available technology had allowed the design and manufacture of equipment and systems that recorded, processed, and handled color video signals in their analog component form. That approach offered a number of advantages (especially in the domain of magnetic videotape recording). Working with component signals meant:

- circumventing all unavoidable distortions generated by the color-coding process.
- facilitating the introduction of new recording methods.
- enhancing the gamut of signal manipulations and special effects.
- extending the opportunities for downstream processing.
- reducing the differences between the existing color standards to the single difference of scanning parameters.

All these advantages led the broadcasting industry to agree that the only "future proof" approach (i.e. an approach that can stand the test of time) would be to digitize component signals. In the 1970s such a decision had a price tag attached—digitizing component signals meant obtaining considerably higher bit rates that were more difficult to handle, with corresponding equipment that was harder to develop and more expensive to manufacture.

The next step was the definition of basic digitization parameters: the sampling frequency and the number of quantization levels (number of bits per sample). At that time the developers had quite a modest number of initial input parameters:

- the Nyquist criterion and its empirical extension, stating that the sampling frequency had to be somewhat higher than the Nyquist limit

- the theoretical assumption that a higher sampling frequency and a higher number of bits per sample meant a better and finer definition of the signal
- a practical certitude that a higher bit rate required a wider bandwidth and meant more complex and expensive recording and processing equipment
- good engineering practices, which implied that the selected digitization parameters must be cost-effective by offering an optimum balance between the signal quality and the importance of the bit rate to be handled

Such a meager input could generate a huge number of different values of the basic digitization parameters and consequently initiate endless theoretical discussions. To prevent such a situation, and to remain faithful to good engineering principles, both groups started by defining a kind of test bed against which all proposals had to be measured. After a detailed investigation, a theoretical standard production chain was adopted. In fact it was a cascade of different pieces of equipment, which generated, processed, manipulated, recorded, dubbed, and reproduced the program signal. This chain was meant to faithfully replicate an average real-world production and postproduction facility. A combination of the commercially available and purposely built experimental digital equipment was assembled and used in different laboratories to demonstrate the span of processing operations that could be performed almost transparently with digital signals issued from different sets of basic digitization parameters. The criticality of different pieces of equipment or processing methods was assessed in the process, and it was discovered, for example, that among those test operations, chroma keying* was the most critical one. It was also recognized that such a chain was incomplete since one of its most important components—the digital videotape recorder, believed to be the cornerstone of a future all-digital studio—was missing. The EBU and the SMPTE were already working on the development and standardization of a professional digital videotape recorder, but its completion would take several more years.

The next step on the road toward an international standard was the definition of the relationship between the sampling frequency for luminance and the one used for the digitization of the color difference signals: the sampling frequency for color difference signals was to be two times lower than the one used for the luminance signal. This decision was based on knowing that color difference signals have, by definition, a narrower bandwidth than the luminance signal

---

*Chroma keying, or chroma key effect, consists of positioning a subject or an object that has to be in the foreground in front of a monochromatic background, usually blue or green, and then with the help of a special piece of equipment—*chroma keyer*—replacing that monochromatic background by a still or moving picture from another picture source.

and that the human visual system is less sensitive to color than to brightness differences in the area of small details.

At that stage of the standardization process it became apparent that different digitization parameters for different television applications would be useful. That finding led to the definition of the international digitization standard as a *family of standards* consisting of three tiers, where the central tier was intended for all mainstream television applications. Fully defined, that particular level featured a 4:2:2 ratio between selected sampling frequencies for the luminance and the two color difference signals. The upper tier was just barely sketched out as the one in which all three components would be sampled with the same frequency (4:4:4) and where it would be possible to use a higher number of quantization levels, all of which could be necessary for some special processing procedures requiring the highest possible signal quality. The lower tier was only hinted at. Even the relationship of the sampling frequencies for that member of the family was ambiguously defined. Two possible approaches to defining the relationship of the sampling frequencies were investigated. One advocated a further lowering of the sampling frequency for color difference signals (4:1:1), and the other proposed to keep the same sampling frequency for the color difference signals but to include a sequential approach where the luminance signal would be digitized in each line and the color difference signals in alternate lines (4:2:0). It is interesting to note that this "neglected" lowest member of the digital family became very important in the design and construction of consumer and electronic news-gathering (ENG) digital camcorders, as well as in the development of digital bit-rate reduction methods.

The skeleton of the future standard was therefore in place. The next parameter—the number of quantization levels for the 4:2:2 (middle-tiered) member of the family—was defined rather easily, although some manufacturers complained that the selected 256 levels (or 8 bits per sample) were not enough for some critical television-processing operations.

The most contentious issue was the selection of the luminance sampling frequency. A lot of time was spent and a number of arguments exchanged before a consensus was reached. At that time European experts were favoring 12 MHz for the luminance signal, while their U.S. counterparts preferred 14 MHz (which for them had an additional advantage of being very near to 14.31818 MHz, representing four times the NTSC subcarrier used for the digitization of composite NTSC signals). After a long and fierce debate, the joint EBU/SMPTE Task Force recommended the adoption of a single set of sampling frequencies—13.5 MHz for luminance and 6.75 MHz for each of the two color difference signals. A close look at that set of adopted figures (and their subsequent fate) clearly shows that they are the result of a serious study. The goal was to define a single set of parameters for both 625 and 525 television systems and to preserve at the same time in both cases the *orthogonal* sampling structure, that is, a structure in which samples

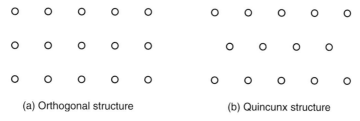

(a) Orthogonal structure   (b) Quincunx structure

Figure 5.5   Sampling structures: a) orthogonal; b) quincunx.

have identical positions in individual lines and can be represented as aligned in vertical columns, perpendicular to the horizontal rows. Another sampling structure, called *quincunx*, is one in which samples are disposed like the black fields of a chess board (see Figure 5.5). An orthogonal sampling structure can be achieved only if the sampling frequency is an integer multiple of the horizontal scanning frequency, and 13.5 MHz is the only value between 12 and 14 MHz which represents a full multiple of both 625 and 525 line frequencies. The selected set of values was clearly a very wise compromise.

The EBU and SMPTE agreement meant that the international digital standard, common to both the 625/50 and 525/60 (525/59.94) worlds, was in place. The subsequent codification of those same parameters in 1982/1983 by the International Radio Consultative Committee (CCIR) as its Recommendation 601* transformed that agreement into a worldwide standard.

The essential parameters of the 4:2:2 level of the worldwide digital-coding standard as agreed to by the EBU and the SMPTE and defined by Recommendation 601, are as follows:

- **coded signals**: luminance (Y) and the two color difference signals (C_r and C_b)
- **sampling frequencies**: 13.5 MHz; 6.75 MHz, and 6.75 MHz. respectively
- **number of samples per digital line**: 720 for luminance and 360 for each of the color difference signals
- **number of bits per sample**: 8
- **overall bit rate**: 216 Mbps (megabits per second) {(13.5 MHz × 8) + (6.75 MHz × 8) + (6.75 MHz × 8)}

It is important to note that the pixel structure of computer displays is somewhat different from the one defined by Recommendation 601. Not only are the number of samples per line and the number of lines and frames different, but also

---

*CCIR – Comité Consultatif International en Radiocommunications (International Radio Consultative Committee) a body of the International Telecommunication Union (ITU), now re-formed and renamed ITU-R.

the sampling grid, which in the computer industry follows strictly the 4:3 aspect ratio of the screen (800:600 as 4:3). Practically, that means that all pixels are not only orthogonal, but also equidistant in both vertical and horizontal directions. Such an arrangement is called *square pixels*. The A/D conversion in accordance with Recommendation 601 creates an orthogonal disposition of pixels but not square pixels, since the number of pixels per line is the result of the selected sampling frequency and the number of lines was inherited from the existing scanning standards. Therefore, to be used for television, graphics prepared on PC-based workstations have to be converted from square pixels to the 601 sampling grid using data interpolation methods similar to the ones described in Section 5.4, "Digital Standards Conversion."

5.6 Convergence

With the adoption of digital techniques, the television industry not only added a number of highly valuable tools to its panoply, it also changed its fundamentals. Television was converted from specific and complex analog signals to digital ones, identical to those already used in the computer and telecommunications industries.

Indeed, regardless of what they represent—static or moving pictures, sounds, a bank account, or any other set of data—all digital signals are identical and can be handled by the same sort of equipment, the only difference being the overall bit rate, which has to be addressed in each case. Almost from its beginning, computing technology has been based on digital signals and techniques. Although the first registered patent in the digital domain was meant for telecommunications, that field adopted digital technologies somewhat later than the computer industry. Finally, with the adoption of Recommendation 601, the digitization of television progressed at a very fast pace. This brought three industries much closer together and led to one of the most important events in present-day electronics—the convergence of television, telecom, and computer technologies into one complex entity known today as *communication and information technologies.*

Convergence means that the same techniques can be used in different areas, the same transport channels can carry any sort of content, and a large number of requirements can be answered by software rather than by the development of specialized hardware. Obviously, as long as all these systems are meant to be used by human beings, the system inputs and outputs must remain different from one another as well as analog (since our eyes and ears are analog sensors and cannot decode digital signals directly). Digital signals have to be converted into analog ones that then drive analog display devices performing the electro-optic and the electro-acoustical conversions.

The convergence process is underway, progressing very rapidly, and its initial stages and the initial hype are behind us. A number of benefits of convergence can now be exploited, but the process has not yet reached the point when, for any application in television or telecom, it suffices to take an off-the-shelf computer and add the appropriate software. There are still a number of requirements in the domain of the processing speed, bit rates and handling, storage capacity, reaction time, and human-machine interfaces, which make it difficult to use standard computer units and require the use of specialized or even specially designed hardware. On the other hand, software is continuously being improved and revised. Often the software gets to be so bloated that it exhausts the capacity of the original hardware, requiring hardware upgrades or replacement (processing speed, storage capacity, etc.) just to keep up.

Despite software problems, computer-based techniques "invaded" television production technology, and standard telecom lines and techniques are increasingly used for the transport of television programs and program materials. Nonlinear editing systems, large central storage systems, graphics engines, video and audio special effects, picture and sound restoration, and regeneration systems and methods—all these highly valuable tools are based on processing techniques developed in the computer industry. The digital telecommunication lines also made possible the so-called "networked production"—a completely new organization of the television production process.

However, the digital transition is far from complete. In the domain of television transmission, all the necessary digital standards have been developed and adopted. But the transition is slow in view of important investments both on the side of program providers and network operators and on the side of consumers who have to acquire new receivers, and even more because of the inertia created by the enormous installed base of analog television sets. In the area of television program production, a respectable number of pieces of analog equipment and even analog production complexes are still operating around the world. At the same time, it is important to stress once more that at the input of the system and at its output there still have to be analog video and audio signals. Consequently, since everything starts with an A/D and ends with a D/A conversion, a good understanding of analog techniques is a must for all those who take part in the television program production process.

6

Digital Compression as the Key to Success

The adoption of Recommendation 601 represented the turning point in the development of digital television. A unique worldwide digitization standard boosted the development of new digital equipment that featured digital inputs and outputs and was ready for integration in all-digital subsystems and systems. The "4:2:2" label became extremely popular and adorned front panels of ever more engines. EBU and SMPTE successfully finalized another key development: the definition of the first worldwide digital videotape recording standard, D1. It seemed that all necessary components were in place for a fast transition to an all-digital future. Yet the transition lagged and the broadcasting market witnessed an avalanche of extremely capable and successful new analog equipment.

6.1 Why Compression?

Some tried to explain that paradoxical onslaught of analog equipment as a rear-guard battle of the analog principle, comparing it to the known fact that the most dramatic improvements in sailing-ship technology occurred in the two decades that followed the appearance of the first steam ships. The main reason was probably the digital component signal itself. With its 216 Mbps, it offered perfect quality. If cascaded D/A and A/D conversions were avoided, that quality could be kept almost intact, regardless of the length and complexity of the production chain and of its different processes. D1 recorders offered an almost unlimited number of transparent generations. However, 216 Mbps is a huge bit rate. It requires almost ten times more bandwidth than composite PAL signals. That fact is particularly critical for transmission but also for the area of magnetic recording where 601-compliant recorders had to be quite complex and very expensive. On the other hand, although it was clear that the digital principle could bring large benefits to the consumer electronics market, nobody even tried to develop camcorders or VCRs operating at 216 Mbps that could be mass-produced and sold at affordable prices.

Obviously it was necessary to find a solution that would reduce such a huge bit rate but leave the quality of the video signal untouched. The overall bit rate is the product of the selected sampling frequency and the number of bits per sample. To reduce the sampling frequency would be to contravene the Nyquist criterion, thereby generating unacceptable aliasing effects. The reduction of the number of bits per sample would produce a much coarser definition of the sampled signal leading to a serious increase of quantization noise and deterioration of picture quality. The only element that remained to be explored was to find some redundancy inside the video signal itself and develop methods for its detection, rejection, and subsequent reconstruction. Bit-rate reduction methods existed already at the time of adoption of Recommendation 601, but they were considered to be inadequate for professional broadcasting applications. It was felt that in the production domain only, uncompressed 601 signals ensured the required broadcast quality.

As with many other technical developments, the advance in compression techniques required almost simultaneous breakthroughs in several areas of communications technology. Three key activities led to the creation of the necessary synergy that opened the way to the definition of efficient and viable compression methods:

- Studies of digital video images showed that they contained a large amount of redundancy and that in the digital domain it should be possible to represent acceptable moving images with a considerably lower bit rate.
- Developments aimed at achieving an all digital HDTV standard for the United States produced complex processing and modulation schemes for the transmission of high-definition signals in narrow conventional television channels. This proved to be beneficial to the development of compression methods for standard definition applications.
- Important advances were made in design and mass-production of powerful digital signal-processing chips.

These and a number of other developments paved the way for the establishment of digital compression that profoundly influenced a number of sectors of the audiovisual industry:

- They made possible the design and construction of practical professional digital camcorders and other high-quality professional production tools.
- They prompted a much more dynamic introduction of computer-based solutions in the video production area.

- They opened the way to fast development of digital television broadcasting standards.
- They were prerequisites for the mass-production of a highly successful series of consumer equipment.
- Finally, without compression, high-definition television (HDTV) would be practically impossible or at least nonviable. The huge bit rates, on the order of 1 gigabit per second (Gbps), cannot be handled easily in production. Even by using a number of clever technical tricks, the transmission of HDTV signals would require use of at least two channels for the transmission of a single program. That is why HD-program production equipment and early HD broadcasts only became truly possible when digital compression left the labs and became an everyday tool.

6.2   Compression Methods and Tools

Digital compression (bit-rate reduction) methods are based on the removal of fully redundant data from video or audio signals, as well as on the elimination of data whose absence will be practically unnoticeable. The net result of these processes is a dramatic reduction of the bit rate and, at the same time, the preservation of an acceptable picture quality (for example, with 2–50 times lower bit rates than the standard 216 Mbps, video signals can still be used for broadcast purposes). It is a clever and intricate process relying heavily on complex algorithms (mathematical transformations) and mathematically computed predictions.

The compression in fact rejects information

- that could be easily reconstructed;
- that is considered nonessential;
- the absence of which will not be noticed by our eyes or ears.

In that respect, compression is not only a generic attribute of digital television since it existed in analog television as well. The interlace principle in itself represents a 2:1 compression since a progressive scanning would require a bandwidth twice as large. The color-coding standards are also a sort of compression because they permit two additional color difference signals to squeeze into the channel designed and of the dimensions for the transmission of a single luminance (black-and-white) signal.

The digital domain, however, offers considerably more opportunities for compression or bit-rate reduction. Compression methods can be divided into two general groups:

1. *lossless compression* – the rejected redundancy is fully recoverable at the moment of decompression.
2. *lossy compression* – this is nonreversible and causes definitive loss of some picture information. However, thanks to the psychophysical characteristics of human vision and its limitations, even a lossy compression can produce video signals whose quality is subjectively assessed as acceptable; in some instances, depending on the compression ratio and on the content of the compressed pictures, that quality can even be very good.

The goal of all compression methods is to achieve a maximum compression efficiency that represents the relationship between the bit rate and the picture quality at the end of the decoding process. *Higher efficiency* could mean better picture quality at a given bit rate or it could mean that a lower bit rate will ensure a given picture quality.

Every signal (or, more precisely, every piece of information) has two parts (see Figure 6.1):

- *entropy* – a part that is unpredictable and that must be kept at all times as complete as possible;

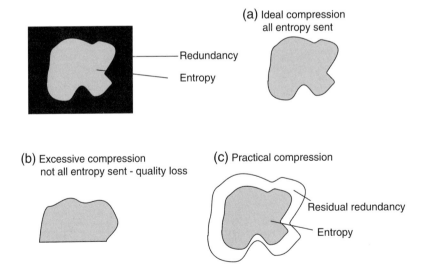

Figure 6.1 The principle of compression (a. Ideal compression, b. Excessive compression, c. Practical compression)

- *redundancy* – a part that has a very high degree of repetitiveness or is highly predictable and can be easily reconstructed from a simple initial indication.

All compression methods function by rejecting as much redundancy as possible while preserving the entropy untouched. In Figure 6.1, entropy and redundancy are represented as two coherent fields for the sake of simplicity, while in the real world, entropy and redundant information are scattered all over the picture area.

Ideally, a perfect compression process would reject all redundancy and retain only the entropy (Figure 6-1a), but such compressors would be very complex and costly. Consequently, the practical ones fully preserve the entropy but also some residual redundancy (Figure 6-1c). Keeping and carrying a part of the redundancy burdens the system with a larger bit rate than absolutely necessary, but such a construction of compressors acts as a security device preventing an accidental rejection of a part of the entropy. If a part of the entropy is lost, visible impairment may appear in the decompressed picture. However, in some applications where the paramount requirement is not the absolute signal quality but rather the economics of the system, higher degrees of compression are used, creating highly visible impairments of the decompressed picture (although those impairments are considered acceptable for these specific applications, for example, video telephony).

In the domain of video signals we can identify three distinct types of redundancy.

1. *Spatial redundancy* is the redundant information inside one single picture or frame. For example, the repetition of the same color information in the case of a large and uniform field of one color, such as a large area of sky or a grassy field. Instead of transmitting all 720 pixels of one television line, only the first pixel is encoded along with that piece of information indicating the number of times the same content has to be repeated along that line. The spatial compression is also described as *intraframe compression* since the totality of the removable redundancy is located inside one single television frame.

2. *Temporal redundancy* represents identical content in subsequent pictures, the extreme example being a freeze-frame lasting a couple of seconds in which there is no change between adjacent pictures. In that case we can encode the first picture and send it along with the information of the number of frames during which the encoded picture remains unchanged. If a change occurs between pictures, we shall encode all pieces of information pertaining to the first picture and then only the information about the difference between that picture and the following ones. Since temporal

redundancy represents identical content in adjacent frames, the compression based on the removal of that type of redundancy is also called *interframe compression*.

3. ***Statistical redundancy*** is constituted by elements that are regularly repeated, including the horizontal and vertical sync pulses, and can be predicted to a large extent. In such a situation it is possible to encode fully only the first repetitive element and then send it with the information about its regular repetition rate, thus reducing the total amount of data to be transmitted.

The amount of redundant content in television pictures is relatively high and sometimes can be over 90% of the overall bit rate. However, the amount of redundancy is closely linked with the picture content. Static shots and a low level of action in a talk show will obviously offer a considerably larger amount of redundant information than the live transmission of a sports event. However, it is not unusual to find in the middle of a "quiet" talk show a fast-moving object suddenly crossing an otherwise calm and steady shot. Obviously a compression method cannot be "universally" successful since the end result—the appearance of the decompressed picture—depends not only on the selected bit-rate reduction technique but also on the picture content of the compressed program material, that most unpredictable aspect of a television program. Compression methods are, therefore, selected and checked to offer the most satisfying results for a majority of the expected situations, accepting in advance that for some particularly detailed or fast-moving critical pictures the results could be less than optimal.

There are a number of bit-rate reduction schemes and methods used today. Some of them are falling out of use, like the DigiCipher, developed for digital transmission of HDTV signals, or JPEG (Joint Photographic Experts' Group), developed for the compression of color stills but later slightly modified to allow the compression of moving images in early PC-based television production tools (such as Motion JPEG that analyzed moving pictures as a series of stills, applying the JPEG compression scheme to them).

However, both compression schemes have a considerable historical value. DigiCipher compression represented the major breakthrough that not only in a way started the subsequent research on video compression, but also changed the character of HDTV, transforming it from a laboratory proposition into a viable television production and transmission standard (see Chapter 14). Motion JPEG was used for the implementation of first-generation nonlinear editing units. As will be explained in more detail in Chapter 11, nonlinear editing represented a considerable step forward in the domain of television postproduction. It permitted editors to combine all the advantages of handling and processing electronic signals with revolutionary new operational features, such as random access to all desired frames, a facility that until then existed only in the domain of film cutting or the possibility to reshape edits inside of a completed program without having to redo all the edits downstream from the place of intervention (see Chapter 11).

In the broadcasting area, two bit-rate reduction schemes are dominant today. It is interesting to note that neither of them was originally developed for professional television production applications. One, the *MPEG standard* (or more precisely, family of standards), was developed by an international group of experts (the Moving Picture Experts Group, or MPEG) under the auspices of the ISO/IEC (International Standardization Organization/International Electrotechnical Commission) for a large number of applications. The other, the *DV compression scheme* (DVC), was the result of a collaborative effort of mainly Japanese manufacturers whose goal was to develop a common compression standard for consumer digital video products.

The first standard to be developed by the MPEG group was MPEG-1. The initial aim was to develop a compression standard that would support recording video and audio on *compact disc* (CD). Given the modest bit-rate capacity of CDs, it was necessary to use very stringent compression means as well as downsampling of original signals. Nevertheless, the result was judged appropriate, and the video CD had some success, although it is now superseded by the considerably better DVD (*digital video disc* or *digital versatile disc*).

The MPEG group then developed the highly successful MPEG-2, aimed initially at applications that notably excluded broadcast-quality production (later developments were to bring a variant of MPEG-2 that was specifically designed to fulfill the requirements of broadcast television production). The group also had the goal of developing a scaleable and multiresolution compression standard. However, final steps in developing that standard (which was to bear the name "MPEG-3") coincided with the finalization of MPEG-2 development, and both works were consolidated in one single standard—MPEG-2.

The next step in compression technology was initiated by the need to provide a compression method that would preserve acceptable picture quality at the higher compression ratios required for the transmission of video signals over narrow channels (like Internet and wireless delivery). The resulting standard (MPEG-4) was more complex than previous standards but managed to achieve a better compression efficiency than MPEG-2. In 2001, the MPEG group and the Video Coding Experts Group of the International Telecommunication Union joined forces to form the JVT (Joint Video Team). The result of that joint effort was the development of the improved coding method known under different names: AVC (Advanced Video Coding), H.264, or MPEG-4 Part 10.

6.3 The MPEG-2 Bit-Rate Reduction Method

The key moment in the development and standardization of bit-rate reduction methods happened in 1988 when ISO/IEC created a working group named MPEG and entrusted it with several basic tasks:

- to produce generic world standards for video and audio compression that offer options designed for different applications;
- to define the transmission features for all likely media;
- to define all relevant elements needed to fully describe a compressed digital signal, or a bitstream, rather than prescribe the exact construction, or architecture of coders and decoders that would be used for the compression and decompression, in order to give maximum freedom to the industry and foster the competition among manufacturers;
- to develop compliance procedures that could be used for checking systems and individual pieces of equipment.

However, their terms of reference did not encompass requirements that are essential for television production applications, such as

- frame-by-frame editing resolution;
- frame-accurate switching and routing;
- multigeneration (successive re-recordings of the same piece of program material) with processing;
- matte and key effects;
- cascading with other compression methods and systems, that is, creating a succession (cascade) of different compression methods to be applied one after another to the same signal.

As described, the first result of MPEG efforts had been the development of the MPEG-1 standard for nonbroadcast applications (low resolution and low bit rate of 1.5 Mbps). The next and the most important result of the group's work was the completion of the MPEG-2 compression format, a means of compressing video and audio signals and packaging the result of that compression. MPEG-2 does not define the equipment that performs the compression nor specify how an encoder should work; it only describes the bitstreams and in that respect could be considered to be a standardized tool kit for compression. As long as a coder delivers at its output a signal that is in compliance with the standardized bitstream, its internal workings are irrelevant. On the other hand, since the delivered bitstream is standardized, it does not reveal the details of the solutions implemented inside the coder. It is important to stress that MPEG found a wide application and acceptance thanks to the fact that it was extremely flexible, offering a set of techniques that could be used for an extremely broad palette of applications, from very low bit rates for telephony or videoconferencing to bit rates considered adequate for broadcast television applications.

The MPEG-2 tool kit removes different types of redundancy by using several compression techniques:

- subsampling
- blanking suppression
- transform coding
- run-length and variable-length coding
- motion compensation
- statistical coding

Subsampling consists of sampling the color difference signals in two ways: 1) with sampling frequencies two times lower than the ones defined by Recommendation 601 (3.375 MHz instead of 6.75 MHz), indicated as the 4:1:1 sampling structure; or 2) by applying a sequential approach that consists of sampling the luminance component in all lines and the two color difference components in every second line only, but with the standard 6.75 MHz frequency (the 4:2:0 sampling structure). Subsampling offers a significant reduction of the bit rate. While a regular 4:2:2 sampling structure results in a 216 Mbps bit rate, both 4:1:1 and 4:2:0 structures will produce only 124 Mbps. It is important to state that subsampling is a lossy compression method since it results in a loss of resolution, which cannot be subsequently recovered. The 4:1:1 subsampling scheme shows a loss of horizontal and the 4:2:0 of vertical chrominance resolution. The 4:2:0 schemes are mainly used with 625-scanning standards where the loss of horizontal chrominance resolution is more critical than the loss of the vertical one. The opposite is true of the 525-scanning rate—the equipment produced for that standard is generally based on the 4:1:1 subsampling scheme. However, regardless of the scanning standard, it is believed that compression schemes encompassing subsampling should be confined to electronic newsgathering applications, while the mainstream production should be based on compression schemes that preserve a full vertical and horizontal chrominance resolution.

Blanking suppression consists simply in removing horizontal and vertical blanking as well as sync information and replacing them with the detailed description of one of each and the exact information concerning their repetition rate. This technique is certainly useful but does not produce spectacular bit-rate savings.

6.4 Exploiting the Spatial Redundancy

The main burden of bit-rate reduction has therefore to be born by *transform coding* that permits the removal of spatial and temporal redundancies. As mentioned above, every television picture contains a large amount of spatial redundancy. The removal of spatial redundancy (the intraframe bit-rate reduction) is a lossless process since the removed information can be restored at the receiving end without any perceptible loss. The essential tool for the removal of spatial redundancy is a mathematical process known as the *discrete cosine transform* (DCT). It is important to stress that the transform by itself does not remove any redundancy from the picture. Its role is to facilitate the detection of the existing redundancy, which will then be removed with other tools. The DCT is not a particularly new technique. It was developed in the mid-1970s for the first major compression standard, the CCITT H261 standard for video conferencing.

The DCT process consists of analyzing a television picture that has been divided into a number of smaller blocks in order to generate specific information, known as coefficients, that fully describe it and, at the same time, allow it to easily detect the redundancy. The detected redundancy is then removed through a quantization process refined further by the subsequent entropy coding.

6.5 Exploiting the Statistical Redundancy—Entropy Coding

The data stream resulting from DCT coding can further be reduced by exploiting the statistical redundancy, that is, by using variable-length coding and run-length coding techniques. A *variable-length code* is a code that uses shorter descriptions (fewer bits) to describe elements that appear most frequently. A good example of the variable-length code is Morse code in which the most frequent letter in the English language ("e") is represented by a single dot. Therefore, the variable-length coding scheme permits allocation of the shortest codes to the most frequently occurring values, with a net result of a serious reduction of the average number of bits needed.

A *run-length code* detects the number of zeros occurring together in a given datastream and assigns a special symbol to that block of zeros. In addition, a very long string of zeros is frequently found at the end of a data block. That long string of zeros can easily and efficiently be replaced by a short end-of-block symbol.

6.6 Exploiting the Temporal Redundancy

As stated earlier, temporal redundancy can be found by comparing two adjacent frames. The bit-rate reduction techniques used for the removal of that type of redundancy are consequently called interframe compression. Considering that two adjacent frames are separated by either 33 or 40 milliseconds, it is clear that in such a short time span not many changes can occur. In its essence the interframe compression technique consists of analyzing two adjacent frames, calculating all the differences that exist between them, and sending further only these noted differences.

Figure 6.2 shows the amount of temporal redundancy existing between two adjacent frames. A careful look at this figure will reveal that the differences are minimal and that most of the content of the first frame is repeated in the second. Therefore, the role of the interframe compression will consist in detecting the differences and coding them accordingly. The first of the two frames shown in Figure 6.2 will be compressed by the intraframe compression methods and all the spatial redundancy will be eliminated; the next frame will consist only of the coded information of the differences between these two frames. The differences between two successive frames are analyzed and quantified by comparing two pictures element by element, that is, block by block.

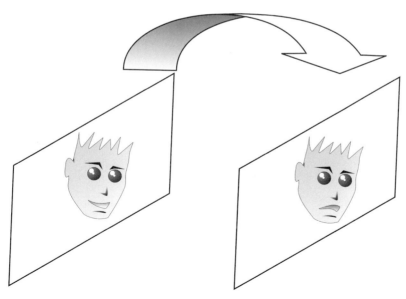

Figure 6.2 Limited differences between two adjacent frames.

However, the simple interframe compression cannot deal successfully with situations when there is a lot of movement in the scene. A moving object will be in two different positions in two adjacent frames, regardless of the fact that the displacement could be very small. If the two pictures are compared, taking as a reference the static background over which an object is moving, the result will be a relatively large difference signal that would have to then be coded. To further reduce the bit rate and facilitate an accurate prediction of all parts of the picture, including the moving ones, it is necessary to apply an additional process known as *motion compensation*. That technique is used to estimate as precisely as possible the location in the previous picture of the block to be coded, and then the difference signal is calculated by using just that area of the previous picture. This process provides motion vectors that describe the location of the block used for the computation of the difference signal in the previous picture. It is important to stress that the inaccuracies in estimating the motion vectors will not distort the decompressed picture but will lead to an increase of the bit rate to be transmitted and less efficient compression.

The goal of motion estimation is to detect horizontal and vertical motion vectors that will provide the minimum error for the block to be coded. In that respect the most important parameters are the search range and the hierarchical search algorithms. The *search range* defines the number of pixels over which the motion-estimation process will check for block matches. A larger search range means a wider span of motion speeds that can be evaluated. However, here again a technical optimum has to be found. If the search range is restricted, the motion-estimation process will not track all fast movements or small moving objects and the compression will be less efficient. On the other hand, a full search range permits the checking of all possible vector displacements, but it requires considerable processing capacity. One way to reduce such a stringent computational requirement is to implement *hierarchical search algorithms*. The hierarchical search is a series of consecutive search procedures. The first pass investigates possible motion vectors and defines the best one. The subsequent stages are refinements centered on the vector that was defined in the first pass. Compared with an exhaustive search, this system is certainly a compromise since there is no assurance that the first algorithm will find the best possible vector, but it leads to considerable savings in the processing capacity of the encoder chips.

After the application of compression tools described above, an MPEG-2 data stream will consist of several types of compressed frames:

- *I-frames (intra)* use only intraframe compression (i.e., all the spatial and statistical redundancy existing inside that same frame is removed). All the necessary information for decoding these frames is contained in the frame itself and does not require referencing to any adjacent one. For that reason decoders use I-frames as a starting point for decoding a group of pictures that also contain other types of frames.

- *P-frames (predicted)* use the nearest preceding frame (either an I- or another P-frame) as a base for the computation of their predicted content. Such a content calculation is called *forward prediction*. P-frames offer a considerably greater compression ratio that I-frames, but they cannot be used independently since I-frames are needed in the decoding process.
- *B-frames (bidirectional)* are computed by means of bidirectional prediction, that is, on the basis of both the previous and the next adjacent frame. As such the B-frames are even more efficiently coded than P-frames but cannot be used as a base for predicting other frames. B-frames bring an important contribution to the efficiency of the bit-rate reduction, but their decoding requires more storage capacity in the decoder and this makes it more expensive.

In principle, the predicted frames will be more efficiently compressed than the intraframe compressed frames, and it could seem advantageous to constitute a data stream composed mainly of such frames. However, to start its operation, a decoder must encounter an I-frame and start decoding from that point. If there is no reference I-frame, an error introduced in the first predicted frame would propagate along the datastream. To overcome these problems the MPEG coder controls the number and frequency of I-frames in the data stream, defining the length of a group of pictures (GOP).

A *group of pictures* (see Figure 6.3) is a set of compressed I-, B-, and P-frames, or pictures that start with an I-frame and extends to the frame preceding the next I-frame in the sequence. A GOP is *open* when the last P-frame in it is referenced to the first I-frame of the next GOP, and *closed* when all the pictures in the group are referenced to the first I-frame of that same group and when the last picture in the series is a P-frame.

The MPEG coder is also responsible for the definition of the number of B-frames in one GOP and for the order of transmission, which should be such as to permit a correct decoding of the stream. For example, if a GOP contains B-frames, the decoding efficiency will be greatly enhanced and the decoder design simplified if the B-frame is sent after and not between the two reference frames used for its prediction. The normal display order is then re-established before the output of the decoder.

Such a bit-rate reduction method, or more precisely set of methods, produces a bitstream of a variable bit rate reflecting the variable picture content. However, transmission and recording channels usually require constant bit rates, and, for that reason, at the end of the MPEG encoding process the compressed signal is

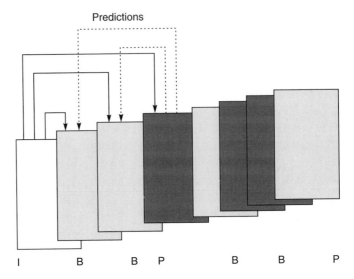

Figure 6.3   MPEG-2 group of pictures.

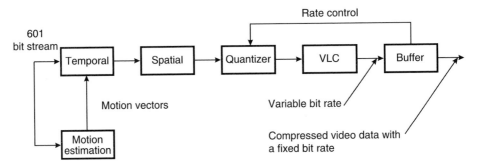

Figure 6.4   Workflow of MPEG-2 coding.

fed to a "smoothing buffer" and the data are subsequently read from the buffer at a constant data rate (see Figure 6.4). At the same time the buffer controls the amount of stored data and sends control signals back to the coder. If the buffer is too full, the control signal pushes coding to a higher level thus reducing the output bit rate. When the level of data in the buffer becomes too low, the control signal switches the coding to a lower level and this results in a higher bit rate at the output.

6.7 Compression Levels and Applications

The MPEG-2 compression system is certainly very efficient and offers excellent results. But it is perhaps even more important to stress that it is inherently a very flexible system offering a number of different combinations resulting in different bit rates and stream structures. The same set of basic techniques can be used for a very wide gamut of applications from video conferencing, through digital broadcast, to the most demanding television production applications. MPEG-2 is therefore systematized in a number of profiles and levels. The *profiles* represent a given subset, or tool kit, of the complete MPEG-2 repertory, while the *levels* define constraints influencing the resolution of the picture. In principle, a decoder designed for a given level should also be capable of decoding the lower levels.

In addition to high, main, and low levels and profiles, the MPEG standard defines a *scaleable profile*. The coder used for scaleable profiles produces two separate bitstreams. One is a regular MPEG stream, which can be decoded as such by a standard decoder ensuring a given quality level. The other is a special stream, which cannot be decoded individually but, if received by a special, more complex, and expensive decoder and added to the standard stream, will enhance the quality of the decoded signal by increasing its resolution or the signal-to-noise ratio.

The most widely used MPEG 2 option is the Main Profile@Main Level (MP@ML), since it is part of practically all television transmission applications and it constitutes the preferred source-coding method for current standard-definition digital television transmission standards (DVB*ATSC**). Its basic parameters are

- 720 pixels per line, up to 576 (626/50) or 480 (525/60) lines
- 4:2:0 sampling before coding
- DCT coding
- adaptive frame and field motion prediction
- I-, P-, and B-frames structure
- 15 Mbps maximum bit rate

The ATSC standards for HDTV are also based on MPEG-2 compression schemes but, considering the higher resolution that has to be handled, it was

---

*DVB (Digital Video Broadcasting) is a standard developed in Europe but used worldwide for broadcasting digital television signals over terrestrial and satellite transmitters as well as for distribution over cable systems. It was recently enhanced to encompass transmission to handheld devices as well as transmission of HDTV signals.

**ATSC (Advanced Television Systems Committee) is the name of a standard developed in the United States for broadcasting digital television signals over terrestrial transmitters. It is also the name of the body that codified it.

necessary to use the Main Profile@High Level (MP@HL) resulting in a bit rate of about 19 Mbps.

The intrinsic qualities of MPEG-2, its flexibility, and the quality of decoded pictures prompted broadcasting professionals to envisage its usage throughout the broadcasting chain—from acquisition through postproduction to transmission. However, as stated above, with its 15 Mbps, MP@ML could not respond to the most important requirements of broadcasting production. To overcome these limitations and at the same time make it possible to use MPEG-2 throughout the whole broadcasting chain, a new profile was proposed and eventually standardized—the 4:2:2 Profile@Main Level (422P@ML), also called *professional*, or *studio profile*. Its main parameters are defined as

- 720 pixels per line, by 608 (625) or 512 (525) lines
- 4:2:2 or 4:2:0 sampling before coding
- DCT coding
- adaptive frame and field motion prediction
- I-, B-, and P-frames allowed
- 50 Mbps maximum coding rate

Although all types of frames (I, B, and P) are legal in the 422P@ML it should be stressed that due to editing and switching requirements only two versions of that standard are generally encountered: one with GOP of only one frame (obviously an I-frame) and the other with two frames (I and B).

It is important to stress that the MPEG coding schemes were initially developed for transmission applications. Consequently, regardless of the level and profile used, the MPEG encoders are considerably more complex and more expensive than the corresponding decoders, which is an excellent solution for the point-to-multipoint transmissions in which a limited number of encoders can send signals to innumerable decoders. In television production applications, however, this particular feature of MPEG does not offer any advantage whatsoever.

6.8   DV Compression

The main incentive to develop the DV compression scheme came from the area of consumer video recording and editing. A consortium of 10 mainly Japanese companies agreed to develop a common standard for such applications, thus creating a level playing field for all manufacturers and offering to users the long-awaited full compatibility of all the competing products on the market. During the development process a number of other companies joined the consortium thus ensuring from the onset very large support for the standard.

That newly developed recording standard, named originally "DVC" (digital videocassette, shortened later to "DV"), also included a compression scheme. Basically it was an intraframe compression based on chrominance subsampling and DCT coding, resulting in a constant bit rate of 25 Mbps, which proved to be extensible to 50 Mbps and over. At the same time, since it was developed for videotape-recording applications, the standard responded to the specific demands of that domain:

- the compression had to be limited to the rejection of spatial redundancy and entropy coding;
- the resulting bit rate had to be constant;
- each frame had to have the same number of bytes.

These essential characteristics make DV compression attractive for professional applications, and several contemporary broadcast-quality recording formats are based on it (DVCPRO 25, 50, and 100, and DVCAM).

The DV compression system is not radically different from MPEG-2 and consists of the following operations (see Figure 6.5):

- raster transformation (for 25 Mbps)
- shuffling
- DCT coding
- entropy coding

The first operation—the *raster transformation*—is a filtering procedure that consists of transforming a standard 4:2:2 signal to a 4:2:0 or a 4:1:1 subsampled one.

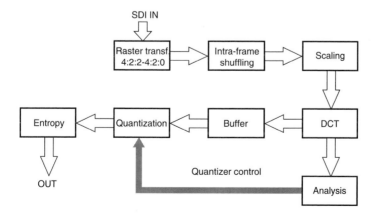

Figure 6.5 Block diagram of a DV compression system resulting in 25 Mbps bitrate.

As in MPEG-2 compression, the picture is divided into a number of smaller blocks. These blocks are then *shuffled* to redistribute complex image information that is usually concentrated in several distinct parts of the picture over the entire picture area. As a result the compression process is never overloaded with an excessive amount of data, and the more and less complex blocks are compressed together, which can ensure a more consistent quality level after compression.

The next step is the same DCT coding described above in the explanation of the MPEG compression method, followed by the quantization process. However, the complexity of the video signal is not constant but varies depending on the content of each frame. If a static quantization table is used, the net result of the compression process will be a variable bit rate—higher for more complex pictures and lower for the simpler ones. Such a variable bit rate is acceptable if the compressed signal has to be stored on a DVD or a hard disk, but it is inadequate or even unacceptable if the signal has to be transmitted over a channel of a given bandwidth or to be recorded on a videotape.

For videotape recording it is necessary to ensure that the compressed signal to be recorded has a constant bit rate. To fulfill that demand it is necessary to act upon the quantization process and make it variable. Such a control can be achieved either through a *feedback control* system used in MPEG-2 or a *feedforward control* system.

The MPEG-2 feedback control system (see Figure 6.6a) consists of compressing the incoming signal (through DCT coding, quantization and variable length coding), then to buffer the compressed signal in order to extract the information on the bitrate variations and feedback it to the quantizer, obtaining as a final result the desired constant bitrate.

The bit-rate control through a feedforward system used in the DV compression scheme is represented on Figure 6.6b. The incoming signal is DCT coded and the coding product is analyzed. The resulting information is forwarded to the quantizer to regulate dynamically the coding so that a constant bit rate is ensured already at the input of the variable length coder. This method requires a considerably higher processing power since it is based on the analysis of noncompressed signals in real time.

The last step, entropy coding, is again practically identical to the process described above in the Section 6.5.

6.9 The MPEG-4 Compression System

The MPEG-4 compression is most frequently described as an object-based compression method, where an object is any part of a picture that can be assessed and

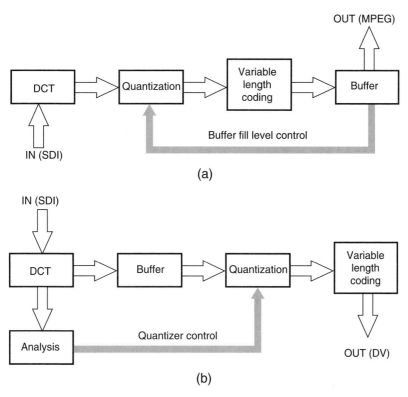

Figure 6.6   a) Feedback and b) feedforward control of the quantization process.

processed independently. By using a larger number of additional lossless prediction tools, this compression system achieves a considerably higher efficiency than its predecessors. In the case of MPEG-2 and other previously described compression methods, the whole picture content is described with pixels creating fields and pictures. MPEG-4 has a different approach based on additional tools used for image description, and it requires a whole set of new definitions, almost a new vocabulary. Therefore, before offering a short explanation of the workings of that complex compression system it is necessary to explain the basic definitions of that new vocabulary:

- *Video object* is a planar pixel array of any shape that changes its shape or position with time.
- *Video object plane* is the equivalent of a picture in MPEG-2. In MPEG-2 a moving object changes its position from one picture to another, while in MPEG-4 a video object intersects object planes.

- *Still object* **or** *sprite* is a planar pixel array that does not change with time.
- *Texture* is the appearance of a part of the picture.
- *Mesh object* is a 2D or 3D shape that changes its position and shape with time. By using computer-based processing methods it is possible to apply a texture on the mesh (the warping process) and obtain rendered images.
- *Face and body animation* is used in transmissions at very low bit rates, such as videoconferencing or video telephones where it is used to recreate facial and body movements at the decoder.

The MPEG-2 compression method achieves a considerable bit-rate reduction by using motion-compensated prediction and creating P- and B-frames. The motion compensation is based on detecting movement in regular fixed-size areas of the picture called *macroblocks*. If a moving object is not aligned with the boundaries of a macroblock, the desired smoothness of the movement rendition and the overall decoded picture quality require the transmission of a higher residual bit rate, which lowers the efficiency of the compression process.

In the case of MPEG-4, moving objects are assessed separately as arbitrary shapes and processed separately from the background. In that way considerably less residual data are transmitted. Namely, in the MPEG-2 encoding system, the first frame is encoded, then the differences in the consecutive frames that are the result of the object's movement are detected, encoded and sent forward together with motion vectors whose role is to interpret correctly the movement itself. In the case of MPEG-4 encoding only the first frame is coded and then the moving object in the following frames is described by movement vectors only, which obviously will require less bits. Several moving objects as well as the background can be separately assessed and processed. The data resulting from these separate processes are multiplexed and sent as a single bitstream. At the other end, the decoder acts as a *multilayer compositing vision mixer*. It receives the background data, decodes it and keys in the texture of processed moving video objects and mesh objects. If the background shifts due to camera movements, it can be treated as another video object and shifted at the decoder by using information from motion vectors.

MPEG-4 is a very complex and very successful bit-rate reduction method featuring a large number of different tools. Some even believe that a codec equipped with all options offered by this method will never be built. Therefore, the following is not a full explanation of all essential MPEG-4 compression aspects but rather presents a general description of the video object coding method as a sample explanation of the workings of several MPEG-4 compression tools.

As shown on Figure 6.7 the incoming picture is analyzed, and the moving video object (object 1) is detected. A *bounding rectangle* is defined around the moving object, encompassing the entirety of the object. The coordinates of the bounding

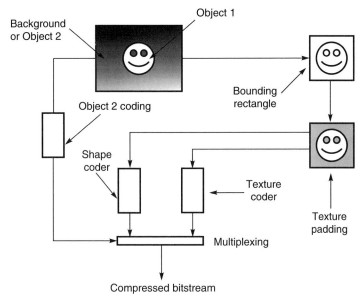

Figure 6.7 MPEG-4 video object coding.

rectangle are then coded. The bounding rectangle can change from one video object plane to another, in line with the object movement. Inside the bounding rectangle all original pixels outside the shape of Object 1 are replaced by *texture padding* data. Padding data are selected in such a way as to produce minimal DCT coefficients that can be discarded in the process, leaving only the texture contained inside the boundaries of Object 1. The shape of the video Object 1 is then coded in a shape coding process known as *context-based coding*, which relies heavily on prediction, while the texture of the object is coded separately using a conventional DCT coding process. At the same time, the background is coded either as a still sprite or as another object (Object 2) that can also change over time. If the background is a still picture, it can be coded by using a wavelet-based compression. The *wavelet transform* is a mathematical formula—a process that, like the DCT coding, explained earlier, does not perform the bit-rate reduction but simply represents the picture in a form that facilitates the detection of redundancy, which is then rejected by other means. The name "wavelet" is a literary translation of the French word "ondelette," coined by French mathematicians who were instrumental in developing this mathematical formula.

In this way, the shape data and the shape movement as well as the texture data and texture movement of all objects and backgrounds are separately analyzed and coded, and the result of all these separate coding processes are *multiplexed* (combined to represent a single signal) to create one single MPEG-4 bitstream.

At the decoder side, all multiplexed bitstreams will be separated and separately analyzed to recreate the background and to key into it the video objects.

Besides video object coding, the complete set of MPEG-4 compression tools for broadcasting applications also encompasses other sophisticated methods that can ensure important additional savings in bit rate. The use of all these tools ensures an impressive compression efficiency.

The latest extension of MPEG, the H.264 AVC (advanced video coding), can be considered a sort of extreme refinement and great improvement of MPEG-2 and MPEG-4 compression tools. H.264 is not based on object coding but on the revision and ultimate refinement of all previously developed solutions. It is an extremely complex system requiring a considerably greater processing power both on the coding and decoding sides, but offering as a reward two to two-and-a-half times better compression efficiency than MPEG-2. Although H.264 or the proprietary Windows Media 9 compression methods offer considerably higher compression efficiency than MPEG-2, they are not meant to replace it in existing applications. In the domains of standard-definition digital broadcasting or television production, MPEG-2 is firmly implanted, and it would be difficult and probably counterproductive to change all the adopted standards. In addition, you have to take into account that the number of pieces of equipment produced in accordance with that compression method is really impressive. On the other hand, new applications such as DVB H (transmission of video content to handheld devices) or some areas of HDTV production are domains that could benefit from these new highly efficient methods.

6.10 Compression and Picture Quality

As explained above, compression systems and methods are essential for the achievement of viable television production tools, affordable consumer products, and economical transmission channels. However, compression is not a panacea. While offering all the listed advantages, compression also introduces a number of distortions and limitations. For example, all compression methods are based on redundancy removal, and at the same time all error concealment systems are based on creative usage of the redundancy. Therefore, compression should be used only when it represents the only way to achieve results in a sensible and cost-effective way. Even then it is necessary to apply a rule of thumb: use the mildest compression rate that will yield the desired results.

It is difficult, if not impossible, to establish a precise and exact relationship between the application, the required picture quality, and the equivalent bit rate. The quality of the compressed program material depends not only on the level of compression and on the compression method used, but also on the content of compressed pictures. Static or almost static pictures will display a brilliant quality at relatively modest bit rates while pictures containing a lot of details, sudden lighting variations, and critical movements will display artifacts and distortions even at bit rates usually considered sufficiently high for a given application. Therefore the following application boundaries for standard-definition signals compressed by MPEG-2 bit-rate reduction methods should be considered only as an approximate indication:

- **1–2 Mbps**: browsing quality used for proxy clips (copy in low resolution used for viewing purposes) in different media asset management systems
- **4–6 Mbps**: adequate for transmission to the viewer via one of the existing standards (DVB, ATSC, or ISDB*)
- **4–8 Mbps**: recommended bit rate for digital satellite newsgathering; also acceptable for the exchange of news
- **25 Mbps**: preferred rate for news acquisition and postproduction
- **50 Mbps**: minimum rate for mainstream television production
- **216 Mbps**: full 601 quality

6.11 Concatenation Loss

In a way, all compression processes are to some degree lossy processes. The output of a decoder is never absolutely identical to the picture as it was prior to compression. Fortunately, in the case of one pair of compression-decompression processes these differences are either irrelevant or made invisible by the actions of the compression-decompression process itself. However, if the signal has to be recompressed again, then the result of putting one after the other a number of compression-decompression processes, of that concatenation (literally putting some elements in a chain) of codecs, may produce visible artifacts—a quality degradation known as *concatenation* or *generation loss*. The reasons for such quality degradation are multiple. MPEG does not define the coder but only the MPEG stream, therefore it is difficult to find two identical coders. The second coder can take different estimations and make different decisions than the ones during the first encoding. The second coder can take a former B-frame from the decoded stream and code it into an I-frame, opening the way to a series of erroneous decisions. In addition, if a signal is processed after decoding (editing, special

---

*ISDB (Integrated Services Digital Broadcasting) is a standard developed in Japan for broadcasting digital television signals and other services over terrestrial and satellite transmitters and for distribution over cable systems.

effects, etc.), the change of the value and the position of pixels may lead to completely different decisions of the second coder.

In general terms, concatenation should be avoided whenever possible although palliative methods have been developed (the generation of a set of coding information during the first encoding process and its use for the control of all further recompressions). MPEG systems feature a number of levels and profiles resulting in different bit rates, and in a television environment it is frequently necessary to convert from one MPEG bitstream to another. The worst solution would be to fully decode the signal and then to re-encode it, as it would unavoidably lead to a generation loss. In such circumstances it is advisable to use a recompressor, but also to limit that sort of processing to situations when a signal with shorter GOPs is to be recompressed into a signal with longer GOPs and featuring a lower bit rate. Going in the other direction brings the risk of a serious concatenation loss.

Digital Audio Compression Methods

All audio compression methods and systems rely on the application of the perceptive coding model based on the exploitation of specific characteristics of the human auditory system. For this reason, a thorough understanding of the workings of the human ear-brain combination is a prerequisite for grasping the rationale of different analog and digital audio solutions. Before discussing the details of digital audio implementations, we will examine the basics of the mechanisms of human hearing.

7.1 Human Auditory System

The *human auditory system* (HAS) is the combination of the three parts of the human ear (outer, middle, and inner), the brain, and the neural connections between the inner ear and the brain. The parts of the ear receive the sounds that surround us and transform them into neural impulses, which are conducted to the brain where they are decoded and interpreted. The *ear-brain system* is another phrase for the HAS.

Sounds are vibrations of air particles (molecules) whose frequency and amplitude are within the limits of the human auditory system's perception capabilities. The sensitivity of the human ear to different frequencies of the audible spectrum differs from one individual to another and in principle has the tendency to degrade with the age of the listener. Statistically, the average audible frequency range is from 20 Hz to 20,000 Hz (20 kHz), which corresponds to a span of ten octaves—where one octave represents the doubling of the frequency (20–40–80–160–320–... 20.520 Hz). At the same time, it is important to underline that the HAS is not equally sensitive to all frequencies of the audible spectrum. The highest sensitivity is to the middle frequencies in the range of one to several thousand Hz. Sensitivity diminishes toward the lower as well as the higher frequencies, as can

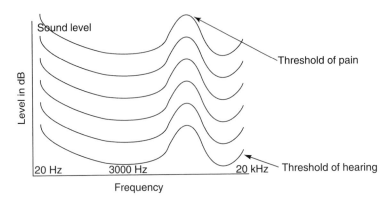

Figure 7.1   Equal loudness curves.

be seen on Figure 7.1 representing the *equal loudness curves*. These curves show that to obtain the same subjective loudness sensation it is necessary to use higher levels of sound at low and high frequencies than at those located in the middle range (2000 – 5000 Hz). Take, for example, the lowest curve, the *threshold of hearing*, which represents the levels of sound needed at different frequencies to start perceiving the existence of sound. The distance from the base horizontal line to any point on that curve indicates the level of sound that has to be used at that particular frequency to start hearing the sound—the larger the distance, the higher the necessary sound level. The curve clearly demonstrates that for the perception of the existence of a sound, higher sound levels are needed in the low and high part of the sound frequency spectrum than in its middle.

As indicated earlier, the lowest curve in Figure 7.1 represents the threshold of hearing—the lowest intensity of sound vibrations the HAS is capable of detecting at a given frequency. At the same time the HAS will assess sounds of different absolute amplitudes as equally loud provided they have different frequencies. That is why the curve that shows different absolute amplitudes that are perceived as sounds of equal loudness is called an *equal loudness curve*. The highest equal loudness curve in Figure 7.1 represents the loudest sound a HAS can support, a level that will cause a painful sensation in the human ear.

The frequency-discrimination capability of the HAS is directly linked with the constitution of the human ear. The ear is composed of three basic parts:

1. **The outer ear** includes the visible part of the ear, which plays an important role in the detection of the direction from which a sound arrives, and the auditory canal ending with the eardrum, or tympanic membrane.
2. **The middle ear** includes the three bones, or ossicles (malleus, incus, and stapes), that transmit the vibrations of the tympanic membrane caused by the incoming sound vibrations to the inner ear.

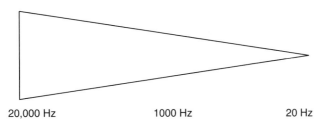

20,000 Hz   1000 Hz   20 Hz

Figure 7.2 Simplified representation of the uncoiled basilar membrane and its frequency-sensitive areas.

3. **The inner ear** includes the cochlea, which is filled with a liquid and encapsulates the basilar membrane. The basilar membrane is the *transducer*, or sensor, that transforms the sound vibrations into neural impulses. It extends from the base end of the cochlea—the end where the ossicles transmit sound vibrations from the eardrum through the oval window to the liquid in the cochlea—to the opposite end of the cochlea. As shown in Figure 7.2 the basilar membrane has a changing shape that can be approximated as a triangular one. Different parts of the membrane will resonate at the different frequencies of the liquid oscillations. The part resembling the base of a triangle (left part on Figure 7.2) will resonate at the highest audible frequencies, while the part looking like a peak of a triangle (right on the Figure 7.2) will resonate at the lowest ones. All other parts of the membrane between these two extreme parts will resonate selectively at other frequencies of the audible spectrum. In this way the basilar membrane is able to discriminate different frequencies within the audible range. The organ of Corti (running through the middle of the basilar membrane) contains hair-shaped cells (hair cells). The vibration of a given part of the basilar membrane causes the deflection of the corresponding hair cells of the organ of Corti, and these deflections trigger nerve firings that are then conducted to the brain by the auditive nerve.

When a single-frequency sound is transmitted to the cochlea, a specific portion of the basilar membrane surrounding the precise point that is sensitive to that particular frequency will start to resonate. However, as shown in Figure 7.3, the basilar membrane does not have the capacity to separate precisely one single frequency, since it can not resonate with only that one infinitesimal part of itself that corresponds precisely to that frequency. In reality, the resonance area will be larger. That area is called the *resonance envelope*, and its maximum amplitude corresponds to the input single frequency. The size of a resonance envelope depends on the loudness of the incoming sound. When sound is composed not

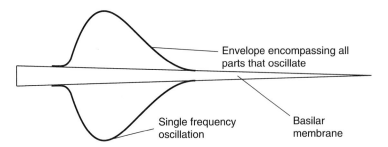

Figure 7.3   Resonance envelope at the basilar membrane.

of a single frequency but of one frequency component of a high intensity and a cluster of lower intensity components at neighboring frequencies, the same sort of resonance envelope will be formed, but within that envelope sounds whose intensities are less important than the one at the peak of the envelope will not be detected by the HAS—they will be inaudible. As will be discussed later in Section 7.4, that characteristic of the HAS will be used as the basis for audio bit-rate reduction methods.

Knowing that HAS features also a number of other specificities, such as the fact that parts of the spectrum will be variously assessed at different loudness levels, that sound assessment is heavily biased by the listener's subjective perception, that the ear can detect minute distortions, and so on, it is easy to conclude that the ultimate quality control of an audio system is unavoidably a subjective evaluation. As beauty is in the eye of the holder, sound is in the ear of the listener. In technical terms that means there is a need to establish a relationship between measured values of different parameters and the subjective assessment of these same values. Once defined, such a relationship is called the *weighting factor*.

7.2 Analog-to-Digital Conversion of Audio Signals

Since the human auditory system is a very sensitive and delicate mechanism, the digitization parameters have to be carefully selected in order to ensure high-quality digital signals. The basic analog-to-digital conversion process follows the same sequence for audio as for video signals (sampling to quantizing to coding), and the two most critical parameters are the sampling frequency and the quantization resolution.

As mentioned in Chapter 5, the first patent dealing with digital signals, or PCM (pulse code modulation) signals, was aimed at digital telephone transmissions and consequently dealt with low telephone bandwidths (less than 3000 Hz) and point-to-point communications. Later on, when digitization entered the field of professional audio, the signal to be digitized was the full audio bandwidth signal of 20 Hz to 20,000 Hz, and in accordance with the Nyquist criterion, the sampling frequency had to be higher than 40 kHz. At the same time it appeared that the available audiotape recorders were not capable of handling signals of such bit rates in a viable way. The only alternative in the late 1970s was to use the existing videotape recorders developed to handle much larger bandwidths and higher frequencies.

As will be explained further in Chapter 10, videotape recorders use rotary heads enclosed in a drum to scan a magnetic tape wrapped around that same drum. During one pass over the tape, the video head records one track containing all active lines of one television field belonging either to a 525 or 625 scanning standard. (Videotape recorders are built to handle both scanning standards; that feature is achieved by modifying the recording and playback processing circuitry and slightly changing the tape speed.) Therefore, the usage of videotape recorders for the recording of digital audio signals implied a formatting of digital audio signals to be recorded in such a way as to create a sort of digital pseudovideo signals. In practical terms it meant selecting a sampling frequency that would generate such a stream of audio samples, which would accommodate an integer number of samples in the time span of one active video line in both scanning systems. Such a sampling frequency proved to be 44.1 kHz, and that became the first standard sampling frequency implemented in early tape recorders and in the manufacture of music CDs.

The larger introduction of digital technique brought with it the use of digital terrestrial point-to-point wireless communication links (called microwave links because they use as information carriers signals having very short wavelengths) for the transmission of digital audio program signals from the radio station to broadcast transmitters. Since FM transmitters had their frequency bandwidth limited to 15 kHz, it was logical to limit to the same extent the bandwidth of the signal transmitted over terrestrial lines. For an aliasing-free sampling of a 15 kHz signal, it is sufficient to use a 32 kHz sampling frequency. Another standard was born. Finally when the European Broadcasting Union (EBU) and Audio Engineering Society (AES) joined forces to fully document a single professional audio digital standard, they selected a new sampling frequency of 48 kHz, with the following characteristics:

- That value had a simple relationship with both 32 and 44.1 kHz, which made the transcoding from one to another sampling frequency relatively easy.
- It was sufficiently high to facilitate variable-speed operations.
- It facilitated the generation of a round number of 960 samples per video field in 50 Hz video-recording systems; in that way all video and audio samples

pertaining to one video frame were confined inside the boundaries of the video frame (two vertical blanking periods), which was a precondition for a correct editing (see Chapter 11).
- The only drawback was the need to implement special processing for the NTSC 59.94 Hz field rate (again for editing purposes).

The structure of audio signals and their perception by the HAS require a considerably finer quantization than in the case of video signals. While for the mainstream video applications it is sufficient to use 8 bits per sample leading to 256 predetermined quantization levels (see Chapter 5), audio signals will require at least 16 bits per sample leading to 65,536 quantization levels. The figure of 16 bits per sample was therefore adopted by the EBU and AES as the minimum number, while for the whole acceptable range of bits per sample they adopted the span of 16 to 24 bits per sample (when there are more than 16 bits per sample, the additional bits can be used either for a finer definition of the audio signal itself or for the transport of auxiliary information).

7.3 Digital Audio Compression

A standard EBU/AES digital audio monophonic signal has a total bit rate of 768 kbps (kilobits per second), while a stereo signal has 1.536 Mbps. When compared to the 216 Mbps bit rate of the video signal, the digital stereo audio rate seems negligible and the need for compression questionable. However, if the audio signal is analyzed separately, it becomes evident that such a signal will require more than 800 kHz of transmission bandwidth compared to the modest 50 kHz required for the transmission of a similar analog stereo signal. At the same time it is easy to calculate that the content of a 60-minute CD would require 630 MB of hard-disk storage space. In addition, video signals in television applications are generally handled in their compressed form, featuring bit rates ranging from 1.5 to 50 Mbps. Compared to such video bit rates, the 1.5 Mbps stereo audio signal is far from negligible and has to be compressed.

However, digital television broadcasting is not the only area where audio compression is necessary or simply useful. It is required or represents the foundation of a number of technologies or technical solutions:

- Compressed audio signals can be transferred over ISDN lines, thus eliminating the need to lease expensive dedicated broadband circuits.
- Using compression, it is possible to transform the four digital audio channels of contemporary digital videotape recorders into multichannel units particularly well suited for multilingual operations.

- Compressed audio is at the base of digital radio broadcasting standards such as DAB (Digital Audio Broadcasting) or DRM (Digital Radio Mondiale).
- Highly effective surround-sound systems for movie theaters are based on the use of compressed audio signals.
- In the domain of consumer products, the MiniDisc records compressed audio, and the whole area of MP3 applications is based on the use of compression.

7.4   Audio Compression Methods and Standards

Like video compression methods, audio counterparts are also based on the rejection of redundant and irrelevant parts of the signal. The audio signal contains by definition a very low level of redundancy, and the compression has to rely heavily on the detection and coarse definition or rejection of irrelevant components. Although a number of audio compression methods feature different technical solutions, all are based on the application of the perceptive coding model derived from the specific characteristics of the HAS. As can be seen from Figure 7.1, the human ear is the most sensitive to sounds at around 3,000 Hz and then its sensitivity falls rapidly toward the lowest and highest parts of the audible spectrum, which can therefore be more coarsely quantized, thus producing some reduction in bit rate. Another, particularly important characteristic of the HAS is the *masking effect*. The presence of a loud sound at a given frequency will mask all other quieter sounds existing at nearby frequencies—it will practically prevent them from being heard. As shown in Figure 7.4, a loud sound elevates the threshold of

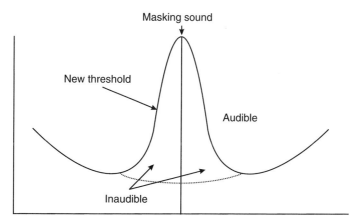

Figure 7.4   Masking effect.

hearing in its vicinity, and all sounds whose amplitude is lower than the changed curve of the threshold of hearing will be inaudible for all practical purposes. Consequently those inaudible sounds can be considered irrelevant information that can be rejected in the compression process.

All compression processes have to fulfill the following basic requirements:

- ensure a sufficiently low bit rate that satisfies the demands of transmission, processing channels, and equipment
- ensure that the compression is performed in real time with minimum delays
- achieve reduced bit rates with a minimum of perceived loss of quality due to distortions or to audible noise

Obviously, as long as the masking effect covers the noise and distortions, the compression process can be considered to be *transparent*, that is, the output analog signal will be accepted as practically identical to the analog sound present at the input of the system. The limit of perceived transparency is called *perceptual entropy*.

One of the major ways to ensure transparency in the compression process is to keep the noise under the limits of the masking effect. The most important component of overall noise is quantization noise. Every time a quantization process is applied to an audio signal, the amplitude of each sample is compared to one of the 65,536 predetermined discrete levels (16-bits quantization). Whenever the amplitude of the sample does not correspond ideally to one of those levels, it is rounded up lower or higher to the level nearest the actual amplitude (see Figure 7.5). The difference between the real amplitude and the selected predetermined level is the quantization error, and it appears in the decoded signal as noise. Obviously the cascading of coding and decoding processes will unavoidably contribute to the accumulation of quantization noise and bring down the limit of transparency.

All these compression methods exploit the characteristics of the human auditory system and are essentially based on the use of transform coding and predictive coding, both in combination with subband coding. *Subband coding* consists of separating the whole processed audio bandwidth into a number of narrower subbands (usually 32), thus replicating, to a certain extent, the critical bands of the human auditory system described earlier. Once the bandwidth is divided into subbands, the quantizing process is conducted and the masking effect evaluated inside those subbands.

As in video compression, the transform coding consists of applying a mathematical transform to ensure the transformation of an audio signal waveform from a time-domain into a frequency-domain representation and to generate

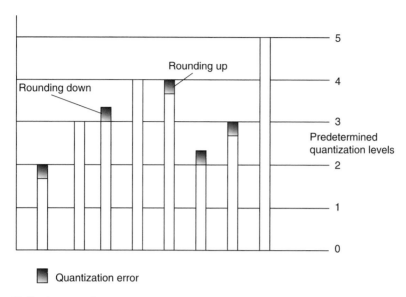

Quantization error

Figure 7.5 Source of quantization noise.

coefficients, which will subsequently be quantized, applying more bits per sample to more important or more audible components.

The *predictive coding* consists in analyzing the value of a number of consecutive components and, on the basis of that analysis, predicting the value of the next one. In the next step, the real value of the predicted component is measured, compared to the prediction, and if there is a difference (positive or negative), that difference is taken as the *prediction error* and only that information is forwarded to the decoder. In the decoder a similar process is performed: a series of components is analyzed, the value of the next component predicted, and the prediction error is added to it, thus providing a correct output value (see Figure 7.6).

In the domain of audio compression, there are a number of different systems and methods. Some of them are part of international standards while others are proprietary schemes. The most important and most widely used international standard was developed by the MPEG group and consists of three layers (1, 2, and 3), which must not be confused with the video compression standards MPEG-1 and MPEG-2. On the proprietary side the most widely used is the AC 3 system developed by Dolby Laboratories and adopted as a standard for some of the digital television broadcasting formats.

When ISO/IEC created the Moving Pictures Experts Group, it was entrusted with the task of developing video compression methods. However, very soon it became apparent that it would be beneficial if the same body would tackle

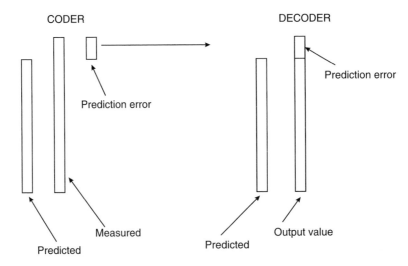

Figure 7.6 Principle of predictive coding.

the problem of audio compression as well, and the Audio MPEG SubGroup was formed. That SubGroup did not start its work from point zero but based its investigations on previous work done by a number of research institutes and manufacturers' research and development laboratories. At the time, two compression systems were fully developed:

1. **MUSICAM** (masking pattern-adapted universal subband integrated coding and multiplexing) developed jointly by the French research laboratory CCETT, German research institute IRT, and the Dutch manufacturer Philips.
2. **ASPEC** (adaptive spectral perceptual entropy coding) developed by AT&T Bell Labs, the German Fraunhofer Society, the manufacturer Thomson, and the research institute CNET from France.

After a careful study of these systems and a number of tests and experiments, the MPEG group combined tools and solutions from the two systems to create three distinct levels or layers, optimized for different areas of application.

MPEG Layer 1 is a sort of simplified MUSICAM compression method delivering mild compression ratios (4:1) at low cost. It accepts as its input all three sampling rates (32, 44.1, and 48 kHz) and processes the 20 kHz stereo signals in 32 subbands using a limited number of compression tools.

The MPEG Layer 2 audio coding method is practically identical to the MUSICAM compression method and was originally developed for DAB (Digital Audio Broadcasting—a new standard allowing digital radio broadcasting over existing FM channels). Later on, the same MPEG Layer 2 was adopted in the framework of the DVB standard for the compression of television sound signals. MPEG Layer 2 also accepts all three sampling rates and processes audio signals in 32 subbands, but it uses more complex compression tools to achieve higher compression ratios.

MPEG Layer 2 is used for the encoding of five channels of a surround-sound system (right, left, center, left surround, and right surround) in a single backward-compatible stereo mix. Namely, one bitstream is coded as a backward-compatible signal carrying all necessary information for the representation of the stereo downmix of a five-channel system. The same bitstream will also contain some additional information, which the simple stereo decoders will not interpret but will simply reject. However, that additional information, called *multichannel extension*, is aimed at special decoders that can interpret it as the necessary data for the reconstruction of a full multichannel sound image from a stereo downmix.

The main fields of application of the MPEG Layer 2 coding method are

- audio source coding for DAB (Digital Audio Broadcasting—digital radio developed in Europe by a consortium of broadcasters and manufacturers)
- coding method for the exchange of program material in broadcasting operations
- audio source coding for DVB (Digital Video Broadcasting)
- audio coding method for DVDs aimed at the European market (although it seems that the AC 3 compression scheme is becoming dominant in the worldwide DVD market)

MPEG Layer 3, probably the most widely known under its "MP3" name and for its controversial application for downloading music from the Internet, represents a complex combination of MUSICAM and ASPEC compression tools and allows the achievement of the highest compression ratios. It was specifically developed for all applications where the bandwidth is the most critical element.

In the process of defining the three MPEG layers, one of the starting assumptions was the need to ensure a certain backward compatibility among the three layers. Although interesting in terms of practical applications, such a requirement restricted the use of all available compression tools and the achievement of high-quality audio reproduction at higher compression ratios. That was the reason that pushed the MPEG audio group to continue its work and develop an advanced coding system—the AAC (Advanced Audio Coding) that is not compatible with the previously described layers but offers superior quality at lower bit rates. At the same time, the AAC supports not only the compression of mono, stereo, and surround-sound systems but also of multichannel ones up to 48 channels. All compression tools, including those used in layers 1–3 and the newly developed ones, are grouped as modules in three profiles of differing complexity and efficiency:

- the main profile that uses all the tools from the AAC repertoire and consequently has the most complex coder
- the low-complexity (LC) profile that has more modest requirements in terms of memory and processing complexity and is composed in such a way that LC-coded signals can be decoded by main-profile decoders
- the scaleable sampling rate profile (SSR) that offers a specific solution based on the splitting of the input audio into four frequency bands and a separate processing of each of these bands (resulting in a separate bitstream). At the decoding side it is possible to select one or more of these bitstreams and obtain reconstructed signals of a reduced bandwidth.

The advanced characteristics of the AAC compression method and its non-compatibility with earlier MPEG coding schemes recommended it for some new applications:

- audio source coding for the latest digital audio broadcasting standard DRM (Digital Radio Mondiale—digital broadcasting standard for AM radio broadcasting)
- audio source coding for ISDB (Integrated Services Digital Broadcasting) standard
- in a somewhat expanded form (featuring some additional tools), the audio compression method selected to accompany MPEG-4 video coding
- possible compression format for a new generation of personal solid-state audio players

The AC 3 coding scheme was developed at the beginning of the 1990s by Dolby Labs as a multichannel coding system for the cinema industry. Since its main aim was to offer a coding method for a multichannel sound display in movie theaters it was conceived without any restriction imposed by the need to be compatible with some other, previously developed method. Although it uses somewhat different tools, or the same tools in a different manner, the AC 3 coding method is, like all MPEG layers, essentially based on the use of perceptual coding. The AC 3 coding method is considered to be slightly more efficient than MPEG Layer 2, and its main areas of application are

- compression format for the theatrical display of surround-sound films
- audio source coding for the ATSC (Advanced Television Systems Committee) broadcasting standard
- dominant compression format for DVDs

As was the case with compressed video signals, it is difficult to issue decisive statements about respective qualities and efficiencies of the described audio compression methods. Such a task is made even more difficult by the fact that the appraisal of the quality offered by different coding schemes is based on subjective assessment methods. Nevertheless a number of assessments were made around the world, and some statistical values could be taken as sufficiently representative. Therefore, these tests, conducted with the necessary rigor and in accordance with internationally recommended methods, showed the following results:

- MPEG Layer 2 compression method offers near-transparent quality at 256 kbps for a stereo pair although, in practice, a 192 kbps bit rate for a stereo pair is frequently used for broadcasting purposes.
- Stereo audio signals compressed in accordance with the AAC coding method are assessed as near transparent for bit rates ranging from 96 to 128 kbps, while a comparable quality for multichannel transmission is achieved at rates ranging from 256 to 320 kbps.
- The same near-transparent quality for stereo signals is achievable by the AC 3 coding scheme at bit rates on the order of 192 kbps, and for multichannel transmissions at 384 to 448 kbps.
- Finally, some credible comparative tests show that for stereophonic signals, the output quality is assessed as equal for MPEG Layer 2, AC 3, and AAC coders at 192, 160, and 96 kbps respectively.

At this point it seems necessary to refer to some specifics of the human auditory system (HAS) since in a way these specifics limit the area of possible applications of audio compression methods. The masking effect is the feature of psychoacoustic models used in compression systems. However, the results of masking prove to be quite different in the case of mono and stereo reproductions. The effectiveness of masking is based on the presumption that the masking and the masked sound sources are co-sited, that is, share the same physical location. Although it is not the case in real life, in mono reproduction all sounds come from a single source, and the masking effect can be exploited to its full extent. However, in the case of stereo reproduction, the situation is radically different. It is important to recognize that the HAS is capable of discriminating one sound source in the midst of a multitude of other sources and to enhance its subjective audibility. A stereo sound system creates an artificial audio space where the ear can recognize different locations of different sound sources and therefore, if the HAS decides to use the auditory selectivity to pick one or another, the effect of masking will be considerably reduced. At the same time the HAS is capable of separating main source sounds from sound resulting from multiple reflections (*reverberation*) and constituting what is usually called *ambience*. In the real world environment—say, when listening to live music in a decent acoustical space—the HAS will accept the main sources as the "lead" and the ambience will add fullness, thus enhancing the overall effect. However, in the process of bit-rate reduction, the coder will most frequently decide that the major part of the ambience is under the masking level and will thus simply eliminate it, creating a much "drier" sound reproduction.

It is important to stress that the effects described above are not drastic and that they perhaps limit but do not prevent the use of audio compression. Obviously audio compression remains the preferred approach in a number of applications, from digital radio and television transmission systems through some recording applications to the whole span of MP3. However, it explains why in the domain of production of high-quality recording, where the goal is to reproduce as faithfully as possible the real-life listening experience, the use of full EBU/AES digital audio signals is still mandatory. Fortunately, as mentioned earlier, the overall bit rate of such signals is well inside the handling capabilities of standard present-day equipment.

8

Exchanging Program Material as Bitstreams

The introduction of digital techniques culminated with the adoption of ITU-R Recommendation 601, which provided the basis for an orderly transformation of analog signals into digital bitstreams. Along with that, Recommendation 656 defined the serial digital interface (SDI) as the most rational way to convey bitstreams from one point to another. The transition to digital certainly represented a huge step forward in the area of making television programs. Initially the digitization offered a possibility of improving audio and video signal quality and of giving considerably larger latitude for creative expression to program makers. But the conversion to digital left practically unchanged the basic flow of television operations. One form of signal (digital) replaced the other (analog), and a digital videotape recorder or production mixer replaced a similar analog piece of equipment.

By the end of the 1990s, broadcasters became conscious of the fact that new digital technologies could offer something more than the preservation of signal quality and the enhancement of creative flexibility. They realized that information technologies (IT) offered new functionalities, initiated a proliferation of distribution channels, enlarged the distributed content beyond the conventional audio and video signals, and opened the way to bidirectional communication in a domain that was traditionally strictly unidirectional; that is, it provided the necessary prerequisites for the development of interactive television services. In such circumstances it was clear that the content remained essential but had to be produced much more efficiently and in such a way as to serve multiple uses. One of the important conclusions was that broadcasting would very soon have to evolve in a networked environment and that the new environment and the new techniques must be used to

- improve the functionality of broadcasting systems
- open up new ways to manage the program materials that represent the main assets of broadcasting organizations
- offer the opportunity to develop new business models

At the same time broadcasters realized that the development of new IT-based technologies was progressing at a very fast pace and if appropriate action was not taken soon, the result might produce chaos instead of a stimulating environment. For example, one of the crucial activities in broadcasting was the exchange of program materials. In the domain of conventional techniques, the exchange was accomplished mainly with packaged media, such as videotapes, for which a number of recording formats coexisted on the market. All those formats were well documented so to ensure the exchange interoperability it was sufficient to strictly adhere to the announced standard. In the case of stored files, the situation was somewhat different since the file format was a logical category and in fact dissociated from its physical carrier and its specifications.

8.1 File Transfer

Computers communicate by exchanging files. A network can be used both for the streaming of content and for the exchange of files. The comparison of these two communication methods shows that both are legitimate and viable, but each has specific qualities as well as advantages and drawbacks. *Streaming* has these characteristics:

- It is viewable during the transfer.
- The receiving side does not acknowledge the reception automatically.
- It is normally synchronized and has specified minimum and maximum bit rates.
- Decoders are always sequential.
- It has a minimum delay, which is particularly important for live broadcasts.
- It is a point-to-point transmission without bottlenecks but is more often used for point-to-multipoint or broadcasting purposes.
- It is a continuous and reliable operation but it can be performed only at real-time speed.
- It always requires an optimum bandwidth closely correlated with the signal bit rate.
- It has to be stored on a dedicated device or processed in accordance with the storage device requirements.

- All accompanying data have to be transferred either as streaming, once the audio and video materials have been streamed, or via some other parallel-transfer means.

On the other hand, *file transfer* has these characteristics:

- It uses packet-based network interconnect.
- The reception is usually automatically acknowledged.
- It is based on a file-by-file transfer with a known start and end.
- It is usually asynchronous, making the transfer and display rates mutually independent.
- It can be performed at a wide range of speeds, from slower than real time to several times faster than real time, all depending on the available bandwidth for transmission.
- It makes it possible to trade off transmission time for transmission cost (if it is operationally acceptable, it is possible to rent a cheaper line with a narrower bandwidth and transfer the material at a speed slower than real time).
- A system can be assembled by using only low-cost standard IT components.
- It can be stored on almost any sort of storage device or media, including magnetic tapes and optical disks.
- It opens the possibility for multiple empowered users to simultaneously access the same program material within a network of a given distributed production.
- It does not introduce any quality degradation of the sound and picture since these signals can be packaged in the file in their native form without any transcoding or recompression.
- It has the ability to package in the same file all relevant materials—not only the sound and vision, but also the accompanying data. The drawback is that it can frequently experience transmission bottlenecks.
- Viewing during transfer is not always possible.
- It is inadequate for live transmission or for final transmission directly to the viewer.
- It is essentially used for point-to-point transfers but can also be used for point-to-multipoint transfers with a rather limited number of reception points.

It is obvious that in a fully digitized environment where a lot of equipment is based on computer processing techniques, file transfer can offer a number of advantages over streaming techniques. However, to benefit from these advantages it is necessary for the systems to be *interoperable*, that is, for the source and destination to understand each other. Unfortunately, standardization was never widely supported in the computer world. Each manufacturer usually developed proprietary standards, and very seldom was the same solution adopted by somebody else. A number of proprietary file formats were developed for data transfer. These formats were usually directly adopted from the IT industry and then used for data transfer or for simpler audio or video applications (such as Quick Time, Audio Video Interleaved, Advanced Systems Format, etc.) and were clearly inadequate for use in the broadcasting environment. The size of files was too small, the formats precluded editing of the content within a file and they were not content agnostic, that is, they were not able to accept indifferently all signal configurations but required a specific signal shape in order to accept it. The only standardized file format was the general exchange format (GXF), developed and standardized by the SMPTE. That format offered a number of features necessary for broadcast applications and was very widely used, but since it was developed at an early stage of the convergence process it could not satisfy all the demands emanating from present-day production techniques.

The need for standardization was recognized by both manufacturers and users. In order to investigate the new paths and determine all actions that had to be taken, the EBU (representing broadcasters) and the SMPTE (representing both broadcasters and manufacturers) decided to join their forces to create the EBU/SMPTE Task Force for Harmonized Standards for the Exchange of Program Material as Bitstreams. In two years of intense work, that group investigated a large number of essential issues from compression methods to the adoption of the serial data transport interface (SDTI), and they performed very important introductory work on the question of file-transfer and file-format standardization. That initial work was later taken over by EBU, SMPTE, ProMPEG Forum, and the AAF Association. Soon after, it bore fruit with the adoption of a standard file format for the exchange of program material as bitstreams—the material exchange format (MXF) file.

Program material used to be and still is, in a large number of cases, stored in the form of packaged media: it is recorded on tapes of different formats and exchanged in the form of a physical exchange of material tapes and cassettes carrying recorded audio and video signals. That program content is always accompanied with additional data that also have to be exchanged, including

- time code (see Chapter 11)
- copyright information
- *dope sheets* (program-related information usually offering a short description of individual shots)
- dialogue

Some of these data are recorded on the same tape (such as the *time code*), but the major part of data is recorded on different supports (from paper to magnetic or optical disks) and transported together with the cassettes. At the point of destination, the program materials can be used in the form in which they were transported—as videotape recordings that are viewed, sometimes processed (dubbing, subtitling, etc.), and then played back. The additional information is reproduced and taken into consideration. However, at that same point of destination, the audio or video content can be transferred to servers. In that case, the additional data can also be ingested in the server. Once ingested in the server, all data can be handled in the form of files. These files will consist of content and its container or wrapper. The *content* is made of audio, video, and data information, called *essence*, and additional data that describes and/or completes essence, called *metadata* ("data about data"). When metadata contain information on rights and when that information indicates that the user has the right to use the content, that content becomes one of the user's assets, since the user can freely exploit that program material, distribute it over his network, sell it or exchange it with other parties—in short draw benefit from that particular piece of content.

The essence is the program material itself. It can take the form of compressed or uncompressed audio, video, graphics, but also data. Data essence are different forms of data that have their own value and are not just a description of an aspect of the audio and/or video essence, such as script, subtitles, or captions.

As its name clearly indicates, the purpose of the *container* or *wrapper* is to contain essence and metadata in different amounts and proportions. Its purpose is also to facilitate the identification of all parts of the enclosed content by defining and describing its structure. A wrapper can be visualized as an envelope containing a videotape (audio, video, and data essence) and one or several pieces of paper that carry data about the essence—the metadata. There is also an inscription on the envelope indicating what is inside. Wrappers are intended to be used for storing content on servers and for transferring files but are also used for streaming the program material across interconnecting lines. The content stored in a wrapper, or as it is sometimes designated, the *payload*, can be in the form of:

- **content component** – representing an individual item of either essence or metadata (for example, a block of video information)
- **content element** – consisting of one type of essence (video, audio, or data) and the metadata related to that piece of essence
- **content item** – made out of several content elements, with metadata associated directly with that group of elements or needed to indicate the way all elements are associated (for example, a video clip)
- **content package** – consisting of several content items and of the metadata related directly to the package or required to associate the items and elements (for example, a complete program including video, audio, and subtitles).

A wrapper can contain any number of different forms defined above. It can contain just a few components or several packages. Although it could seem an attractive proposition, it is impossible to develop a single wrapper format for all applications, a single solution that would satisfy the requirements of all applications and transfer mechanisms such as:

- IP-based streaming
- streaming over Fibre Channel
- streaming in SDTI circuits
- storing on different disk-based storage systems
- file transfer in server systems
- file transfer in editing operations
- transfers in media asset-management systems.

However, an appropriate usage of metadata and of standard templates ensures a full interoperability of all formats that have to be developed for different applications and provides the expected *low-processing conversion capability*—an easy and fast conversion from one file or wrapper format to another.

Considering the complexity of the present-day production environment, with the multiplicity of formats and standards, it is essential that the wrappers, and consequently the file formats, are:

- *compression-format agnostic* so that any compression format or uncompressed signals can be encapsulated with equal ease;
- *platform neutral* so that all machines in use can read them (although not always with equal efficiency) regardless of the type of machine that was used for their creation.

8.2   Metadata

Metadata can be broadly defined as all information within content that is not essence. Or more precisely, metadata is the information that describes different aspects of audio, video, and data essence. Metadata have a meaning or a value only in association with the essence they describe. All information that can be written on a tape label, or printed on a sheet of paper that accompanies the tape in its travels, is metadata. As a term, "Metadata" is a relatively new concept, developed at the moment when having all metadata information became essential for a correct handling and processing of video and audio essence in modern production, distribution, and archiving processes.

A number of pieces of information that are today part of metadata existed long before the merging of broadcasting and computer technologies. In those analog or early digital times different data concepts were developed in order to carry important information along the chain. Such were the time-code or the remote-control protocols. With the increase in the number of compression methods, with more and more software-based pieces of equipment, and with the proliferation of editing solutions, it became virtually impossible to design systems that would be able to handle all possible combinations of different parameters. It was necessary to design a universal mark-up or information-carrying system that would facilitate an automatic configuration of every element in the chain in accordance with the incoming type of essence. Therefore, the industry decided to undertake the task of developing a new architecture for the definition and transport of vital additional information—of metadata. This new architecture had to be open to new developments, to be adaptable to both hardware- and software-based units and processes, and to be effective in mixed analog and digital systems.

The potential varieties of metadata are practically limitless since every participant in the television program processing chain can have particular information needs and demands. To simplify the approach of interpreting metadata, they can be classified in the following categories:

- *Essential metadata* represent the information concerning details that have to be known in order to decode essence (such as audio and video compression formats, number of audio channels, etc.).
- *Access metadata* provide and control the access to essence (such as copyright data and information concerning the right to access the essence).
- *Parametric metadata* carry information on the setup of equipment used to originate essence (such as camera setup information, colorimetric details, etc.).
- *Composition metadata* facilitate the assembling of a number of components into a continuous sequence or offer historic information on how the essence was originated (such as edit decision lists, parameters used for virtual sets or for the color correction process, etc.).
- *Relational metadata* offer the necessary information for synchronizing different content components (such as the time code).
- *Spatiotemporal metadata* deliver information on the position of the source during acquisition and about the date and time of origination (for example, "Downing Street 10, Monday April 20, 2006").
- *Descriptive metadata*, as will be explained later in Section 8.3, offer all the necessary information for cross-referencing essence.

- Any other data that can be needed by the users, that is, data that are left to the user to define them freely and which are not expected to be recognized by other users of the same material.

Depending on their intended length of usage, metadata can be either permanent or transient. *Permanent metadata* is information that will be needed from the moment the material is generated, throughout the postproduction, distribution, and delivery processes, and that will still be needed when the material is deposited in the long-term storage. Typical examples of such metadata are the essential metadata or the embedded decoding information. *Transient metadata* are useful and even valid only during a given process or a series of processes, but there is no need to keep them permanently associated with the material. Typical examples are postproduction detailed information, which are important to all those who take part in the postproduction process, but which became irrelevant once that process is finished.

Metadata can be content driven, generated in order to provide information, which is vital for the exchange of material between different elements in the production, postproduction, archiving, and playout (airing or transmission) processes. The EBU identified this sort of metadata as part of a system-to-system communication that ensures an indispensable high level of interoperability. Typical examples of such metadata are information on

- compression methods used
- number of audio channels
- edit decision lists
- time code
- title of the program

The major parts of these metadata will always be intimately linked with the essence; they will be part of the same files. In order to act as interoperability facilitators, these metadata have to be easily and universally recognizable. They have to be unambiguously identifiable, and to that end internationally agreed-upon dictionaries or encyclopedias have been established. Typical examples of such dictionaries are the *SMPTE RP205—Metadata Dictionary*, or the *EBU Tech 3293—Metadata for Radio Archives*. An operator may also decide to introduce some specific metadata that are closely linked to one or several of its specific needs, but such metadata will not exist in public dictionaries. The approach is legitimate since all systems should be capable of recognizing and separating that information from the internationally recognized ones. For the decoding of such information the user that has introduced it must develop specific custom-designed solutions.

Content-driven metadata can also have descriptive elements, and these pieces of information have to be deposited in separate databases since they are used for search and retrieval purposes. Such metadata are part of electronic catalogues but have to be linked to the metadata embedded in files in order to ensure an adequate retrieval of the essence. To ensure such linkage as well as unambiguous identification of all materials, a unique content identifier—the *unique material identifier* (UMID) has been developed and is updated by the SMPTE. The EBU/SMPTE task force emphasizes in their report the need to develop a feature that permits unambiguous tracking of a single piece of program material throughout the production, postproduction, and distribution processes. It is important not to confuse the *unique program identifiers* (UPID)—simple labels generated through a registration process—with the newly developed UMID. UMID offers a unique identification of each piece of essence and also ensures a vital connection between the identified piece of video, audio, or data with the metadata information that is related to it. The UMID identification is certainly important in a production process, but it is undoubtedly essential for archives (both new digital and old analog ones) because it controls the precision and speed of access to every single piece of stored material. The development of UMID is a brilliant result of the convergence of broadcasting and computer technologies. It offers a bridge between these two industries, permitting broadcasters to use computer-based techniques in order to improve the efficiency of their traditional environment and providing the computer community with a common, internationally agreed-upon standard for material identification.

The UMID provides the identification of a number of essential aspects of the essence. In the standard documents, UMID appears in two forms:

1. The basic form is composed of a minimum number of elements needed to identify a material clip. It does not provide a mechanism for the separation of content units that constitute the clip.
2. The extended form is composed of the basic form followed by information that provides a signature for each content unit and a time component that permits the separation of the enclosed individual content units.

According to the official SMPTE documentation, "the UMID is a unique identifier for picture, audio and data material, which is locally created, but is globally unique" (SMPTE 330M-2000). That apparently contradictory statement is justified by the construction of the UMID, which is formed by one standardized part, unique and kept in the central database, and another part that is generated locally but contains several elements whose combination ensures its uniqueness.

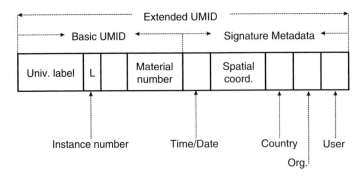

Figure 8.1   Configuration of basic and extended UMID.

As shown in Figure 8.1, the UMID starts with the universal label, developed and documented by SMPTE (where the central database is kept). The *universal label* indicates the character of the following data construction and announces that it represents a UMID but also offers information on the methods used for the generation of unique material and instance numbers that follow. The next section is the *length value* (information on the length of the UMID). The *material number* follows; it is a unique numerical identification for the attached piece of material. However, that number does not indicate the status of the material. In fact, the original and all the copies of the same material will have the same number. The needed differentiation is ensured by the *instance number,* which ensures the identification of each copy. The set of data that follows the instance number is optional and called *signature metadata.* It consists of the date and time of the creation as well as the identification of its creator (country, organization, and user identification numbers).

Business transactions require another category of metadata. These metadata cover the needs of program planning and commissioning, associated editorial work, and promotion and sales of finished programs. Such information is usually dissociated from the essence and kept in separate databases; it is, following the EBU expression, *distributed.* Although kept in separate databases, these metadata have also to be linked in an appropriate way to the essence. As in the case of distributed content-driven metadata, that linkage is ensured by the existence of the same UMID information on the metadata as well as on the essence side.

Besides this kind of linkage, ensured by the use of the same UMID in both storage places, the essence and its related metadata can be linked in a number of other ways. Metadata can be directly embedded with the essence. That is the case with essential metadata in ITU-R 601 or MPEG-2 bitstreams. Another method is to enclose the essence and metadata in the same wrapper, as in the SDTI content package and in the case of a conventional videotape recording where the wrapper is the magnetic tape and the link is constituted by the recording format that defines the respective and mandatory positions of video, audio, time code and *cue* tracks, where the latter two carry information that could be identified as metadata. In this and other similar cases, the link between the essence and metadata exists only inside the wrapper and cannot be exported when the essence is taken out of the wrapper.

The defining of electronic metadata systems represents one of the essential elements in the design of new television facilities and the renewal of those already in existence. As mentioned above, metadata are standardized to a very large extent, but the standards do not offer simple, easy, and "packaged" solutions; they only offer basic material that have to be used as building blocks in the course of a carefully planned design and development action. Each broadcaster and each video production facility has to study, define, and carefully conduct the implementation of a metadata system. Usually such a move is linked with the decision to streamline production activities, improve the business flow of information, reduce the operational and production costs, or simply to rethink the whole system when an overhaul is needed. But whether the initiative for renewing the facilities comes from business interests or engineering needs, it is necessary to base all decisions on a careful joint study of the whole problem. Careful analysis of the potential creative and financial repercussions of introducing an electronic metadata system is a very important component of this study.

Probably the most important step on that road is to study all current processes and workflows and determine which of them have to be changed and how they could be improved. The redesigned processes and workflows must be open to future needs and changes and must be evaluated in terms of potential costs and savings. Once the new processes and workflows are designed and adopted, it is necessary to make a careful plan for their gradual introduction. This work will offer the basis for the next step, the definition of all pieces of information needed to run these processes efficiently, the definition of the complete set of necessary metadata—of a *metadata scheme*. The following steps offer an opportunity to define precisely all the relevant details, investigate the extent to which the existing standards can be applied, define metadata that will be embedded and those that will be externally linked, and, in short, generate all the elements out of which a complete evaluation model can be created and used for the assessment of offered solutions.

The introduction of electronic metadata is usually linked with the decision to partially or fully base the content transport on files. As mentioned earlier, a number of standardized file formats have been developed for different applications. From the point of view of television production operations, certainly the most important ones are the advanced authoring format (AAF) and the material exchange format (MXF).

8.3   Material Exchange Format—MXF

The MXF file format is the fruit of a joint effort of users and manufacturers grouped in several international associations such as the EBU, the AAF Association, and the ProMPEG Forum. It is a response to the need, defined as urgent by the EBU/SMPTE Task Force, to develop and standardize a file format that would be used throughout the industry for content exchange over different transfer media.

In order to respond to these expectations, the MXF format has to fulfill a number of requirements. Some of them are related to the basics of the format itself, or stem from the need to accommodate the differences of streaming and file transfer, while others are related to the specifics of different areas of the wide field of content production and distribution. For example, a file format designed for streaming must have the essence arranged in the body in a directly playable order or must carry a sufficient amount of metadata information to facilitate full recognition of the transported payload. On the other hand, different parts of the content production and distribution process have different requirements. In acquisition it is necessary to generate different categories of metadata information depending of the type of program (the "who, what, when, where, and why" of the news operations or the "shot, take, and location" information for the documentaries, drama, children or music programs). That phase of content production may require reconciling the recommendation to keep the original recorded format unchanged with the need to use circuits that do not offer an adequate bandwidth for the transfer of the shots in their native form to the base. The postproduction part of the process is distinguished by a huge amount of metadata information that has to be generated, handled, and stored—from the edit decision lists, edit history, and ownership to all other postproduction-related information. In addition, at the end of that phase it is important to store a copy of a finished program as "work in progress" in order to facilitate later refinements and the production of derived works. The storage, distribution, and subsequent archiving of finished works demands considerably less additional information, but it must contain information on program ownership, content usage, and all cross-referencing data needed for an easy retrieval. At the same time the content has to be stored in an easily streamable form.

The design of MXF files is based on a set of guidelines derived from a number of user requirements, with the result that MXF files are

- easy to understand and apply by adequately trained technical staff
- compression agnostic (i.e. they accept all signals regardless of the compression method used to generate them)
- an open system (i.e. a system that can be easily interconnected with other systems)

- capable of providing an adequate identification of the payload
- extensible and scaleable (i.e. a system that can be extended in the future and that can be used in configurations of different complexity)
- usable on all major platforms
- adapted to a partial file transfer
- independent from a transport and storage mechanism
- easily convertible between stream and storage versions

It should be added that the participants in the development process took note of the results achieved in the domain of AAF system definition, and of the role that this file format could play in complex postproduction processes, and concluded that not only must a very high degree of interoperability be ensured between the two file formats, but also that MXF must be developed as a subset of the AAF system.

An MXF file is a very complex file format. That complexity is undoubtedly the result of the need to respond to the numerous demands of the content-creation environment and of the intricacies of a mixed conventional and IT-based technical production systems. Consequently, the description of an MXF file in this book must suffer from oversimplification as it will be unavoidably limited to a sketchy exposition of its most prominent features.

The basic definition of an *MXF file* is that it is a physical implementation of a data or logical model. As symbolically represented in Figure 8.2, an MXF file is composed of a header that starts the file, carries the metadata necessary for the identification of the content, and timing and synchronization information. The header partition also contains labels used to determine the compliance of the decoders. The MXF system is designed in such a way that every MXF decoder must be capable of reading the header and reporting the file content regardless of whether or not it is capable of decoding that particular content.

The next part of the file is its body where the essence container stores picture, sound, and data essence that can be considered to be the basic material of the file content. The essence container also indicates that the basic material has been packed in a file in an interoperable way. Picture and sound information may be stored in the essence container in different ways depending on the intended use of the file. In addition, several essence containers can be placed inside a single file. These essence containers are then separated by *partitions*, (not visible on

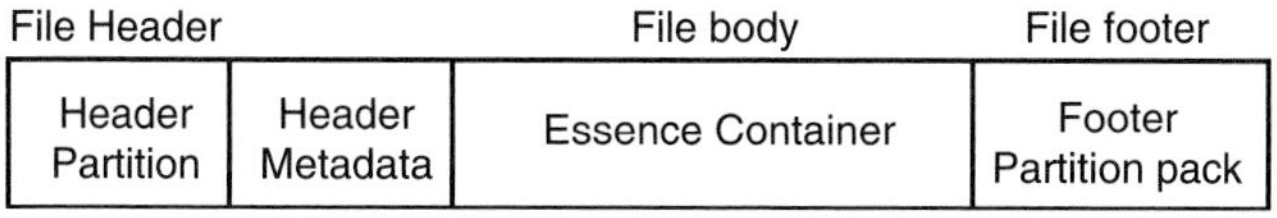

File Header		File body	File footer
Header Partition	Header Metadata	Essence Container	Footer Partition pack

Figure 8.2 Symbolic representation of the construction of an MXF file.

Figure 8.2) which facilitates the use of MXF files for *playlists* (i.e. electronically generated lists of program items that automatically controls their playout in a predetermined order at predetermined times).

Additional data are included in the header to make the file as versatile and flexible as possible. For example the *index tables* and the *random index pack* define the position of all partitions inside a file making random access to the material placed inside a file easy and unambiguous. Other housekeeping information, like the data that define the position of the file footer, completes the file content.

All elements enclosed inside an MXF file are coded in a special way by KLV coding (key, length, value). Because of that code, all MXF decoders and processing units can simply ignore items they do not recognize and continue processing the recognized ones. Simultaneously the KLV code offers an opportunity to develop further the file format by adding new features (for example, compression methods unknown today or innovative metadata schemes), knowing that such additions will not disturb the functioning of the existing equipment (which will just ignore these additions and process the recognized elements).

Metadata content defines the logical construction of the file. It also defines and describes different essence types that exist inside the file. The logical metadata representation is very compact, and its size does not depend on the size of the essence it represents. It is possible to identify two main types of metadata: structural and descriptive metadata.

Structural metadata are defined and standardized by appropriate SMPTE documents and are used to define first the number of basic essence parameters such as picture size, rate, aspect ratio, audio-sampling frequency, audio quantization, and so on. Structural metadata will carry information about the compression scheme used in the video and in the audio essence and consequently will offer information on the type of decoder needed for decompression. Structural metadata also describe the mutual relationships of different essence types.

Descriptive metadata offer additional information to those defining the structure of the file and its components and can be read by either humans or machines. Such metadata existed before files and file transfer. They were simply present as pieces of paper accompanying videotapes or cassettes. Obviously the amount of information on those papers (or sometimes even diskettes) varied from one organization or production process to another. Sometimes the information was implicit, as when operators recognized the recording format simply by looking at the physical appearance of the cassette. However, in the file domain everything has to be documented, and the list of items that might have to be documented could be endless. For that reason a descriptive metadata scheme 1 (DMS-1) was defined by selecting the number of descriptions usually accompanying magnetic tapes and cassettes and adopting that list as a standard that should cover most of the requirements of content production, distribution, and archiving. Descriptive metadata cover a very large span of production-related information. Such metadata can provide essential information concerning the title of the program or the details of the producer and can also offer detailed information on different editorial aspects of a given clip and on its position inside a complete production plan. It is important to stress that a number of pieces of descriptive metadata information can be generated automatically. For example, a camcorder or a camera can have circuits that generate GPS coordinates, have the name of the cameraperson and of the production company already programmed, produce instructions concerning particular shots, as well as a number of other details that will be extremely useful during postproduction. All these pieces of information could be generated as descriptive metadata in line with the adopted DMS-1 vocabulary. These metadata will be stored in the MXF file with the captured essence and therefore be available throughout the whole life cycle of the essence.

There is another metadata expression connected with MXF files that deserves a couple of words—*dark metadata*. That expression describes all types of metadata that are not recognized by a given decoding application—they are "dark for it." Such metadata could be nonstandard user-generated information that requires a specially developed decoder or new metadata standardized after the construction of the decoder in question or simply standard metadata that are irrelevant for a particular decoding application.

8.4 AAF and Other File Formats

AAF was developed by a group of manufacturers and users as a file format for multimedia authoring and postproduction. It was intended for the exchange of the essence and a very rich set of associated metadata. Originally the complex production process was based on the exchange of essence and part of the metadata on videocassettes. In that process, other metadata were occasionally exchanged as recordings made on separate supports and the nonlinear editing was almost an isolated island. The introduction of the concept of networked production imposed the development of new workflows where the metadata generated in the preproduction were already available during acquisition, where rich metadata flew from acquisition to different stages of a complex postproduction, and where the need to distribute the same content to different channels and different media was taken into account at a sufficiently early stage and so initiated the generation of different versions for different outlets (see more details in Chapter 12). All these aspects required a completely new approach to the organization of the interchange of essence and metadata, an approach where these two sets of data would be encapsulated in a single container, where they would be part of a single file system. The result of this new approach was the development of the

AAF format that, in a way, benefited from and superseded several previous attempts to facilitate the exchange between different parts of a postproduction process.

The AAF format facilitates an easy exchange of essence and rich metadata between different platforms and applications. It is structured for the exchange of pieces of material, where the essence can be stored on a physical carrier (tape or film) or inside a file in a computer-based storage system. In addition, in the AAF system, metadata are always encapsulated in the AAF file while the essence can be in the same file or in an external file. In that case, as in the previously described situations, the metadata and the essence are linked by unique identifiers (e.g., UMID). When two postproduction tools share the same storage (as, for example, do all nonlinear editing units [NLEs] and graphics or special-effects tools that are connected to the same server), the AAF file contains only metadata while the essence is directly exchanged between the tools. That approach avoids the need to build large AAF files and speeds up the operation, but it also offers an added flexibility since the external files can be other AAF files, MXF files, or even different elementary streams of compressed video. When postproduction tools do not share the same storage, it is necessary to generate AAF files that contain both the essence and the associated metadata.

The AAF is particularly well adapted to all possible aspects of present-day, complex postproduction operations. For its part, the MXF file system is developed as a subset of the AAF and adapted to the task of simple interchanges of intermediate, partially complete, and/or fully finished content. Both systems share the same data model, that is, they use an identical method for describing the organization of the essence, which ensures full interoperability of the two systems and makes them complementary rather than competing solutions, as represented in Figure 8.3.

In addition to the recently developed AAF, the broadcasting industry still uses a number of heritage file systems. Some of them, such as the open media framework (OMF) were used as a starting point for the development of the AAF. Others, like the general exchange format (GXF), were and still are widely used for the transport of finished material to the playout systems or for the transport of finished commercials or news clips. A number of these file formats still offer an adequate service inside a given limited field and remain in use in isolated "island" areas. However, none of them can be used for intercommunication between different islands or communication with systems that use the AAF. Such communication requires a neutral and advanced format that can be converted from and to any of these heritage systems with the minimum computational complexity. The MXF file appears to be such a neutral format that it can be successfully used for island intercommunication as well as for the communication between these islands and the AAF-based postproduction systems (see Figure 8.4).

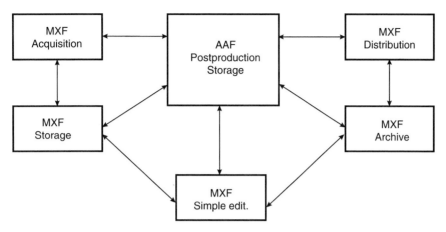

Figure 8.3 The relationship between the AAF and MXF formats.

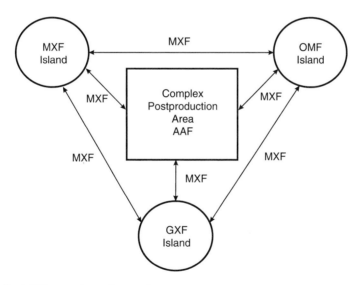

Figure 8.4 MXF as an interchange format.

There is another interesting file exchange format, although it lies somewhat outside the boundaries of television technology—the digital picture exchange (DPX) format. The DPX is developed for the specific needs of the film industry, where it fulfills the role of exchange format in the newly introduced area of the digital intermediate.

In the filmmaking process, scenes are shot on negative film in the studio or the field and then developed; a working copy is made and used for editing. When special effects have to be introduced, an additional optical print is made and sent to special-effects departments or independent houses where the effects are created in a complex and difficult way. The advent of electronic imagery and especially the introduction of computer-based image-generation and processing techniques displayed the enormous potential that such a technology could bring to the domain of special effects. However, the equipment for electronic special effects was initially based on television standards and was consequently inadequate for the film industry (insufficient resolution, interlaced scanning standard, etc.). To successfully introduce the *digital intermediate* process (where original camera negatives would be scanned into digital electronic form, processed in that form in the special-effects facility, and then returned to the form of a duplicate film negative enriched with all the desired effects), it was necessary to develop special tools and techniques. These new ways of working would respect the requirements of film and ensure a seamless connection between electronically processed scenes and scenes that went through a conventional optical filmmaking process only. To achieve that goal it was necessary to develop

- telecine machines that would progressively scan the film negative and generate digital video signals featuring the high level of resolution needed
- a digital coding method that would overcome the negative consequences of two cascaded lossy optoelectric and electro-optic conversions
- a new file format for the transport of film frames and the accompanying information
- equipment for generating special effects that would operate at very high definition
- film recorders for the reverse conversion from electronics to film

The adaptation of existing equipment for the handling of very high resolution for progressively scanned pictures proved to be within the capabilities of the available technology. A new coding scheme was developed based on the encoding of different print-density values, thus ensuring minimum quality degradation in the cascaded conversion processes. The missing link was the electronic content transport mechanism that would permit an unrestricted exchange of material between the film originators and different facility houses. Since different facility houses unavoidably used equipment coming from different manufacturers, it was obviously necessary to standardize the material exchange system. The standardization process was conducted by the SMPTE and resulted in a specific file format able to transport a large number of information fields organized in separate headers that would facilitate a rapid interpretation and processing of the encapsulated images.

The images, generated through a telecine optoelectric conversion and a digital coding process, were transported on a frame-per-file basis. Therefore each DPX file contained a large amount of information (at the time of the definition of the DPX format, these added pieces of information were not yet called "metadata") and one single film frame in its digital form, but with no restriction concerning the image format. The file supported different aspect ratios, pixel shapes, and spatial resolutions, provided that the information data section adequately described all these parameters.

The box-office success of the movies based on special effects prompted the expansion of electronic intermediate techniques and generalized the use of the DPX files in the film industry.

Television Cameras

9

Being at the front end of the television production chain, television cameras not only perform the basic functions of converting optical into electrical energy and generating the video signal, but also set the upper limit of picture quality that the chain is able to offer. All subsequent units that handle the video signal in different ways (amplifying, distributing, recording, or using it to achieve some special effects) cannot improve its quality; they can only introduce some more or less objectionable degradations. These degradations are particularly apparent in the case of analog production and distribution chains. The quality of the picture signal is, in principle, better protected in all-digital chains, but bear in mind that even these chains are not 100% transparent, especially if they encompass cascaded compression codecs. Consequently, to assess the quality, or the level of transparency, of any given television production and distribution chain, it is the video signal at the output of the camera to which we should compare the picture at the output of the system.

Electronic cameras are designed and built with their intended application in mind. The performances, robustness, and richness of operational features are different for a consumer model produced for the mass market than for a top-of-the-line camera developed to fulfill the most demanding studio or out-side broadcast (OB) applications. However, regardless of their intended area of application and of their respective level of sophistication, the construction of all these cameras, all these complex electro-optic devices, follows the same basic pattern. To facilitate description, this basic pattern will be divided into three subsystems:

1. optical system
2. sensor (electro-optic converter)
3. electronic processing circuitry

9.1 The Optical System

The *optical system* consists of two parts:

1. a lens that accepts the light reflected from the scene and projects a focused optical picture on the next element of the system
2. the light-splitting block that separates the received light into three primaries—red, green, and blue—and transfers them to the three associated sensors

Today practically all electronic cameras use zoom (variable focus) lenses. A *zoom lens* is a construction of a number of fixed and movable glass lenses whose task is not only to pick up the incoming light and to project a focused picture on the splitting block but also to offer the possibility of continuously changing the focal length while at the same time preserving the focus (see Figure 9.1). The change of focal length results in the continuous change of the angle of view and of the image size. The name "zoom lens" comes from the strong impression the viewer has of looking through the front window of an airplane zooming skyward. High-quality lenses used in television are very complex and rather expensive units that have to satisfy a number of sometimes conflicting requirements.

The front element of a zoom lens, the *focusing group*, consists of several glass lenses; its task is to receive the incoming light and, by adjusting the relative position of the elements in the group, to ensure the focusing of the picture projected on the sensor plane. The next two elements are the variator and the compensator. They are moving elements: the *variator* changes the image size and the *compensator* moves along with the variator to preserve the focus. The compensator encompasses also the *diaphragm* or *iris*, which is an adjustable opening regulating the amount of light that will reach the optoelectric sensor. To achieve an optimum brightness of the generated picture the diaphragm can be adjusted manually or

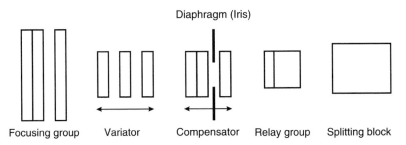

Figure 9.1   Schematic representation of a zoom lens.

automatically. As the focal length of a zoom is changed by moving the variator and the compensator, the angle of view is changed accordingly. At a short focal length, the viewing angle is large and the camera sees a wide area in front of it. By increasing the focal length, the viewing angle becomes smaller and smaller and the camera has a more and more "selective" view of the scene—it concentrates on a detail of the whole scene and magnifies it (see Figure 9.2).

When a lens is focused on an object that occupies a flat plane perpendicular to the optical axis of the lens, then all elements positioned in front and back of that object, within a certain range, will also be in focus. The distance between the first and the last element in focus is called *depth of field*. That parameter is very important as it determines which elements of a given scene will be sharply represented and which ones will remain in a sort of haze. The depth of field is also an important creative tool since the director and the director of photography can use it to achieve a number of dramatic effects.

The following features define the depth of field:

- A smaller iris opening gives a greater depth of field.
- A shorter focal length (the lens zoomed out) offers a greater depth of field.
- A greater distance of the subject from the camera again offers greater depth of field.
- The depth of field is bigger behind than in front of the subject.

The compensator is followed by the *relay group* whose task is to transmit the light from the compensator to the optical splitting block and to define the size of the picture that will be projected on the opto-electric sensor. The final element represented in Figure 9.1 is the *splitting block*, which is the final part of the optical system, but is not part of the zoom lens. The splitting block is part of the camera

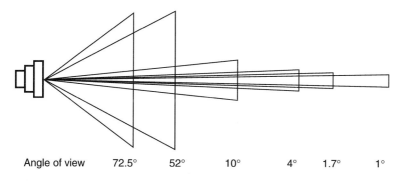

Angle of view   72.5°   52°   10°   4°   1.7°   1°

Figure 9.2 Focal lengths and viewing angles.

and, as it will be explained in more details later in this section, has the task of splitting the incoming light into three primary components.

The specification of a zoom lens is constituted by a number of key parameters. All of them are important, but some are essential for the evaluation of a lens or for the assessment of the appropriateness of a given lens for a planned application:

- **Image size**. The image projected by a lens is in fact round, and the image size is the size of a 4:3 or a 16:9 rectangle inscribed inside that circular image. The image size must correspond to the size of the sensor installed in a given camera.

- **Focal length**. For a *single lens*, the *focal length* is the distance between the center of the lens and the point on the optical axis where all deflected light rays will converge (see Figure 9.3). The focal length of a *compound lens*, that is, a lens made of a number of single lenses, is defined as the distance between a defined point inside the compound, called the *principal point*, and the point of intersection of deflected light rays.

- **Angle of view.** The *angle of view* is defined as the angle between the principal point and the image plane, measured in horizontal, vertical, and diagonal directions. The angle of view and the focal length are closely interrelated: a shorter focal length gives a wide angle of view and vice versa (as was shown in Figure 9.2).

- **Zoom ratio.** A zoom lens has by definition a variable focal length and consequently a variable angle of view (from the wide angle to the telephoto angle). That span between the longest and the shortest focal length (or between the two extreme angles of view), which is defined by the construction of the zoom, is called the *zoom ratio,* and it defines the rate of change of the picture size on the output monitor.

- **F-number.** The aperture of the diaphragm (iris) can be changed by changing the size of the opening, that is, the amount of light flux and consequently the brightness of the image projected by the lens on the sensor. The *f-number,* which is calculated on the basis of the focal length and the effective aperture of the lens, describes the brightness of the projected picture—a smaller f-number indicates a brighter picture. Obviously with a change of a focal length, the f-number should change also; however, the construction of modern lenses minimizes or fully compensates for that effect, but if a focal range extender is inserted in the lens, the brightness of the projected image will drop visibly and the aperture of the lens will have to be adjusted in order to preserve the quality of the output image.

- **Modulation transfer function (MTF)**. The capacity of a given lens to transmit fine details can be described by indicating its resolving power, which

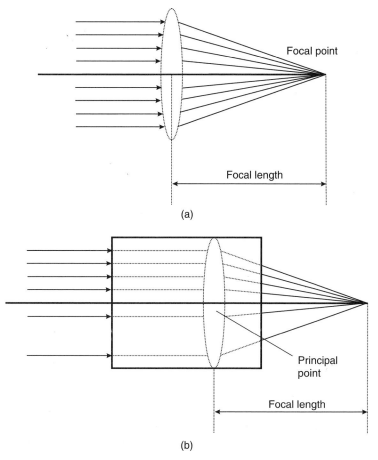

Figure 9.3 Focal length: (a) single lens and (b) compound lens.

is determined by photographing a test card showing a number of parallel black lines of different widths on a white field; the number of differentiated lines indicates only the limit of lens capability (that is, the finest lines it can resolve) and not its behavior throughout the whole range from the widest to the thinnest lines on the chart. Television cameras and the television system as a whole have a limited bandwidth that limits the transmittable fineness of details. Therefore, the important factor in evaluating a zoom lens is the quality of reproduction, the range of contrast offered at values below the bandwidth limit set by the camera, and the television system. That information is offered by the *modulation transfer function* (also called the *optical transfer function*), which describes the total performance of a lens in transmitting fine details over the whole range defined by the system bandwidth.

- **Back focal length and flange back**. The *back focal distance* is the distance between the last glass element of a given lens and the plane of the sensor. That distance is usually converted to a more practical *flange back*, which indicates the distance between the flange surface of the lens and the image plane on the sensor, taking into account the characteristics of the light-splitting block. Every zoom lens has the possibility of a slight adjustment of the flange back, but the range of adjustment is usually small and it is necessary to use a zoom lens whose flange back corresponds to the camera for which it was intended.

- **Minimum object distance (MOD)**. The *minimum object distance* is the closest distance from the first front-glass element of the lens to the object being photographed. Zoom lenses developed for studio cameras usually have short MOD in order to facilitate their use in small studios where the camera has to be positioned close to the subject.

- **Aberrations**. *Aberrations* are departures from ideal lens behavior that have as a result visible deteriorations of the picture quality, and they are unavoidable. There are a number of aberrations that together have a negative influence on the achievable sharpness of focus, but the construction of modern lenses provides solutions for minimizing the visibility of all these defects.

- **Distortions**. While aberrations influence the sharpness of focus, *distortions* are related to the overall geometry of the projected picture. If you consider an ideal rectangle to be the goal of a given lens, distortions will be represented as the percentage of departure from the real- to ideal-picture dimensions (see Figure 9.4).

The light-splitting block separates the incoming light into the three primaries—R, G, and B—and projects them respectively on three associated sensors. The light-splitting block has a crucial influence on the faithfulness of color reproduction of any television camera, and consequently a special attention has to

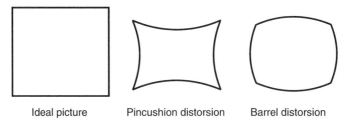

Ideal picture   Pincushion distorsion   Barrel distorsion

Figure 9.4   Geometric distortions.

be paid to its construction and adjustment. Most modern cameras use a splitting block made of a combination of prisms. The contact surfaces between two adjacent prisms are covered with a complex coating consisting of some 10 to 20 layers of different characteristics and acting as a special sort of optical filter known as a *dichroic mirror*. Dichroic surfaces or dichroic mirrors have the ability to reflect one of the primaries while allowing free passage to the remaining components of the incoming light. As can be seen in Figure 9.5, an appropriate disposition of dichroic surfaces allows the splitting block to separate the three primaries and to project them on designated sensors.

A *trimming filter* is inserted at each exit side of the prism between the glass surface and the sensor. The function of these filters is to free the selected primaries from unwanted residues of other colors and improve the selectivity of the light-splitting process.

9.2 Sensors

The function of the sensors is to transform the received photo energy into electrical signals. Just as the camera itself defines the upper limit of quality achievable by a given production chain, the sensor will determine the highest quality achievable by a given camera.

The development of different sensors has been one of the decisive factors in the overall development of television. The advent of electronic sensors in the late

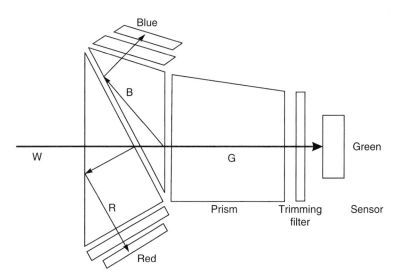

Figure 9.5 Schematic representation of a color-camera light-splitting block.

1920s opened the way to the development of television as we know it today. Fifty years later the reduction in size of electronic sensors and the improvement of their overall characteristics facilitated the construction of portable cameras, a new production tool that created a radical change in the methods of television program production and in television language itself.

From the early days of the first electronic sensors to our present time, we have seen the development of many models based on different technical solutions, but although they differed widely by their construction and by their overall performances, they all belonged in fact to only two large "families" of sensors, defined by two fundamentally different operating principles:

1. pick-up tubes
2. solid-state sensors

9.2.1   Pick-Up Tubes

Although it is conceivable that tube cameras may still be in operation somewhere in the world, pick-up tubes are definitively part of television history. However, for more than 60 years, pick-up tubes were the only available sensors. As such, they determined a number of elements that are still part of television systems. A brief description of their functioning and a short list of major landmarks in the history of their development will help explain their legacy.

Pick-up tubes are electronic tubes essentially made of a photosensitive plate (having the property of changing its electrical state under the impact of the incoming light) and a heated cathode (emitting a cloud of electrons, which are then focused in a beam). That electron beam scans the photosensitive plate, thus generating an electrical current that faithfully represents in the electrical domain the light picture projected on the plate.

The development of pick-up tubes was based on two nineteenth-century discoveries:

1. *Photoemission* is the capacity of certain materials to radiate free electrons under the effect of the incoming light. The number of these electrons is directly proportional to the intensity of the incoming light.
2. *Photoconductivity* is the capacity of some materials to change their resistance to electrical currents under the effect of the incoming light. Here also the resistance of these materials at any given point is inversely proportional to the intensity of the incoming light.

These two phenomena will serve as a basis for the development of all sensors used in television cameras from the late 1920s until the end of the 1980s.

The first two electronic pick-up devices were developed almost simultaneously during the 1920s. One of them, the Image Dissector, was patented by Philo Farnsworth and the other, the Iconoscope, by the Russian-born scientist Vladimir Zworykin. The Iconoscope was considerably more sensitive than the Image Dissector, although its sensitivity was rather poor by today's standards—it required some 10,000 lux for normal operation. That low sensitivity demanded large iris apertures, which in turn considerably diminished the depth of field. At the same time, the noise level was rather high. Nevertheless, the Iconoscope was a tremendous step forward in the development of television. It made possible the achievement of an all-electronic television chain and facilitated the start of the first regular television services in the mid-1930s.

By the end of the 1930s two new tubes appeared—the Orthicon and the CPS Emitron. These two sensors introduced a most important novelty: a transparent photosensitive plate. Such a plate was able to accept the light on one side and the scanning beam on the opposite side. This feature allowed the construction of pick-up tubes in the shape of a straight glass tube.

A major step forward occurred after World War II, with the appearance of a considerably improved version of Orthicons—the *Image Orthicons*, whose development was prompted by the general advancement of electronics during the war. The basic capabilities and performances of Image Orthicons conditioned their rather long life in television exploitation. Appearing by the late 1940s, they were used until the gradual phase-out of black-and-white television service in the mid-1960s.

Almost in parallel with the development of Image Orthicons, another family of tubes was conceived based on the effect of photoconductivity. The first member of that family, the Vidicon, used a photoconductive transparent plate, was smaller than the Image Orthicon, required less complex electronic circuitry, and offered a decent sensitivity and noise levels, but had a very high propensity to memorize light images and a high degree of *lag* (blurred outlines trailing behind moving objects). These shortcomings almost prevented the use of Vidicons in the professional environment.

In the early 1960s the Dutch manufacturer Philips put the first broadcast-quality photoconductive pick-up tube on the market, the Plumbicon. This sensor represented a considerable step forward compared to the Image Orthicons and Vidicons. It was smaller and had higher sensitivity, less noise, less inertia, better resolution, and was, in short, a device that opened the way for the implementation of a new generation of television cameras and gave an important boost to the development of color television.

The Plumbicon was followed by a number of other photoconductive tubes: Vistacon, Leddicon, Saticon, Newicon, and so on. All these tubes were based on the same operating principles, and the main difference (setting aside some

Figure 9.6 Plumbicon and CCD chip.

details in their construction) consisted in the formulation of the photosensitive plate. Vidicons had been based on antimony trisulfide; Plumbicons, Vistacons and Leddicons on lead oxide; and Saticons on a compound of selenium, arsenic, and tellurium.

Over the years, the performances of Plumbicons and other photoconductive tubes improved significantly. The formulation of the photosensitive plate was changed, a number of details in the internal construction of the tubes modified, and their mechanical concept redesigned. The diameter of the tube and its overall dimensions decreased gradually from 30 mm and 25 mm to 19 mm and then to 12.5 mm, thus allowing the construction of portable color cameras.

The pick-up tubes were continuously developed and improved over 50 years of television history, but their development capacity was limited by a number of shortcomings, deficiencies inherent to the basic construction and operating principles on which all of them were founded. That incited researchers to try to replace pick-up tubes with solid-state sensors. Many avenues were investigated, and the most promising appeared to be the charge-coupled device (CCD), which represented an important step forward in the development of television technology.

9.2.2 Solid-State Sensors

The CCD sensors operate on the principle of photosensitive cells where the incoming light creates electrical charges proportional to the light's intensity.

Under the effect of a control voltage, these charges are coupled and transferred toward the processing circuitry. The first prototype camera equipped with three CCDs was shown publicly in 1975 by the U.S.-based company RCA. First-generation CCD sensors displayed an inadequate resolution and a very poor sensitivity (in order to produce a standard television picture, the camera required a light intensity of a fantastic 30,000 lux, almost 100 times higher intensity than the one we usually experience in our offices). It took 10 additional years to produce commercially available CCD sensors with adequate performance. Once basic performance became acceptable for professional applications, CCD sensors quickly phased out pick-up tubes, thus ending the pick-up tube's undisputed 60-year reign. The CCD sensor's rapid and sweeping victory can be easily explained by simply listing the inherent advantages of these new sensors:

- Pick-up tubes have a definite life span. Over time their essential performance gradually degrades, and when they fall under an acceptable level, the tubes have to be replaced. Theoretically the life span of a CCD should be limitless. In practical terms it is safe to state that a CCD sensor features an incomparably longer life span than a pick-up tube.
- All pick-up tubes show an amount of lag, or blurred outlines of moving objects. *Punctual* highlights (highlights having high intensity and very small physical dimensions, like a point) on the scene create a comet-tail effect in the picture—a sort of halo behind the highlight spot that looks like a comet tail. If the highlight is very intense it can even *burn* the photosensitive plate, that is, leave a permanent visible mark. Thanks to their operating principle, CCD elements are not prone to lag or comet-tail defects and cannot be burnt by extreme highlight spots.
- Due to their construction, all tubes are mechanically sensitive and affected by outside magnetic fields. If the camera is exposed to powerful sound vibrations, for example, as in live rock-music productions, the internal mechanical elements of a tube may start to vibrate in resonance, creating a very annoying degradation of the output picture. CCD elements are unaffected by even the most turbulent environments.
- It is recommended that the pick-up tube not be put in a vertical position with the photosensitive plate at the bottom. During the normal operation of the tube, some debris may appear inside; if the tube is turned upside down, this debris may fall on the photosensitive plate and stick to it, creating *blind spots*. CCD sensors can operate in any position.
- In spite of all developments, pick-up tubes are still too large for the manufacture of small and handy portable cameras, as each tube has to be accompanied with a set of deflection coils to control the scanning movements of the electron beam. Solid-state sensors are small, they do not require

deflection coils, and they are glued directly on the light-splitting block, which ensures an excellent and immovable superposition of the three (R, G, and B) images (a parameter known as *registration*).

- The electron beam in the pick-up tube is generated by electric heating of the cathode. At the same time it is necessary to generate a number of control voltages, some of which are rather high. All these factors result in relatively high energy consumption, which is a critical factor in the construction of battery-powered hand-held cameras. Like all solid-state devices, the CCD elements have considerably lower power requirements.

- Present-day CCD sensors generate considerably less noise (which shows up as "snow" on the resulting picture) than pick-up tubes. As with any other electronic component, CCD elements will generate a thermal noise as well, but it is possible to considerably reduce the amount by adequate cooling of the sensor.

- Cameras equipped with pick-up tubes have to be regularly adjusted. Before operating it is necessary to control and correct a number of parameters such as beam current, geometry, registration, shading, and so on. By comparison, CCD cameras require virtually no adjustments.

9.2.3 Operating Principles of CCDs

A CCD sensor is made up of a number of photosensitive semiconductor sensors that create electrical charges proportional to the intensity of the incoming light and of *analog shift registers* (a type of a chain of logic electric circuits used mainly for storage of data and their transfer from one to another end of the chain) that move these charges to the output of the device. The photosensitive part of the CCD sensor, its area imaging device, is a mosaic of several thousand photosensitive cells. Each of these cells corresponds to one element of the picture—that is, to one pixel. It is obvious that the resolution of a given CCD sensor will depend directly upon the number of its photosensitive elements. For standard definition television, it is usual to have 500 to 1,000 cells in each row. The number of rows is dictated by the number of lines of a given television system.

Each element of the mosaic consists of a specially treated silicon plate (called *P-type silicon*) on which a thin layer of silicon dioxide is applied. That insulating silicon dioxide layer bears an electrode connected to the voltage source. If the voltage applied to the electrode is positive, then a region of low potential energy (a *depletion*) is created just under the junction of two silicon layers (see Figure 9.7). That low potential energy region acts as a sort of well or empty container attracting all free electrons in the region. The higher the voltage applied to the electrode, the deeper the depletion and therefore the more attractive the well will be.

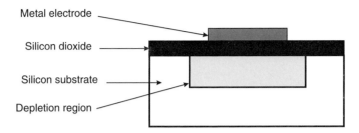

Metal electrode

Silicon dioxide

Silicon substrate

Depletion region

Figure 9.7   The CCD cell.

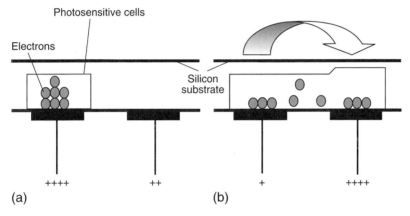

Photosensitive cells

Electrons

Silicon
substrate

++++   ++   +   ++++

(a)   (b)

Figure 9.8   CCD operation: (a) storing the charge and (b) coupling and transfer of charges.

Free electrons appear in the silicon substrate under the impact of light. The number of free electrons is proportional to the intensity of the incoming light. All these free electrons will be attracted and the depletion will store the accumulated charge, acting as an analog memory device (see Figure 9.8a).

The next step in the CCD operation is the coupling and transfer of charges. As we mentioned earlier, each element of the mosaic has its own electrode. However, the elements share the same P-type silicon substrate. If we decrease the positive voltage on the first electrode and apply a higher voltage level to a neighboring one, the free electrons will start to migrate from the first to the second element (Figure 9.8b). At one point, all electrons will be transferred to the second element of the mosaic. By applying a similar procedure to electrodes of the following elements of the mosaic, we enable the negative charge induced by the effect of light to travel through all elements organized as analog shift registers.

According to the organization of registers and the way of transferring charges, we can differentiate three main groups of CCD sensors:

1. frame transfer CCDs (FT)
2. interline transfer CCDs (IT)
3. frame interline transfer CCDs (FIT)

Frame transfer CCDs were developed for professional applications. They are constituted by three *zones* (three groups of elements) forming three registers (see Figure 9.9a). The first zone—the *image zone*—is exposed to the incoming light. The other two zones are always protected from any incoming light. The image zone is made exclusively of active, photosensitive elements. The incoming light consequently creates charges in each of these active elements that are proportional to the intensity of light falling on that particular element. During the vertical blanking interval, a mechanical shutter, similar to the one installed in film cameras, interrupts the light flux from the lens to the sensor. At the same time, transfer voltages are applied to the electrodes and all charges are transferred from zone one to zone two—the *memory zone*. At the end of the vertical blanking interval and at the beginning of the next field, the shutter is open and the light falls again on the active surface. Meanwhile, and for the duration of the whole field (1/50 or 1/60 of a second), the charges from the memory zone are transferred, line by line, into the third, horizontal, or *read-out register*, which delivers the resulting video signal to the output terminal.

Interline transfer CCDs were initially developed for consumer cameras (see Figure 9.9b). Each active photosensitive element of the mosaic has an associated element belonging to a shift register and protected from the impact of light. Active and register elements create a number of parallel vertical columns. During the vertical blanking period, all charges from active elements are transferred to the register ones. During the next field, while the light impact creates new charges in photosensitive and unprotected cells, the charges accepted by the shift register cells during the previous vertical blanking are transferred "downward" along vertical shift register columns and transmitted to the horizontal read-out shift register.

The main drawback of the FT CCD sensors is the necessity of implementing a rotating shutter in an all-electronic camera and of coping with the inconvenience created by that mechanical device (necessity to implement a shutter and its motor in the body of the camera, to solve the problems of vibrations, inertia, noise created by the rotating blade, and so on). On the other hand, the IT CCDs also has drawbacks. The surface of such a sensor is made up of not only active, light-sensitive elements but also of nonphotosensitive register elements. That solution diminishes the number of photosensitive cells that can be

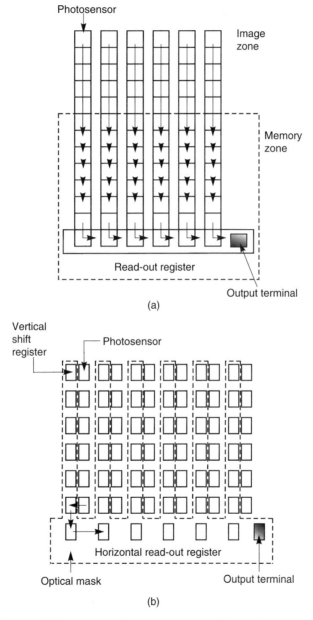

Photosensor

Image zone

Memory zone

Read-out register

Output terminal

(a)

Vertical shift register

Photosensor

Horizontal read-out register

Optical mask

Output terminal

(b)

Figure 9.9 Types of CCD sensors: (a) frame transfer, (b) interline transfer, and (c) frame interline transfer.

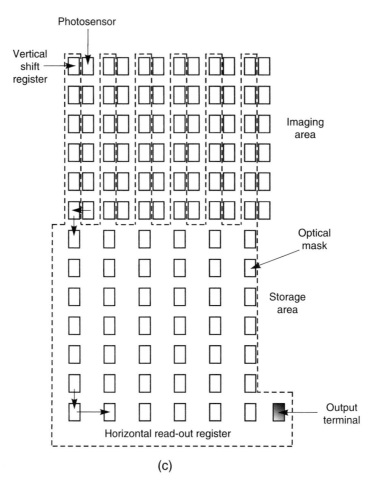

Photosensor

Vertical
shift
register

Imaging
area

Optical
mask

Storage
area

terminal

Horizontal read-out register

(c)

Figure 9.9   Continued.

installed on the CCD surface, thus limiting the resolution power of such a sensor.
When the scene in front of the lens contains important highlight areas, the active
elements of the sensor that receives these highlights are saturated and some of the
generated free electrons are "spilled over" into the neighboring elements of the
mosaic. Since these electrons are not the result of the light falling on the concerned
element or of a controlled transfer, they generate a clearly noticeable spurious
red or pink vertical line in the reproduced picture. This effect is called *smear*.
To diminish this unpleasant effect, later IT CCD sensors have been equipped
with an additional horizontal shift register whose role is to drain the overflow
of free electrons resulting from highlights and to prevent the saturation of active
elements.

Frame interline transfer CCDs are, in a way, a combination of both FT and IT transfer methods and operating principles (see Figure 9.9c). At first glance, FIT sensors look like FT ones since they each have three zones, or areas—the image area, open to the impact of light, and two other, permanently protected areas. The image area, composed of active and shift register cells, looks very much like an IT sensor. The incoming light creates electrical charges in active photosensitive cells. During the vertical blanking interval, these charges are transferred from active cells to shift register cells. While in the case of IT sensors, the transfer from the shift registers to the horizontal register is done continuously (at a line rate within one field, that is, for the duration of one television field), in the case of FIT sensors, a memory zone, protected by an optical mask from the incoming light, is inserted between the active field and the horizontal register. Thanks to the addition of that memory area the charges in vertical shift registers can be rapidly transferred to the memory area (during the vertical blanking interval, that is, 60 times faster than in the case of IT sensors). Once in the memory area, the charges are transferred at a line rate to the horizontal read-out register, in the same way as in FT sensors.

The net result of such a charge-transfer process is the elimination of the mechanical shutter and the considerable reduction of the unwanted smear effect. As indicated above, the smear is the result of the over-saturation of a given photosensitive element and the subsequent overflow of the charge to the neighboring elements. In the case of IT sensors, the charges are transferred line by line from vertical registers to the horizontal one, and that relatively slow transfer rate is convenient for the propagation of the smear. Considering that the transfer from vertical registers for FIT sensors is 60 times faster, the visibility of the smear effect should be diminished in the same proportions. The line-by-line transfer is performed in the memory zone that acts as a buffer between the very fast transfer (which helps eliminate the smear) and the fixed transfer speed defined by the line-repetition rate of a given scanning system.

FIT sensors also offer the opportunity to implement an "electronic shutter." If an additional vertical register is installed on the reverse side from the shift register, it can act as a sort of electron "drain," discarding charges instead of conducting them toward the memory zone. The modification of the speed of change of the control voltage is in fact the modification of the *integration time* in active cells, which is equivalent to the exposure time of photo cameras. The integration time can vary from 1/100 to 1/1000 of a second, allowing an excellent rendition of fast-moving objects. However, the price of introducing this feature is a certain loss in sensitivity.

From the time of their introduction, CCD sensors have progressed tremendously. Some of their initial limitations (such as the lack of resolution, relatively low sensitivity, smear, hypersensitivity in the area of red wavelengths, and the response nonuniformity) were successfully overcome by appropriate solutions. *Hole-accumulated diode* (HAD) sensors dramatically increased sensitivity and reduced the visibility of smear. *Hyper-HAD* sensors introduced micro lenses applied over each cell of the photosensitive mosaic. These micro lenses increased the efficiency and sensitivity of the CCD by collecting the light that otherwise would be scattered over nonsensitive parts of the sensors. *High-definition CCD* sensors became a standard product. For the moment it seems that this type of solid-state sensor still has considerable development potential.

9.3 Camera Processing Circuitry

The signal-processing part of the camera has to perform a number of operations whose ultimate goal is to produce the best possible output signal. The output signal, depending on the user requirements, can be analog component, analog composite, or digital component in its parallel or serial form. However, practically all present-day cameras use digital signal processing (DSP). At the output of the sensors, and after preamplification (which is the first amplification stage and is usually an integral part of the sensor), the R, G, and B signals are digitized and all subsequent operations conducted with digital signals. The A/D conversion (see Section 5.2) is usually performed with a 10- or even 12-bit quantization that ensures high-quality signal processing. At the end of the processing chain, and before the output, the R, G, and B signals are converted to the standard digital components (Y, R-Y, and B-Y) complying with Recommendation 601. Compared with traditional analog signal-processing techniques, digital signal processing offers a number of advantages:

- considerable reduction of the influence of signal-processing circuits on the signal quality
- introduction of additional signal corrections, which are difficult or impractical to perform with analog techniques
- easy-to-memorize settings and use of same settings on several cameras.

CCD cameras with digital signal processing are extremely stable and require few setup alignments. In practical terms this means that a CCD camera will be ready to operate several seconds after being switched on. However, there are a number of corrections that have to be performed in order to optimize the output picture or to adapt the camera to the lighting conditions. Some of these corrections are automatic and automatically triggered. Others are automatic but have to be manually started, while some corrections are still fully manual.

The signal goes through a number of processing stages after preamplification:

- The *master gain* (overall and simultaneous gain adjustment of all three R, G, and B channels) is manually controlled in order to increase the signal amplitude in case of extremely low light levels when the voltage of the signal generated by the sensor is too low for further processing. Increasing the gain results in an unavoidable increase of noise level.
- The fully automatic *shading control* is meant to correct the nonuniformity of response over the whole image surface, which could be the result of lens errors or of differences in sensitivity of particular cells of the sensor.
- *Color correction* is used to adjust the correct colorimetry of the reproduced picture. The spectral sensitivity of the R, G, and B camera channels has to be adjusted to match the spectral curves of the screen phosphors. Although it is possible to compute a theoretical optimum, many broadcasters have their own colorimetric preferences and consequently, camera manufacturers offer switchable preset values (e.g., EBU, BBC, RAI, etc.). At the same time, studio and outside broadcast (OB) cameras are equipped with manual gain controls that support matching the appearance of pictures delivered by several cameras in a multicamera production.

Like their predecessors the pick-up tubes, CCD sensors used today have a *linear transfer characteristic*, that is, a linear relationship between the generated electrical signal and the incoming light—throughout the whole range of illuminations, equal changes of the intensity of the incoming light will generate equal changes of the amplitude of the electrical signal. However, for correct color reproduction it is necessary that the whole production, transmission, and reception chain be linear. The last element in that chain, the cathode-ray tube, is not a linear device. Consequently, to ensure a linear operation of the system a *precorrection* has to be introduced at the front end of the chain. The linear characteristic of the sensor must be made nonlinear but complementary to the transfer characteristic of the display. The addition of the sensor and of the display characteristics will produce an overall linear response (see Figure 9.10). That precorrection, known as *gamma correction*, usually has several manually controllable preset values.

The finite number of photosensitive cells in a CCD sensor as well as the presence of the optical prefiltering result in a loss of resolution. To compensate for this loss, a special manual control called *contour correction* is introduced to artificially improve the crispness of all transitions. This correction ensures better and sharper pictures but must be used with great care. Its application leads not only to an increase of the basic noise level but also to too much contour correction, which may produce unnatural-looking pictures in that they are much sharper than real ones.

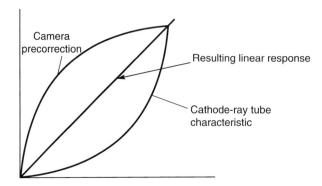

Camera precorrection

Resulting linear response

Cathode-ray tube characteristic

Figure 9.10   Gamma correction.

As was explained in Chapter 2, white lights from different sources have characteristics, expressed as different color temperatures, which unavoidably influence the color rendition of photographed objects. Consequently, to ensure a faithful reproduction of the whole color spectrum under given lighting conditions, it is necessary to adjust the relative values of the R, G, and B channels accordingly. That adjustment is known as *white balance* and has to be performed prior to any shooting and whenever the lighting conditions change (shooting indoors vs. outdoors, etc.). To adjust the white balance, the operator has to point the camera toward a uniform white surface exposed to the ambient light and then manually initiate the automatic adjustment circuitry.

Studio or OB cameras usually have three separate subassemblies, which together represent the camera chain:

- **camera head** – optics, sensors, viewfinder, and the associated circuitry
- **camera control unit** or CCU – containing the major part of the processing circuitry
- **operational control panel** – remote controls of the iris, black level, white level, and individual R, G, and B channel controls, allowing a continual control and adjustment of the photographic quality of the output picture.

A camera cable connects the camera head and the CCU. Since every cable introduces a degree of attenuation and distortion of the transmitted signal that is directly proportional to the length of the cable, it is necessary to introduce a precorrection that will compensate for the expected losses. The amount of precorrection depends on the length of the cable, and there is a limit of length over which no correction is possible. That maximum length depends on the type of cable and on the type of camera, but generally it is around several hundred meters for multicore cables and several thousand meters for "triax" cables (special type of coaxial cables where the central or axial conductor is surrounded by two concentric and mutually isolated mesh-tubular conductors, which act also as radiation shields) that carry all relevant signals both ways in a multiplexed form.

All modern cameras feature a number of other controls and corrections. Some of them are essential; some are an "added value" that differentiates one camera from the other on the market. The selection of a camera has to be based on the evaluation of objective quality parameters, operational features it offers, and price, but all have to be weighed against the intended use of that piece of equipment.

9.4 Basic Quality Parameters

To select one among many cameras offered on the market, or to select the most appropriate camera for a given application, it is necessary to assess its performance. This can be evaluated either by a subjective assessment of the quality of the produced picture or by an objective measurement of a number of critical parameters. Subjective evaluations are attractive but highly unreliable and difficult to reproduce since they involve, by definition, highly variable subjective factors. In addition, the comparison of two subjective assessments of two cameras, or of the same camera, requires a very precise definition and control of all subjective assessment conditions, and that would be a very complex and delicate task. On the other hand, an objective measurement can be easily repeated as many times as necessary. However, meaningful and usable measurement results can be obtained only if measurements are conducted in accordance with known and well-defined procedures and methods. While the departure from the results of a subjective assessment is normal and practically expected, different results obtained from two objective measurements of the same parameter indicate immediately that something is wrong either with the measurement itself or with the measured piece of equipment. A careful check of the measurement procedure can easily give a quick and unambiguous answer to that dilemma.

A single, objectively measurable parameter offering a good representation of the quality of a given camera does not exist. Such an assessment can be obtained only by taking together the results of a number of measured parameters. While a good part of these results are directly related, or practically equal to the performances of the sensors, others are the result of a combined action of the sensors and the camera processing circuitry.

9.4.1 Noise level

Every electronic component generates a certain quantity of unwanted, chaotic, and uncontrolled electron movements in the form of noise accompanying the signal. The noise in the case of the video signal is visible in the form of small points (unrelated to the picture) that randomly move across the screen and that are commonly called "snow" due to their resemblance to snow flakes. Once generated, the noise will accompany the signal throughout its path. Other elements on that path will add their own noise, and every time the signal is amplified, the noise is amplified as well. Since the sensor is the first element in the picture chain, its own level of noise defines the minimum noise level achievable by a given system. Usually we do not measure the absolute level of noise, only the ratio between the peak-to-peak value of the signal and the mean value of the noise. The signal-to-noise ratio is expressed as a logarithmic computation, and its unit is a *decibel* (dB).

9.4.2 Resolution

The *resolution* is the capacity to differentiate small picture details and sharp transitions. Higher resolution means finer and sharper pictures—in short, a better reproduction of the real world. The maximum picture resolution is limited by the basic parameters of a given television system—the overall frequency bandwidth and the number of scanning lines. The resolution of a sensor, or of the whole camera chain, is measured in a way that is similar to the measurement of resolution of photographic systems: by the number of parallel black lines on a white surface that the system is capable of reproducing as identifiable separate lines. Beyond the resolution limit, parallel separate lines will be reproduced as a uniform gray area.

The resolution of a sensor, or of a camera, is usually expressed as *modulation depth*. To understand that parameter, suppose that a camera is pointed at a test chart constituted by a number of "packets" of equally-spaced black lines on a white surface. The first packet is made of rather wide black lines and all following ones are made of thinner and thinner lines.

As shown on Figure 9.11, after the optoelectric conversion, an electric signal is obtained where wider pulses correspond to wider lines and, at the same time, these pulses have a higher amplitude. With the decrease of the line width, the pulses become narrower and their amplitude is reduced. This loss in amplitude is called loss of modulation depth and it is quantified as a percentage of the widest pulse amplitude, which is equal to the maximum amplitude featured by the television system. The smaller the pulse amplitude, the more difficult its reproduction on the screen will be. Therefore, a resolution expressed as 35% at 400 lines indicates that 400 black and white lines will be reproduced with an amplitude representing 35% of the maximum amplitude. The source resolution can be degraded by inadequate quality of the television production chain. Lines transmitted with a modest modulation depth may be identifiable as separate lines

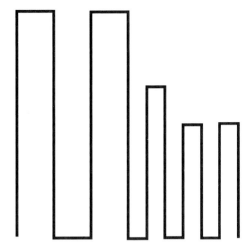

Figure 9.11   Modulation depth. A.) wide, high amplitude pulses corresponding to wide lines; B.) medium pulses corresponding to medium sized lines; C.) narrow, low amplitudes pulses corresponding to thin, narrowly spaced lines.

on the monitor connected to the camera output. However, all subsequent elements in the video signal path will add their amount of noise to the original signal. At a certain point the overall noise level will mask the parts of the signal whose amplitude is small, and it will become impossible to identify separate lines. The area will appear to be a uniform gray. In practical terms, this means that at the end of the chain, the viewer will experience a picture with less resolution and less sharpness than the one observed on the monitor in the studio control room.

9.4.3 Spectral characteristic

Every sensor has its own *spectral characteristic*, that is, it offers different responses at different wavelengths of the visible spectrum. While in the time of black-and-white television the spectral characteristic was not of such importance, it became very significant with the advent of color. It is desirable today that the sensitivity of sensors to different parts of the visible spectrum coincides as much as possible with the equivalent sensitivity (or spectral characteristic) of the human eye, so that the reproduction of colors satisfies our appreciation of them.

9.4.4 Sensitivity

The *sensitivity* is defined by the lowest lighting level that allows the generation of optimum-quality pictures. In order to transpose this definition into a system of objective, measurable entities, it is necessary to define

- the meaning of "optimum picture quality"
- the conditions under which that optimum quality is assessed (light intensity, reflectance of the surface in front of the camera lens, settings of the camera optics, etc.)

The response of a camera depends on the level of the light illuminating the scene in front of it. Reducing the light level that falls on the sensor also reduces the amplitude of the electrical signal generated by it. A lower signal level means a decrease of the signal-to-noise ratio (S/N ratio). A lower S/N ratio is assessed by the viewer as increased noisiness of the picture and interpreted as a loss in quality. Consequently, the signal-to-noise ratio can be used as the necessary objective and measurable parameter expressing the picture quality.

In order to make measurements and assessments as objective and repeatable as possible, the measurement conditions have to be precisely defined. It is necessary to define not only the light level and color temperature but also the reflectivity of the surface at which the camera is pointed. Since the adjustment of optical parameters of the zoom lens determines the quantity of light projected on the photosensitive surface of the sensor, it is important to state exactly what the iris opening, or the f-stop was during the measurement.

Following is an example of the sensitivity of a given camera showing the parameters that should be expressed:

- 2,000 lux at a color temperature of 3,200 K
- aperture at f/8
- uniform white surface with a 90% reflectivity
- signal to noise ratio of 60 dB.

Many camera specifications give additional information with the sensitivity data, such as "minimum illumination" or "usable picture at XY lux." The quoted illumination is usually strikingly low. However, that indication has to be taken with a great degree of caution since it usually corresponds to noisy pictures that can be obtained with a full iris opening. Such pictures can be used if the footage is aimed for a news program and if its topicality is extremely high. In short, the level of "usability" of such pictures depends on their "news value" and not on the results of any sort of quantifiable assessment method.

10

Video Recording

Videotape recorders (VTRs) appeared in broadcasting studios in the late 1950s and quickly became quintessential tools for television production. They played a key role in acquisition, they were pivotal engines in postproduction, and they were essential in transmission. But at the beginning of the new millennium, after almost 50 years of undisputed rule, they seem to be at the end of their life cycle. Tape is being replaced more and more by other information carriers as the recorders gradually cede ground to IT-based servers and storage systems. However, that technological cross-fade, that transition from videotape recording to other forms of storing video and audio signals, will take some time. It also seems that despite all new developments, acquisition and long-term archiving will continue to use VTRs or tape-based solutions for years to come.

10.1 The Evolution of Videotape Recorders

On December 1, 1898, the Danish inventor Valdemar Poulsen filed for a patent protecting a device that permitted magnetic recording of electrical signals on a steel wire. Early models of Poulsen's device were shown at the World Exhibition in Paris in 1900, where they aroused a considerable interest (see Figure 10.1). Unfortunately, the time was not yet ripe for such an invention.

Although Poulsen's device dropped rapidly from the attention of a wider public, engineers continued to investigate and develop this new technique. A string of important improvements and discoveries accumulated until 1935 when the German company Telefunken introduced the first audiotape recorder, which used a paper magnetic tape, to the market.

After World War II, television services reopened and grew at an incredibly fast pace. The developing media saw all the advantages of a magnetic recorder that could record not only audio signals but also moving pictures. That was especially the case in the United States, where three large national networks covered

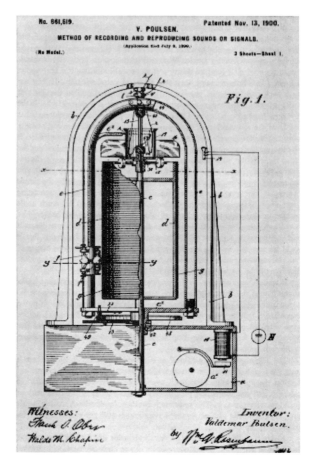

Figure 10.1   Facsimile of Poulsen's patent.

a continent divided into four time zones. For both programming and financial reasons it was important to have "prime time" programs aired at prime time in each zone, in other words, to have a device offering a delayed replay of the same program in different time zones.

Unfortunately, the development of a videotape recorder had to overcome considerably more difficult obstacles than the ones that challenged the design and construction of an audiotape recorder. According to the laws of physics, the head-to-tape speed has to be proportional to the highest recorded frequency. If we compare the highest video frequency (5 MHz) to the same limit of an audio signal (20,000 Hz), it is clear that video recording requires a head-to-tape speed 250 times faster than the one used in audiotape recorders. On the other hand, the maximum span of frequencies that can be recorded with one magnetic head corresponds to 10 octaves (where an octave represents a frequency bandwidth with an upper frequency limit exactly double the lower frequency limit). For example, if the lowest frequency that has to be recorded is fixed at 20 Hz, the limit of the first octave will be at 40, the second at 80, the third at 160, the fourth at 320, and the tenth at only 20,480 Hz, a far cry from the 5,000,000 Hz of the video signal.

The first demonstration of the recording of video signals was done by an engineering team financed by the well-known movie star Bing Crosby. In 1952 the team showed a machine with 12 stationary heads recording 16 minutes of program with the highest frequency set at only 1.7 MHz; the result was a very poor picture.

The leading manufacturer of that time, RCA, set a goal to create a recorder that would be able to record and reproduce color television signals. In 1953 the first prototype, using six stationary heads, was demonstrated. The new machine did indeed record color video signals, but its tape speed was so high that a 50 cm diameter reel had a recording capacity of only four minutes. The second model of the same system showed a reduced tape speed leading to a recording capacity of 15 minutes. Although such a capacity was very small and the quality of the recordings rather marginal, the NBC network, owned by RCA, introduced several such machines in its studios and can be considered the first broadcaster to use videotape recording.

A number of manufacturing and designing teams were simultaneously working on magnetic videotape recording. One of those, a small team led by young engineer Charles Ginsburg, assembled and financed by a modest audiotape-recorder manufacturer, Ampex, concluded as early as 1951 that recording video signals with stationary heads was a blind alley, and that the problem of recording the extremely high frequencies of the video signal could be solved by rotary video heads: if the video head rotated and the tape was transported in its normal translational way, these two velocities will be added together to achieve the required head-to-tape speed. The next and crucial breakthrough accomplished by the Ampex team was the introduction of frequency modulation in the videotape recording process (see Figure 10.2).

To overcome the limitation of 10 octaves, the Ampex team decided to frequency-modulate a "low" carrier (i.e. a carrier whose value is low by comparison to the highest frequency of the modulating signal) with the incoming video signal and to record the resulting FM signal on tape. That approach preserved the whole 0-5 MHz frequency bandwidth, and, in a way, transported it into the range of higher frequencies—the tip of the sync pulse was at 4.95 MHz and the peak white was at 6.8 MHz, a little less than one octave.

In the spring of 1956, Ampex introduced its videotape recorder at the annual National Association of Broadcasters (NAB) show. The response of

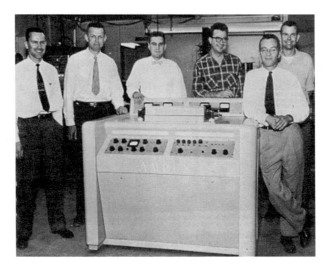

Figure 10.2   The Ampex team and the first professional videotape recorder.

the broadcasting industry was enthusiastic—the problem of recording video signals was solved. In the autumn of that same year, the first *quadruplex recorders* (named for their four video heads installed on a rotating disk) or *transverse scan recorders* (so named because the four heads rested on tape tracks that were almost perpendicular to the direction of the tape motion—commonly called *quads*) were delivered to the CBS network and went on air in Los Angeles for time-delaying the highly popular *Douglas Edwards and the News* program.

10.2   Basic Principles of Magnetic Recording

Some metallic materials, called *ferromagnetic materials*, can be magnetized under the effect of a magnetic field and then remain permanently magnetized after the switching off of the external magnetic field. The utilization of the described properties of ferromagnetic materials is based on the following laws of physics—the electromagnetic principles:

1. When an electric current passes through a conductor, it creates a magnetic field around that conductor. It is a tangential field, and its direction is determined by the right-hand rule: when the thumb is aligned with the conductor, showing the direction of the current, the folded fingers show the direction of the induced magnetic field.

2. Every magnetic material can be magnetized by a magnetic field generated by an electric current passing through a conductor wound in a coil.
3. When a magnetic field is changing in space or time, an electromotive force will be induced in the electric circuit located in that field and will result in an electric current through that circuit.

The magnetic induction depends on the intensity of the external magnetic field and does not depend on the duration of the field activity. Although extremely fast, the speed of magnetization has a finite value. Thanks to the selection of materials used and the construction principles applied, the achivable speed of magnetization allows today unimpaired recordings at very short wavelengths, that is, the recording of frequencies as high as 20 MHz.

The magnetic induction will change with the increase of the magnetizing force but not linearly or continuously. In other words an increase of the magnetizing force will not cause a corresponding increase of the magnetic induction (for example, doubling the magnetizing force will not double the magnetic induction). The magnetization process is nonlinear, that is, after an initial slow increase, the magnetic induction will rise more rapidly with the increase of the magnetization force. Eventually the magnetic induction will reach a saturation point when an increase in magnetizing force will not result in any increase of induction. If at any moment the magnetizing force is slowly reduced to zero, the value of induction will not drop to zero but a certain amount of magnetization will remain. That remaining magnetization is known as *remnant magnetization,* or *remanence.*

When a magnetizing force of an opposite direction is applied to the same magnetized material, its induction will start to decrease and eventually drop to zero. The value of the demagnetizing force required to reduce the induction to zero is called the *coercivity* of that particular material, and it indicates the magnetized material's resistance to demagnetizing forces.

Two kinds of magnetic materials are used in magnetic tape recording:

1. "hard" magnetic materials that have very high remanence and coercivity and are used in the manufacture of the recording medium—magnetic audio- and videotapes
2. "soft" magnetic materials characterized by very low coercivity (ideally the coercivity of such materials would be zero) and used for the construction of magnetic read/write heads

Although all components of a magnetic tape—the plastic base, the binder, and the active material—have their roles in overall quality, the active magnetic material is the most important. Its characteristics determine not only the maximum achievable recording quality but also the limits of the recording capacity of a given format. The active material obviously must present excellent magnetic characteristics, but it also has to fulfill a number of mechanical requirements. Over the years there have been many types of magnetic recording materials on the market. Among the many materials used for the active layer, gamma ferric oxide (γFe_2O_3) is the oldest and was certainly the most widely used magnetic material. Developed by Pfleumer in the early 1930s (and later improved by the German chemical giant I.G. Farben), it is still one of the most widely used recording materials. Gamma ferric oxide particles are packed on tape by coating techniques that resemble conventional painting—a dispersion containing the oxide, binder, and solvent is coated on a base film of polyethylene terephthalate (better known by its brand names Mylar, Celanor, Estor, etc.). Before it dries, the tape is exposed to a magnetic orienting field in order to physically align all particles in the same direction. That orientation has great importance in improving recordings at high densities since the coercive force of a particle depends on the angle between the applied field and the particle's long axis. Over the years, different substances, such as cobalt, were added to the basic gamma ferric oxide to improve its coercivity.

Chromium dioxide was also used for the manufacture of magnetic tapes. It had very high coercivity and better remanence (since its particles could be almost perfectly oriented) but was more expensive than the gamma ferric oxide.

To reach higher values of coercivity, ferric oxide or chromium dioxide particles have recently been replaced by particles of pure iron. These *new metal particle tapes* had one order of magnitude higher values of coercivity and remanence than the ferric oxide tapes. The production process of such magnetic tapes had to ensure not only the creation of very small needle-shaped uniform particles but also the creation of a protective layer over each particle, as the pure iron is *pyrophoric*, that is, has the tendency to ignite spontaneously when exposed directly to air.

It was known for years that thin metallic films had excellent magnetic characteristics promising outstanding recording performances, but their development was crippled by the need to solve basic mechanical problems of wear, corrosion, and friction. Once these problems were successfully resolved, magnetic tapes were manufactured by directly exposing the plastic base to metal vapors that created a thin metal layer. This increased the *packing density* (the amount of information recorded on a surface unit) and heralded the introduction of new recording formats.

Audio and/or video signals applied at the input of a magnetic recorder are processed and then recorded on tape through a *magnetic head*. A magnetic head consists of a core of magnetic material (that cannot be permanently magnetized) and a number of windings of an electrical conductor (see Figure 10.3).

When an electrical current flows through the coil, it generates a magnetic flux in the core of the magnetic head. As that core is not entirely homogenous, a leakage of magnetic flux will appear at the discontinuity (called the *nonmagnetic gap*).

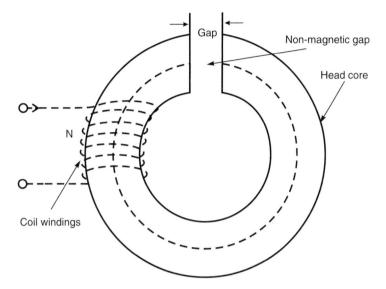

Figure 10.3   Magnetic recording/reproducing head.

If a blank magnetic tape passes across this gap, it will shunt that magnetic leakage flux, that is, the magnetic active layer of the tape will connect the two magnetic poles offering a considerably better passage to the magnetic flux. Each magnetic particle contained in the tape's active coating (which is in contact with the head) will become permanently magnetized to a degree proportional to the intensity of the magnetic flux flowing in the head gap at that moment (see Figure 10.4a). If the current that flows through the windings of the magnetic head changes over time, the generated magnetic field and consequently the remnant magnetization on the tape shall follow the same pattern of change. When such an electric current is the analog representation of a video signal, the remnant magnetization on the tape will represent the magnetic recording of the video image.

The transformation of the remnant magnetization into an electric current is known as the *reproduction process* (or *playback process*). It is based on the principle of electromagnetism, which states that the change over time of the magnetic flux shall induce (generate) an electric current in a conductor located in that field. In the reproduction process, the tape moves past the gap of the magnetic head, acting as the dynamic carrier of recorded information. In consequence, the magnetic flux recorded on tape will pass through the the core of the magnetic head. Due to the movement of the tape that flux will change over time and, in accordance with the mentioned principle of electromagnetism, will induce in the windings of the head coil an electric current that follows the pattern of the remnant magnetization on

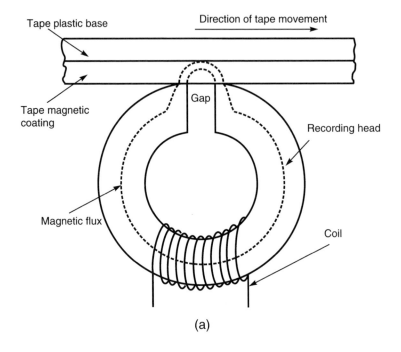

(a)

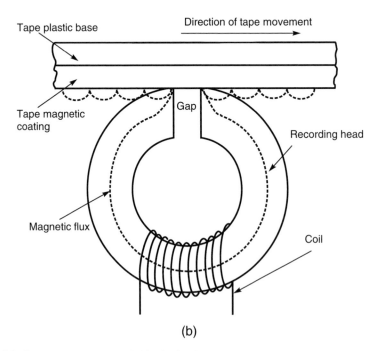

(b)

Figure 10.4   (a) Recording and (b) playback processes.

the tape (see Figure 10.4b). That induced current will be the replica of the current that passed the windings during the recording process and induced the remnant magnetization.

10.3 Practical Recording Characteristics—Losses

The process of magnetic recording and reproduction is far from ideal. It has to cope with a number of losses, which are the consequence of the immutable laws of physics. It is not possible to eliminate all these losses, although clever technical solutions have minimized them, or more precisely, alleviated the limitations they impose. Among all the losses that burden the magnetic recording process, the two most important ones are the spacing loss and the wavelength or gap losses.

The *spacing loss* is caused by lack of close contact between the magnetic head and the active coating of the tape. The existence of a space between the magnetic head and the magnetic tape leads to considerable losses in the signal output, to a dramatic drop of the amplitude of the reproduced signal. Such a loss can be so important as to outweigh the sum of all other losses. The spacing loss is best described by the Wallace law, which states that the loss is directly proportional to the spacing between the head and the tape and inversely proportional to the wavelength of the recorded signal, which means that the spacing loss is more acutely felt at higher frequencies than at lower ones. Since the recording of video signals means recording very high frequencies, it is obvious that the close contact between the head and the tape is of the utmost importance.

The *wavelength loss* or the *gap loss* is caused by the fact that a given magnetic head has a predefined and fixed non-magnetic gap. The highest and the lowest frequencies recordable by a given recording system are determined by the width of the head's nonmagnetic gap. Figure 10.5 shows two extreme cases, that is,

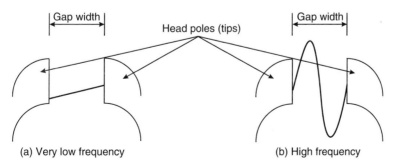

Figure 10.5 Wavelength losses.

two signals of different frequencies confronted with the same magnetic head and its fixed gap. The first one represents a signal of a very low frequency whose wavelength is very long when compared to the gap width. In that case the variation of the induction from one edge, or tip (*head pole*) of the gap to the other is barely perceptible and consequently a magnetization transfer cannot occur. In the second case the wavelength (which corresponds to a signal of relatively high frequency) is practically equal to the gap width. Since the variation of the magnetic induction from edge to edge is equal to one full cycle, and the positive and negative lobes are equal, the resulting magnetization is zero and there is no magnetization transfer. Therefore, the relationship of the momentary wavelength of the signal to be recorded and the fixed width of the head gap will determine the importance of the wavelength loss.

A given gap width determines precisely the span between the lowest and the highest frequencies that can be recorded with that head. A larger head gap will record lower frequencies but will also lower the highest recordable frequency. With a narrower gap the situation will be reversed, but in both cases there is a definite recordable frequency range. Theoretical studies and practical experiments have shown that the recordable frequency bandwidth with any given head gap corresponds always to 10 octaves. The given gap width determines only the precise values of the lowest and the highest recordable frequency but whatever their individual value are, they always represent the limits of a span of 10 octaves.

10.4   Specific VTR Problems and Their Solutions

To design and build a VTR meant not only to discover how to ensure the necessary head-to-tape speed and how to record a signal whose bandwidth was much larger than 10 octaves, but also how to find an adequate solution for several basic problems common to all VTRs:

- good tracking, that is, following recorded tracks correctly
- stability of the time base of reproduced signals
- coping with unavoidable dropouts

As described in Section 10.1, the problem of ensuring a relatively high writing speed is solved by the introduction of rotary video heads. Such heads record on tape a series of parallel tracks, which can be almost perpendicular to the direction of the tape motion (or more simply to the tape edges) or be at any other angle. Considering that rotary video heads have to record video signals on tape that runs at a certain speed in front of these heads, video signals will be recorded on a number of parallel slanted tracks and, not like analog audio, on one continuous track parallel to the direction of the tape motion and to the tape edges—a *longitudinal track*. To correctly reproduce the recorded information, the playback heads have to precisely follow the recorded tracks. Any tracking error, that is, any situation in which the playback head departs from the previously recorded track, will result in visible distortions of the reproduced picture because the playback head will not reproduce the useful information recorded on the video tracks but will scan the space between two adjacent tracks (the *guard band*) or simultaneously and partially scan two adjacent tracks, which results in indecipherable information for the reproduction circuits (see Figure 10.6).

To avoid such errors it is essential that tape and the video heads run at constant, precisely defined speeds, which have to be both absolutely identical during the recording and the playback processes and interlocked. Self-regulating electro-mechanical driving systems (*servo systems*) control these speeds and their mutual relationship. They receive a stable reference signal as well as the information on the speed (tape or head) to be regulated. The information is compared and the resulting data used for the correction of the controlled speed.

The operation of servo systems can easily be seen at the moment a VTR starts in the playback mode. After receiving the start command, the tape begins to run and the video heads to rotate, but the reproduced picture is unusable until the moment when the servo systems establish full control of these two speeds and ensure that video heads scan the previously recorded tracks correctly. This stabilization time, commonly called *preroll*, varies from a fraction of a second to several seconds in different models.

Time-base stability describes the overall stability of the reproduced video signal. It indicates if the signal is stable over time (if the lines and fields follow their

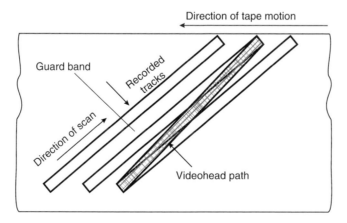

Figure 10.6 Mistracking.

standard rate with a high degree of stability) or if there is some oscillation around standard values.

In the case of VTRs, the lack of time-base stability is the result of several factors: slight but more or less unavoidable imprecision in the operation of the transport system, the instability of the signal-processing chain, and also the change of mechanical dimensions of magnetic tapes due to environmental conditions. As a result of all these factors, the reproduced video signal is not sufficiently stable to be forwarded as such to the downstream elements of a television chain. Do not be misled by the fact that, most frequently, a reproduced uncorrected video signal can be displayed without any apparent problem on a directly fed video monitor. The normal operation of the production, postproduction, transmission, and emission chain requires a considerably higher time-base stability than the one that would satisfy the demands of a video monitor.

Consequently, any professional VTR has to have not only a very precise and stable mechanical system and a similarly performing signal-processing chain, but also has to be equipped with specifically designed electronic circuits (called *compensation circuits*) that can correct and reduce to an acceptable level the residual time-base instabilities of the reproduced video signal.

If the compensation circuits are not switched on during the playback process, occasional shorter or longer, black or white disturbances in the reproduced picture will be noticed; they will look like scratches similar to the ones displayed during a film projection. These scratches, these momentary local imperfections of the reproduced picture, known as *dropouts*, are the result of errors in the magnetization process during recording or in the reading process during playback.

When during any of these two processes a short inadequacy in the head-to-tape contact occurs, the resulting tape magnetization (during the recording process) or the head magnetic induction (in the playback process) will dramatically drop. That drop will be translated after demodulation as a loss of a part of one or of several television lines, as a spark, scratch, or dropout (see Figure 10.7).

Dropouts may be caused by a number of irregularities, which can be roughly systematized in three major groups:

1. The surface of the tape may not be ideally smooth. The active layer can occasionally contain small lumps (*asperities*), which will be detrimental to the head-to-tape contact. Since modern tapes have a very thin active layer, all imperfections of the base film will emerge at the surface of the tape and occasionally influence the head-to-tape contract.
2. In spite of all precautions and technical solutions, the tape surface will always be charged with static electricity that attracts dust and ash particles, other debris, and some oxide particles that have detached from the active layer. These particles may, at any moment, appear between the head

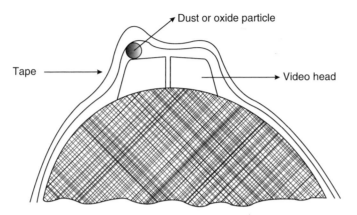

Figure 10.7 One possible cause of a dropout.

and the tape and cause a momentary loss of contact that will in turn cause a serious drop in the transfer of the magnetic flux (see Figure 10.8).

3. The active surface of the magnetic tape can be scratched or damaged, and part of its active layer destroyed; such deteriorations are quite common as a more or less unavoidable consequence of multiple passages of the tape

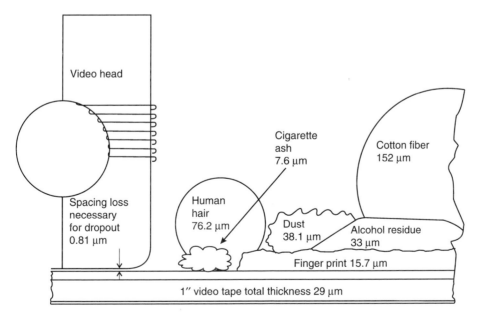

Figure 10.8 Enlarged view of different debris on tape.

through the transport system of many recorders, or of the effects of the tape aging process.

Regardless of why they happen, dropouts always impair the overall quality of the reproduced picture. In extreme situations when the damage of the tape is serious they may even lead to the complete loss of picture or continuity. To diminish the visual effect of these errors, special correcting devices called *dropout compensators* were developed very early in the history of the development of videotape recording techniques.

When a dropout appears in one of the lines, the compensator prevents that line from reaching the machine output and replaces it with the previous line kept in memory. As these are two adjacent lines, our eyes will not notice that they have identical content. Present-day digital videotape recorders use the same approach although with greater sophistication. When a dropout is detected, all pixels surrounding the missing ones are assessed; out of their values the most probable content of the missing information is computed, and the computed value is forwarded to the output. However, it would be dangerous and counterproductive to rely heavily on correction devices. It is strongly recommended to take all possible preventative actions, mainly in the "ecology" domain, that is, keeping the tapes, the operating and storage areas, and the recorders themselves as clean as practicable so as to eliminate the causes rather than to correct the effects and consequences.

It is important to stress here that the design of a modern VTR not only has to solve all of the aforementioned problems but also has to ensure the availability of a number of operational features. Back in 1956, broadcasters were happy to see a machine that would simply facilitate continuous recording and immediate playback of a television program. Today no recorder can be accepted by the market if it does not offer large and flexible editing capabilities, stunt modes (slow motion, freeze-frame, and fast motion), a recognizable picture in shuttle speed, and so on. These features influence the design of a given recorder and sometimes influence even the basic definition of a new recording format.

10.5   Videotape Recording Formats

A videotape recording format is a set of technical data that, taken in their entirety, ensure that all machines built in accordance with them would be compatible, that is, that a recording made on any of these machines must be replayable on any other machine of the same format. The tape format defines the type of scan, tape width, head-to-tape relationship, and pattern of tracks recorded on tape and their respective content, as well as the essential parameters defining the signal processing in the recording chain. All these elements are usually agreed upon, or at least documented, by international technical organizations.

The first among the parameters listed is the *type of scan*. Today practically all VTRs use the *helical scan principle*. Two video heads rotate inside a drum around which the videotape is wrapped. The tape is wrapped around the drum in a spiral, or, more precisely, following a curve known in mathematics as a *helix*. The angle of wrap around the drum varies from one format to another. Due to such head-to-tape configurations, these heads record long, slanted video tracks, that is, tracks whose angle to the tape edge is rather small. The position of video tracks, as well as the tape path around the drum, gave the generic name to all recording formats using it—they belong to the family of *slanted track* or *helical scan recorders*, whose first member was developed in 1959 by the Japanese company Toshiba (see Figure 10.9).

The *track pattern* is the next parameter that contributes to the definition of a recording format. In order to achieve the recording of a whole television field with one video head, it is necessary to ensure that the head is in contact with the tape during the period of one television field. At the same time it is necessary to ensure the uninterrupted continuity of the video signal at the output of the recorder. That goal is achieved by using two video heads and a wrap of the tape

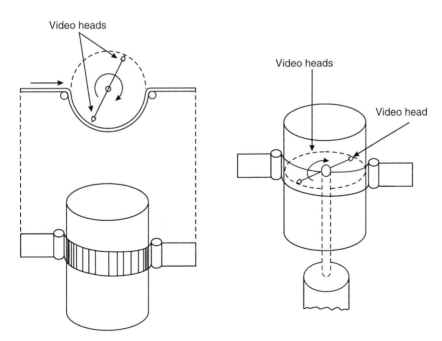

Figure 10.9 Helical scan configuration (Ω wrap).

around the drum slightly larger than 180° so that one of the two heads is always in contact with the tape; a precise timing ensures that the switchover between one head and the other is situated inside the vertical blanking period.

There is, however, another important purpose behind the selection of a wrap angle "slightly larger than 180°": if the wrap is significantly larger than 180°, it is very difficult to develop and build a cassette-based recorder with automatic tape threading.

In addition to slanted video tracks, all track patterns also encompass several longitudinal tracks usually recorded near the tape edges. One or two of them are dedicated to mono or stereo audio signals. The *control track* is a very important track containing a recorded continuous *waveform*, or a series of pulses that provides necessary information on the tape speed as well as carries edit pulses (to be discussed in detail in Chapter 11). Another longitudinal track carries signals used in the editing process—the *time-code track*, which also will be discussed in Chapter 11. An example of a real track pattern (corresponding to the analog component recording format Betacam SP) is shown in Figure 10.10.

If the videotape recording format is based on the recording of one whole television field in just one slanted track (one field per scan recording), it opens the way to the implementation of the *stunt modes*, that is, stable signal

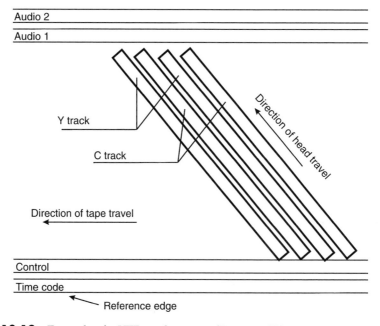

Figure 10.10 Example of a VTR track pattern (Betacam SP).

reproduction at speeds other than normal (slow motion, freeze-frame, fast motion, and reverse motion).

Recording one field per slanted track means that it should be possible to change the speed of reproduction by repeatedly scanning the same track or tracks, thus repeating at the output the same picture several times in a row, which should offer a subjective appearance of a slowed down motion or a freeze frame. However, to achieve these effects, it is not sufficient just to change the tape speed (to obtain at the output a slow-motion effect) or to stop the tape (expecting that the head will scan over and over again the same video track to display a freeze-frame at the output). As shown in Figure 10.11, video tracks are recorded in a dynamic process. During that recording process both the video head and the magnetic tape run at their nominal speeds, and consequently the recorded track will take a different position than the one that would result from the scanning of an immobile tape.

Therefore, to achieve broadcastable slow-motion and freeze-frame effects requires development and installation in the head-drum of an additional video playback head that can be deflected in order to follow precisely the recorded

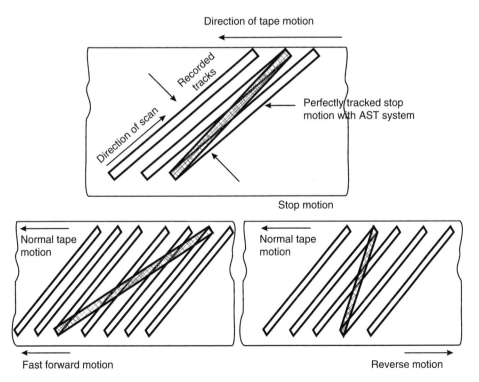

Figure 10.11 Tracking in stunt modes.

track even when the tape speed departs from its standard value. This additional playback head is not mounted rigidly on the rotational arm or disk but on a piezoelectrical bimorphic crystal support, which is, in turn, fixed to the rotational arm or disk. The piezoelectrical material has the property of generating electrical current when bent (a capacity used for the construction of "crystal lighters", where the pressing of the lever bends the piezocrystal, which generates an electrical spark that ignites the butane) or to bend when a current is applied to it. The polarity and the intensity of the current define the direction and the amount of bending (see Figure 10.12).

In the case of VTRs, the electrical current used to control the bending of the crystal is derived from the head-tracking error. Namely, if the video head departs from exactly following a given track, the amplitude of the reproduced FM signal will drop and that drop will be proportional to the amount of mistracking. A special circuitry will detect that change and generate a DC control current, proportional to the amount of the drop, that is, proportional to the amount of mistracking. Since that current offers the information on the amount of mistracking but not on its direction, additional means are used to detect that component. Both pieces of information are fed to the piezoelectrical element that bends accordingly and by doing so, returns the head to the center of the recorded track.

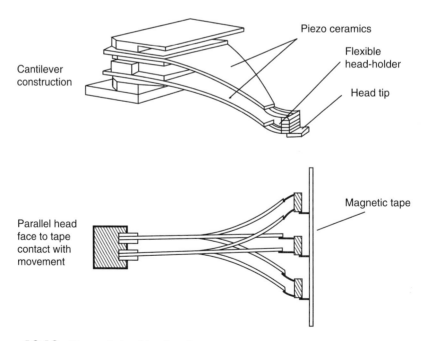

Figure 10.12 Dynamic tracking head.

Automatic track-following system (ATS) or *dynamic tracking (DT)* was first introduced on open-reel, one-inch helical scan recorders of the format C. Later that system became a standard feature offered by almost all subsequent recording formats. It is, however, interesting to note that the long-forgotten idea of a dedicated slow-motion machine was resuscitated recently when dedicated engines (based on IT technology and featuring, of course, considerably more operational capabilities than the modest slow-motion machine of the past) were offered to the market as a replacement (with improvements) of VTRs equipped with a dynamic tracking head.

10.6 Videotape Recording Methods

A number of videotape recording formats have been developed since 1956. Some of them were aimed at the professional market; others targeted industrial applications but unexpectedly were "co-opted" by broadcasters while some formats were designed specifically for the consumer mass market. All of these recording formats differed in their designs, a number of mechanical solutions, and also in their respective basic recording principles. Looking backward it is possible to differentiate several recording methods:

- direct composite recording,
- color-under recording,
- analog component recording,
- digital recording,

as well as one additional feature—azimuth recording.

The first quadruplex VTRs, as well as their immediate successors in the professional domain (the helical scan format B and C recorders), were based on the direct recording of composite video signals.

As can be seen in Figure 10.13, that recording process consists of several stages. The input composite signal is amplified and then led to the preemphasis circuitry. *Preemphasis* consists of a selective amplification of the signal: the higher-frequency components are more amplified than the lower-frequency ones. That process is performed to counterbalance the fact that the FM modulation process is less effective at higher frequencies. During the playback, the order of processes is reversed. The signal is amplified after the video head, then demodulated, treated through the *deemphasis circuit* that performs the opposite action of the preemphasis circuit, and finally amplified before the output. Obviously this short explanation describes only the basic principle and intentionally omits a number of other processing circuits.

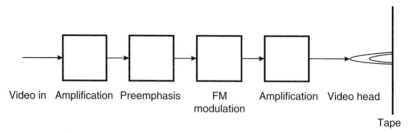

Figure 10.13 Direct composite recording.

By the late 1960s it became obvious that videotape recording techniques were important not only for the professional broadcasting area but also for a number of other industrial and domestic applications. These new markets required a new breed of recorders that would be simpler, cheaper, and easier to use. One of the problems with open-reel recorders was undoubtedly the handling of the videotape (its threading and unthreading through a complex tape-transport system). The newly developed audio compact cassette provided a good example of a device intended for a consumer market. In addition, the cassette offered very good protection of the tape, isolating it from the polluting environment.

To be accepted by the market, the cassette had to be as small as practicable and offer at the same time a decent recording time of about one hour. To design such a cassette it was necessary to use a narrower tape and to find a way to reduce tape consumption. Lower tape consumption meant a lower tape speed, that is, a lower writing speed and therefore the loss of the upper part of the video spectrum, resulting in a noticeable loss of resolution. Since these new cassette recorders were aimed at nonbroadcasting applications, such a sacrifice in picture quality seemed acceptable provided that the chrominance information located in the upper part of the spectrum was preserved to a degree. The solution consisted of introducing a new recording method known as *color-under recording*, and it was generally used for all analog industrial and consumer recording formats such as U-matic, Betamax, VHS, S-VHS, and so on.

The color-under-recording method consists of separating the luminance (Y) from the chroma information at input. Usually labeled "C," the chroma information is the chrominance subcarrier modulated by both the R-Y and B-Y components (see Chapter 4). The luminance signal is led to the direct recording chain described above, and the chroma signal is led to special circuitry that transposes it from its original position (4.43 MHz for PAL or 3.58 MHz for NTSC) to a much lower area on the frequency scale, from 600 to 900 kHz. The transposed signal is then simply added to the FM luminance signal, and together they are led to the recording video heads that record them simultaneously on the same video track.

During the reproduction process, the same playback video head reads both signals. Since they are clearly separated by their respective frequencies, it is easy to differentiate between them and then process them separately. The luminance signal follows the usual process of directly recorded signals, while the chroma signal is converted back to its original position at 4.43 MHz and then added to the luminance signal, thus reconstructing a composite color signal again. This reproduced signal shows a noticeable drop in resolution, but it is an already accepted sacrifice.

Developed by the late 1960s, color-under recorders were aimed at the growing industrial and educational markets. However, by the mid-1970s, the American television corporation CBS (followed very soon by the whole broadcasting industry) introduced electronic cameras and U-matic magnetic recorders into their news operations as a replacement for 16 mm reversal film, thus creating a new television production technology: electronic news gathering (ENG). Broadcasters embraced the ENG methods but were displeased from the outset with the marginal quality of color-under recording and the fact that the recording set consisted of two separate units: the camera and the recorder. In order to build single camera-recorder units (*camcorders*) it was necessary to develop smaller VTRs. However, there is a rule of thumb in the construction of VTRs—the size of the recorder is determined by the size of the tape transport. In turn the size of the tape transport is determined by the width of the tape and the quantity of tape needed to record a predetermined length of program. Therefore, to reach the desirable goal of small and handy VTRs it is necessary to develop systems and formats that will use narrower tapes and feature larger packing densities.

The early 1980s saw the development of a new recording format—the *analog component recording format* based on a narrower (½-inch) tape and on two new solutions:

1. separate recording of the Y, R-Y, and B-Y components
2. azimuth recording

As usual, several competing formats appeared almost simultaneously on the market, but only one of them remained, soon becoming the new universal de facto standard—Betacam SP.

The input of a Betacam SP recorder is presented with the video signal in the form of Y, R-Y, and B-Y components. The Y (luminance) component is led from the input to a conventional direct-recording chain (amplification, preemphasis, modulation, and video head). The recording head records one field in one video track. Compared to the luminance signal, the two color difference signals have a limited bandwidth but the same duration (64 μs in each television line). That makes it possible to use the time-compression multiplex technique that consists

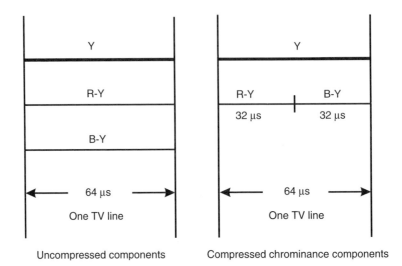

Figure 10.14 Time-compression multiplex principle.

of compressing, in time, each of these two signals by the ratio of 2:1, shortening their duration to 32 μs each and putting them, in a way, side by side in one 64 μs television line (see Figure 10.14) while keeping the overall bandwidth comparable to the one required for handling the luminance component.

The two color difference signals are led from the time-compression circuitry to another classical recording chain (amplification, preemphasis, FM modulation, amplification, and video head). Modulated time-compressed signals are recorded on tape by a separate head co-sited with the "Y" video head, recording also a whole television field in one recorded video track. Therefore, two video heads record two adjacent tracks with no guard band between them. The recording drum is fitted with two pairs of video heads (at 180° from each other). Since the tape-wrap angle is slightly higher than 180°, one head is always in contact with the tape, ensuring the recording of a continuous video signal. The recording medium for Betacam SP is the ½-inch metal particle tape, enclosed in a standard consumer-type Betamax cassette.

10.7 Azimuth Recording

The Betacam SP format was developed with the aim of offering full professional-quality signals at its output. To reach that target it was necessary to ensure the recording of the full 5 MHz bandwidth of the Y and time-compressed R-Y and B-Y signals by introducing a considerably higher writing speed than the one that satisfied the requirements of the standard consumer Betamax format. A higher writing speed meant a higher tape speed and consequently a shorter recording time. To ensure a long enough recording time with a tape length that could be accommodated in the standard Betamax cassette housing, it was necessary to use thinner tapes (to allow an increase in the length of tape enclosed in the cassette) but also to improve the packing density of the recording, that is, to increase the quantity of information recorded on a given tape surface. The development of new active coatings for tape allowed the recording of shorter wavelengths, but the crucial contribution came from *azimuth recording*, a technique that had already been developed and implemented in consumer-grade Betamax and VHS domestic recorders.

In all of the previously discussed recording formats, video signals are recorded on slant tracks separated by guard bands (nonrecorded portions of the tape). These guard bands have a double function. First they prevent crosstalk from one track to another. In communications, *crosstalk* is the unwanted information coming from an adjacent channel and penetrating the channel currently in use. The most obvious example is a telephone conversation: it happens sometimes that unwanted bits of another conversation drop into the channel you are using. In the case of magnetic recording, the magnetic field radiated by one track can be picked up as a spurious signal by the video head while it reads the adjacent track. By putting a greater distance between the tracks, a guard band considerably diminishes the danger of crosstalk. Secondly, when for some reason, the video head slips a little bit off track, it reads a part of the analyzed track and a part of the guard band. Since there is no signal recorded in the guard band, the off-tracking results in an increase of noise in the picture. Without a guard band, the mistracked head would read a part of the adjacent track and instead of an increase of noise, a much more serious picture degradation would appear as a result of mixing two incoherent pieces of information coming from two different tracks.

An important element of the magnetic recording process is the azimuth of the head gap. The *azimuth* is the angle between the head gap and the recorded track or, more precisely, between the head gap and the direction of the head motion (see Figure 10.15). In conventional guard-band recording as well as in longitudinal recording, the azimuth angle of the recording head is 90°—that is, the head gap is exactly perpendicular to the recorded track. If, for any reason, the azimuth of the playback head gap happens to be different, even for a relatively small angle, the level of the reproduced signal will drop dramatically. That *azimuth effect* is detrimental in conventional recording but is used purposefully in a number of recording formats, including Betacam SP, to increase considerably the packing density by abolishing guard bands and recording video tracks one next to the other.

In the case of Betacam SP, the drum contains two video head pairs installed 180° from one another. They record pairs of adjacent video tracks without any

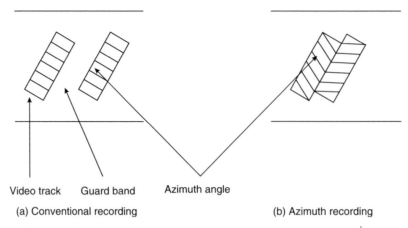

Video track   Guard band   Azimuth angle

(a) Conventional recording   (b) Azimuth recording

Figure 10.15   Conventional and azimuth recording.

guard band. However, one video head has an *azimuth* angle of +15° from the perpendicular position, and the other, −15° from the same reference. If it happens that a +15° head reads the track recorded by a −15° head by accident, the difference between the recording and the reproduction *azimuth* will be 30°. Such an *azimuth error* of 30° will sufficiently decrease the amplitude of the unwanted reproduced signal to make its presence unnoticeable in the output signal.

Thanks to the intrinsic quality of the recorded signals, the long-awaited cassette principle, and the ergonomic characteristics of Betacam SP camcorders, that format very soon became the de facto world recording standard. However, in spite of all its qualities, the Betacam SP videotape recording format was an analog format and consequently suffered unavoidably from the limitations inherent to the analog principle.

The overall video quality of all analog VTRs was limited by the available video recording bandwidth as well as by the noise contribution of the recording chain and of the videotape itself. The audio quality was even more severely limited. In addition to the usual noise contribution of the analog circuitry and of the tape itself, two factors aggravated the situation. On the one hand, the need to achieve smaller and smaller tape transports imposed the use of narrower tapes. To accommodate all the tracks on a smaller surface, it was necessary to reduce the width of the tracks. Narrower audio tracks resulted in a lower signal-to-noise ratio. On the other hand, as mentioned above, the best results were obtained when the magnetic particles contained in the active layer of the tape were preoriented in such a way as to be parallel with the direction of the recorded tracks. Since the recording of high-frequency video signals was more delicate than the recording of audio signals, the preorientation followed the direction of the slanted video tracks, which was not the ideal solution for recording audio signals on their longitudinal tracks.

Any time a copy (a new generation) of the original recording was produced, all of the aforementioned degradation factors would add up. The noise increased, the sharpness of the picture diminished, and instabilities became more and more apparent. In short, every new copy of the previous copy had a lower quality, falling eventually under the threshold of acceptability.

Since linear editing and postproduction in the VTR domain were achieved by copying the original, then recopying the copy, and then recopying again the previously made copy and so on, the limited number of generations limited the creative flexibility of a given recording format. In the analog world, even with the best tapes and applying the best operating procedures, it was difficult to produce more than six or seven acceptable generations. And that was not enough. The number of processings in postproduction could vary from the simplest sequence involving just dubbing on a master tape and using simple cuts thus ending with a second generation recording, to a very elaborate one involving a lot of different and successive operations and requiring a larger number of generations.

Analog videotape recorders receive analog video signals at their inputs and deliver them at their outputs either in composite or in component form. The reproduced analog signals are rather difficult to manipulate, and such limited processing capabilities unavoidably restrict the flexibility of the postproduction process.

All these shortcomings were imposed by the laws of physics and by the fact that video and audio signals were analog. The only way to overcome these limitations was to abandon the analog principle, develop a digital videotape recorder, and switch to the all-digital domain.

10.8 Digital Videotape Recording

By the end of the 1970s, the digital technique, already well established in the computer and communications areas, became more and more present in the world of audio-visual productions. The adoption of a single worldwide standard for the digitization of video signals represented a crucial step toward the achievement of numerous digital engines that generated or processed video signals in their digital form. Starting from modest digital time-base correctors, the family of digital units was growing fast. Digital frame synchronizers, standard converters, noise reducers, special effects, graphics workstations, and character generators followed each other at a very fast pace. However, it was clear that the key element for the achievement of an all-digital production facility was the digital VTR, a machine capable of recording and playing back video and audio signals in their digital form.

Digital videotape recording has the potential to overcome the major problems that burdened analog recording:

- By definition the recording of video signals in their digital form should be almost transparent—it should be possible to reconstruct a digital signal at the output of a recorder that will be virtually identical to the digital signal present at the input during the recording process.
- That transparency should theoretically permit a limitless number of high-quality generations, or, in practical terms, at least over 20 quasi-transparent generations.
- The recording of audio signals in their digital form brings the VTR audio to the same quality level as the one achieved by dedicated audiotape recorders.
- The processing of audio and video digital signals upstream and downstream from the recorder is equally unrestricted.

The first experiments of the feasibility of digital video recording were conducted in the United Kingdom in the BBC and IBA (Independent Broadcasting Authority) laboratories. However, the real start of serious development of digital videotape recording was in 1979 at the Montreux Symposium when three manufacturers, Ampex, Bosch Fernseh, and Sony, demonstrated their feasibility models. Six years later and thanks to the joint efforts of manufacturers and broadcasters, the first digital videotape recording format, D1, was on the market.

Since that time a number of recording formats have been developed. The first generation of digital VTRs was designed to handle uncompressed component (D1 and D5) or composite video signals (D2 and D3), while the second wave benefited from the development of different compression methods.

As can be seen in Figure 10.16, the digital waveform is very simple. It has two states of equal amplitude (Figure 10.16a), and consequently the write current will reverse at the leading and the trailing edge of each pulse, creating a binary magnetization pattern (Figure 10.16b). The reproduced waveform will then have a pattern indicated in Figure 10.16c since, as explained earlier, an output is produced only when the flux in the read head changes.

In spite of that relative simplicity, digital magnetic recording has to solve a number of specific problems. The sources of these problems are inherent characteristics of the digital signal as well as the same characteristics and laws of physics that govern analog magnetic recording. All digital video recording formats differ by the way they handle the following factors:

- overall bit rate to be recorded
- noise
- jitter

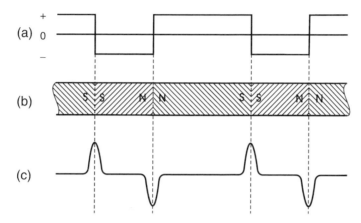

Figure 10.16   The principle of digital recording.

- channel code selection
- error-protection strategy

As explained in Chapter 6, the digital representation of the component video signal requires a considerably larger bandwidth than its analog counterpart, and at the beginning of the current chapter we have demonstrated to what extent the bandwidth and the high frequencies constitute stumbling blocks for the construction of any magnetic tape recorder. The uncompressed video signal with its bitrate of 216 Mbps presents a major technical and economic problem to other parts of the television chain, from the development of processing equipment to the question of channel bandwidth for its transmission.

The appearance of compression methods that allowed a considerably easier handling of digital video signals was both desired and hailed as a major improvement. The first digital recorders handling compressed video signals were based on proprietary compression schemes and featured both mild-compression ratios (Digital Betacam, 2:1) and high-compression ratios (Betacam SX, 10:1). They were followed by contemporary recording formats that embraced standardized compression schemes and ratios.

One of these standardized compression schemes was DV, an international standard created initially by a consortium of 10 companies as a consumer recording format. It uses ¼-inch (6.35 mm) metal evaporated or metal particle tapes as recording support. The DV-based formats use intraframe with adaptive interfield compression resulting in a nominal video data rate of 25 Mbps or 50 Mbps.

The 25 Mbps variant is aimed at the ENG market since it permits simple add-on and insert edits on the compressed signal, avoiding the lossy decompression and recompression process. The overall data rate recorded on tape, including audio, subcode (additional information including time code), and insert and tracking information is about 36 Mbps. The picture quality achievable with 4:1:1 and 4:2:0 sampling schemes is inferior to the one defined for the 601 standard, and the *postproduction headroom* (the extent of postproduction operations that can be performed before visible impairments of the picture quality are introduced) is rather limited (mainly due to the effects of reduced chroma bandwidth and the progressive accumulation of compression artifacts). The main artifacts are the "mosquito noise" effects around fine diagonal details, the spatial *quilting*, (appearance of spurious patterns that resemble in a way the quilt pattern) also noticeable on long diagonals, and some degree of *motion blocking*, or loss of fine details, in the immediate vicinity of moving objects. In spite of the aforementioned shortcomings in overall picture quality, there is unanimous agreement among broadcasting experts that DV-based 25 Mbps formats fully satisfy the requirements of news operations. In addition, the net data-transfer rate and the storage capacity required for a 90-minute program are well within the data-transfer and volume-storage capabilities of modern standard tape and disk based recording equipment, which eases the integration of 25 Mbps DV-based recordings into fully integrated, networked production systems. It is also a consideration that if kept in long-term archives, recordings made at that compression level would be reusable in the foreseeable future. The slight difference that exists between the DV, DVCAM, and DVCPRO formats resides mainly in different codec implementations. Since all three formats use the same mechanical design of video cassettes, all manufacturers who produce DVCPRO- and DVCAM-compliant recorders can offer multiformat players capable of reproducing all three formats.

The 50 Mbps DV-based recorders use the same approach, with the exception of the sampling scheme, which is kept at the standard 4:2:2 level. Since the compression method is frame bound, the format permits frame-by-frame editing. However, as explained in Chapter 11, when edits require access to individual pixels (for wipes, resizing, or other special effects) it is necessary to decompress the signal, perform the edit, and then compress the signal back to the DV format.

The second standard compression scheme implemented in digital VTRs is the MPEG-2 (or, more precisely, the 422P@ML MPEG-2) profile with intraframe compression (I frames only), resulting in a nominal bit rate of 50 Mbps. Developed as the continuation of the Betacam family, this format (IMX Betacam) uses a ½-inch metal particle tape in a Betamax-type cassette, offering an opportunity to build backward-compatible machines that can read all previous Betacam formats (analog SP, digital SX, and Digital Betacam). Conceived for mainstream television production, this format has four high-quality audio channels switchable to eight with a reduced quantization (16 bits per sample compared to 24 bits per sample). This format was developed as a contribution to an all-MPEG production and distribution chain. As indicated in Section 6.11, the concatenation of codecs is detrimental to the final signal quality. Consequently, if the same compression method is maintained throughout the production, distribution, and transmission chain, the need of creating a chain of a number of consecutive codecs is practically eliminated and the chances of preserving an optimum quality are considerably improved.

It is generally believed that the first-generation recording at 50 Mbps is indistinguishable from the full 601 uncompressed signal and that the quality offered after seven generations is still sufficiently high. This level of performance led to international recommendations stating that recorders featuring such a sampling scheme and offering 50 Mbps are adequate for mainstream television productions.

The next element on our list is noise. Digital signals can accept a considerably lower signal-to-noise ratio than their analog counterparts. The noise has a random distribution, and, while it is possible to measure its mean value objectively, it is practically impossible to precisely predict its distribution. As explained above, a digital signal reproduced from tape has the form of a magnetic pole, and it could happen that at a given moment a noise spike reaches an amplitude comparable to the amplitude of the signal. In that case a noise spike could be misinterpreted as a signal, which would cause an error in the reproduced signal. In order to preserve the quality of the recording/reproducing process, it is necessary to implement means to detect and correct or conceal such random errors. Therefore, the definition of the minimum acceptable S/N ratio for a given recording format is a kind of trade-off with the complexity of the error-correction system.

In information theory, the capacity of a given channel is determined by its bandwidth and its S/N ratio. In the case of a magnetic tape recorder, another factor—jitter—has to be taken into account. The *jitter* represents fast oscillations, or timing instabilities, of the edges of reproduced pulses. Both the noise and jitter have a detrimental influence on the correct decoding of recorded signals, but it is possible to treat them together by trading off one for another (a better S/N ratio allows for a greater amount of acceptable jitter and vice versa).

Digital data signals cannot be recorded on tape without previous processing because the interpretation of the details of an analog signal in the digital domain almost always results in a long string or a fast succession of zeros or ones. In fact, long strings of zeros or ones represent DC components that cannot be successfully recorded. A fast succession of ones and zeros theoretically can be successfully recorded but it would be difficult to reproduce them in the presence of jitter. Therefore it is necessary to convert the data to be recorded into a form suitable for magnetic recording, to transform it into a selected *channel code* optimized for that particular channel. Different channel codes are used for different recording formats, but all of them have two basic characteristics: they are DC free and they are self-clocking codes not requiring a separate clock signal that determines the pulse rate of a binary signal.

The essential part of every digital VTR is its error-protection system. The definition of such a system starts with the definition of the potential causes of errors and the goals the system is supposed to achieve. As explained earlier, in digital recording, errors could be provoked by noise, jitter, dropouts, mistracking, and so on. These errors may occur either as isolated random errors or as *burst errors*—massive errors when many bits are simultaneously in error. The most frequent cause of such errors are large dropouts.

In the analog domain, all recording problems, with the exception of dropouts, cause more or less gradual degradations of the key parameters that determine the quality of a reproduced signal (signal-to-noise ratio, chroma amplitude, resolution, etc.). In digital recording, all these problems, starting with the above-mentioned noise and jitter and including dropouts, are translated into bit errors. Consequently, the error-protection strategy is at the same time a great advantage of digital recording, opening the way to quasi-transparent quality and to an impressive multigenerational capability; as such the strategy is a sine qua non of digital recording. Therefore, all previously mentioned digital recording formats have their own error-protection schemes, or strategies, although all of them are in fact different combinations of more or less the same tools:

- error-detection codes
- changing the position of adjacent elements in the stream and on tape
- adding redundancy

An effective detection of all errors is obviously essential for an error-protection system. That target can be achieved by using some of the numerous error-correction and error-detection codes (like the Reed Solomon code). These codes are added to the video and audio datastreams in order to analyze the reproduced signal and detect bits in error. The functioning of these codes is rather complex but can be summarized as a series of comparisons performed on the output signal with the help of predetermined interpretation tables. By comparing the values of different bits and applying the rules from the table, it is possible to detect the bits whose values are erroneous. Up to a certain number of bits in error, the system is able to correct them and ensure at the output a 100% faithful replica of the signal at the input. However, when the error is massive, the system could be overloaded and, instead of correcting the bits in error, would conceal them. The balance between the correction and the concealment is an open question that each developer must carefully investigate because it also addresses the question of balance between the level of transparency of the recording format and its complexity. The error-detection and error-correction codes are added to the program signal thus increasing the overall bit rate to be recorded. At the same time, owing to the effective error-detection codes, it is possible to cope with lower S/N ratios and consequently use higher packing densities in the recording process.

As explained in Chapter 6, television signals and particularly video signals contain a very large amount of redundancy. Even the compressed signals used presently in television production contain enough redundancy to be able to use it to conceal an error. The error concealment, as explained in the case of dropout compensators (see Section 10.4), consists in replacing a missing piece of information (a bit or a pixel in error) by an approximation computed from the values of the surrounding and still-valid pieces of information (the surrounding valid bits or pixels). In order to support the error correction and especially to increase the effectiveness of the concealment process, datastreams are subjected to the interleaving and shuffling processes. The *interleaving process* consists of changing the order of code words in the stream such that adjacent code words are separated from each other, and if a burst error occurs it will not affect the whole code word or a series of them but only individual bits in each of them. In that way a sufficient amount of valid data are preserved for the concealment process.

To improve the prerequisites for concealments, especially in cases of massive burst errors, data are shuffled before being recorded on tape. When a massive burst error appears, it affects a large part of the picture. Without shuffling the result of a concealment process would be visible as a regular pattern of performed interpolations. In the *shuffling processs*, the adjacent data are redistributed over a two-dimensional array. When the above-mentioned massive error occurs, it will affect individual bits in different parts of the picture, and the concealment will be performed as a series of individual interpolations in different parts of the screen. Such concealment is considerably less visible and could even be unnoticeable.

As explained in Chapter 7, audio signals by definition contain a very small amount of redundancy. For the error protection of multiple audio tracks it is necessary to increase the redundancy artificially. Fortunately, audio signals have a more modest bit rate than the video ones, and it is relatively easy to introduce a 100% redundancy by recording all audio streams twice on different positions on tape.

The transition to digital recording offered not only a considerable increase in picture and sound quality but also led to the implementation of a number of new operational features that were difficult if not impossible to implement in the analog domain. Some recorders offer a *pre-read head*, a video head that is installed ahead of the regular record/playback head in order to read the signal from tape, send it to a processing device (for example to the character generator where subtitles are inserted), and then return it to be rerecorded by the regular recording head. In that manner some simple postproduction operations can be conducted with one single machine and more complex operations, including dissolves, with two instead of three units. Others offer connectivity to computer networks by delivering at their output not only digital component signals compliant with the usual interface standards but also audio, video, and metadata packed in files. Some digital camcorders can record automatically, shooting data on solid-state memories integrated in the cassette. These data could be very useful for postproduction operations.

10.9 Tapeless Recording

Digital videotape recording undoubtedly represented a very big step forward in the domain of television production. The quality of the recorded audio and video signals was tremendously enhanced and the operational flexibility of portable and studio recorders very much improved. However, one limiting factor still remained—the moving head—because a good part of the problems in digital recording (such as noise and jitter, two essential sources of degradation) had their source in the head-to-tape system. Further, the presence of two moving mechanical parts (a moving tape and a rotary head) represented a constant threat. These delicate mechanical parts are challenging to build and operate, and they do not offer much promise for improvement. Therefore, tapeless recording seemed to be the next frontier.

The first tapeless recorder was in fact a disk-based slow-motion device developed in the late 1960s. It recorded only 36 seconds of analog video, and its application field was strictly limited to the slow-motion replay, but it was nevertheless the first tapeless video recorder. Later on with the entry of IT technology in broadcasting operations, it seemed attractive to use the same recording support—a hard disk for data and for digital audio and video signals. However, for a number of years the capacity of hard disks was insufficient to handle reasonable recording lengths. Once hard disks had reached the necessary minimum capacity for the handling of compressed video signals, and when almost simultaneously other information carriers offered adequate performances, the development went in two directions. On the one side there were attempts to develop whole families of tapeless recording devices that would cover all applications from acquisition to playout. On the other side, medium- to very large-capacity hard-disk-based storage devices were developed for "stationary" use—for central storage or editing storage applications.

In the first category, three concepts are on the market. Based on the handling of digital signals, these three concepts use different recording media:

- removable computer hard disks or hybrid tape/removable computer hard disk

- rewritable optical disks
- flash memory cards

The first tapeless recorder to appear on the market used a retractable computer-type hard disk with a recording capacity of 4 gigabytes (GB) as a recording media. With the latest versions of this recording system, you can select either to record uncompressed 601 signals or to use a DV-based compression scheme and considerably lengthen the recording capacity. Thanks to the use of hard disks as information carriers, the camcorders of this format offer a number of operational features typical of PC-based broadcast solutions. For example, it is possible to insert a disk package directly into an editing computer and so eliminate the need to transfer recordings from the media to the nonlinear editing system. This type of recording system also offers a number of different editing functions that can be performed directly on the camcorder—features like loop recording, single frame time-lapse recording, and so on. The first version of this format appeared on the market in 1995, and since that time several improved versions have been developed, but none of them has managed to make a substantial impact.

There is an intermediate solution between the tape-based systems and the emerging tapeless ones, a system composed of a DV-based camcorder having both a traditional tape transport and a removable hard disk that can record up to three hours of DV-compressed signals. That disk can be used later for a faster-than-real-time transfer to nonlinear editing units or as memory containing files that are directly accessed by the editing system. At the same time, the tape can be used as a back-up or as a main support when the disk unit is removed and busy with downloading or editing. Such a configuration also has manifold applications, such as dubbing from disk to tape on the same camcorder, using disk recording connected to a laptop for logging the recordings in the field, and so on.

The next "tapeless avenue" currently being investigated is based on the use of rewritable optical disks. The first, and for the moment (in 2005) the only commercially available system of this sort, it is based on the use of 12 cm optical disks (comparable to conventional CDs and DVDs). That disk, enclosed in a dustproof cartridge, offers 23.3 GB recording capacity. Such a huge recording capacity is ensured by a dramatic increase of packing density (five times larger than DVD). Instead of a red laser used in DVD technology, with a wavelength of 780 nm and a numerical aperture of 0.45, this disk uses a blue-violet laser with a considerably shorter wavelength of 405 nm and a larger numerical aperture of 0.85. The recording principle is similar to the one used in other recordable disks—phase-change recording, where the used active substrate material changes its status from crystalline to amorphous and vice versa under the influence of the incoming laser rays. This creates the blind and reflective spots that correspond to the ones and zeros of the digital pulse stream. Manufacturers claim that such disks can be read innumerable times and can support up to 10,000 erase/record cycles.

The disk records files and is consequently compression agnostic, which means that both DV-compressed signals of 25 Mbps (85 minutes of recording time) and MPEG-2 (422P@ML) at 50 Mbps (25 minutes of recording time) can be recorded, provided that the record-processing chain can switch from one to another compression scheme. In addition, it is possible, if the processing circuitry in the record chain is adequately designed, to record full 25 or 50 Mbps program signals simultaneously and their MPEG-4 compressed proxies as browse-quality materials. Four audio channels (with 24- or 16-bit audio) accompany video signals together with a selection of archive and postproduction-oriented metadata. Such a recording principle facilitates not only a full and fast, random access to any recorded frame but also a faster-than-real-time transfer (two-and-a-half times faster for 50 Mbps and five times faster for 25 Mbps). At the same time, the A/V proxy recordings of 2 Mbps can be transferred at 50 times faster than real time. Or there may be no transfer necessary at all because the disks can be taken out of the camera and then inserted into playback units at the nonlinear-editing workstation.

Using such short wavelengths and the high numerical apertures of the recording/reproducing lens makes this disk system quite sensitive to vibrations and shocks. Consequently, when designing a camcorder around this recording technology, special measures have to be taken both in the area of error correction and in the specific mechanical and electronic solutions to ensure a correct recording under the most adverse conditions. If all of the precautions are taken and if the designs of camcorders and accompanying units translate into reality the potential advantages of disk-based recording, it is highly probable that the production workflows of the future will be considerably improved.

The most radical departure from magnetic videotape recording technology represents the introduction of recorders that use flash memory cards as media. The first *flash memory* cards to be used in video recorders are of the *secure digital* (SD) variety and are a form of EEPROM (electrically erasable programmable read-only memory). These are nonvolatile devices, which means that they store information on silicon chips in a way that does not require power to maintain the information on the chip—that is, if the power is switched off the recorded information is retained without power consumption. They offer fast read-access times and solid-state shock resistance, which makes them popular for applications such as storage on battery-powered devices (digital cameras, cell phones, or MP3 players). SD memory cards store information in an array of transistors, or cells. Initially one cell was capable of storing one bit and had some limitations in the domain of erasure flexibility. Modern multilevel cell devices can store considerably more than that and offer at the same time an operational flexibility that is fully appropriate for professional applications. SD memory cards can be programmed and read for practically unlimited numbers of times, but they offer a very high but limited number of record-erase cycles due to the wear that appears on the insulating oxide layer around the charge-storage mechanism used to store data.

These new tapeless machines record audio and video signals directly on SD memory cards thus eliminating the need for any sort of moving parts like tape transport mechanisms or disk drives. The absence of mechanical parts makes these recorders considerably more resistant to environmental conditions. Basic memory units are mounted in special cards that fit into PCMCIA (Personal Computer Memory Card International Association) slots of current notebooks, allowing a convenient and extremely fast data transfer. The same cards can be used to record either 25 or 50 Mbps DV-based compressed video signals. The easy adaptability of SD memory cards to the IT environment has already prompted some manufacturers to claim the advent of a news-broadcasting production technology—the ING for IT (information technology) news gathering. Although the capacity of memory devices develops at a very fast pace, the current cards still have a limited capacity and therefore the camcorders and recorders built around this media carrier have multiple PCMCIA slots in order to achieve a reasonable recording length. In addition, the price of such memory cards is still very high compared to both traditional and more modern media (currently for the same capacity, the ratio is about 1:100). The promoters of SD memory-card-based systems claim that this problem can be fully overcome at this moment by a slight adaptation of the existing workflows, and it can realistically be envisaged that in the very near future the capacity of SD memories will increase and their prices will fall to a more affordable level.

The other type of tapeless recording—high-capacity storage systems—is again based on magnetic recording. The basic information carriers are computer hard disks arranged in specific configurations that have to ensure the reliability of the recovery of stored information.

A *hard disk* is a magnetic disk used to store computer-type data. It is composed of several (at least two) *platters*, a number of *magnetic heads* (one per platter side) attached to *access arms*. Magnetic heads record information in concentric circles or *tracks*, and essentially, the reproducing-recording (read-write) process is identical to the one described at the beginning of this chapter.

The platters are the real carriers of the recorded data. They are made from an aluminum alloy, or more recently from glass or special ceramics that can be made thinner than the aluminum platters and are more resistant to high temperatures. The surface of the platters is either coated with an active magnetic coating or the magnetic material is deposited as a thin film of electroplated (or, in the case of glass and ceramic, evaporated) pure metal. Each platter is coated with a magnetic active layer on both sides, and the number of platters in a drive correlates to the storage capacity. All platters in a drive are separated by adequate spacers and mounted on a single spindle connected to an electric motor. The motor runs the disks at a constant speed, tightly controlled by a servo system.

The data are *transferred*—recorded on the active surface of the platters by recording/reproducing *heads*. The construction principle of these heads is identical to the one explained at the beginning of this chapter. The heads are attached to arms, and all arms are attached to a single *actuator* with the function to move the heads across the platters; its action is also controlled by a servo system. When the platters rotate, a thin film of air is created between the heads and the active surface excluding a direct contact of the head and the active layer; this reduces considerably the wear and lengthens the operational life of hard disks. However, that spacing is so tiny that all impurities shown in Figure 10.8 will cause a serious loss of information as was the case for magnetic tape recording. That is why the hard disk drives are assembled in a "clean room" environment and are afterward sealed in an impermeable housing.

The above description shows that digital data recording on hard disks is in fact just one variation of the overall magnetic recording technology. It is governed by the same laws of electromagnetism as all other types of magnetic recording and can be fully assimilated with digital tape recording, described earlier.

The capacity of a given disk drive depends on the amount of data that can be stored on a single platter and on the number of platters enclosed in a housing. As with magnetic tape recording, disk recording storage capacity can be increased by increasing packing density. To increase the packing density it is necessary to increase the capacity of the active layer and to decrease the recording wavelengths. Over the past several years, packing density has dramatically improved, but there is a theoretical limit to its increase. That limit is set by a phenomenon known as *superparamagnetism*. When the packing density reaches 150 gigabits (Gb) per square inch, the magnetic energy holding these bits in place becomes equal to the thermal energy of the disk itself and as a result, the bits are no longer held solidly in place.

Another possible way to increase the storage capacity of one hard-disk unit is to increase the number of platters. However, for practical, mainly mechanical reasons, the number of platters that can be part of a single drive is also limited and in order to increase the storage capacity of a given unit it is necessary to install in it more than one drive. That is particularly true in broadcasting applications where huge capacities are required for the storage of digital video signals (24 GB for only 45 minutes of program material compressed at 50 Mbps). However, such large storage units usually perform delicate tasks of storing very important or even unique data, and it is essential to ensure the recovery of data under the most unfavorable conditions. If all the installed hard drives were just added to each other, the configuration could accept a massive amount of data but in the case of a failure of one single drive, all data stored on it would be irreparably lost.

A system introduced in 1988 and known as redundant array of inexpensive (or later, "independent") disks—RAID—has been developed to address such a highly undesirable situation.

RAID employs several disk drives in combination in order to increase the storage capacity and, at the same time, increase the reliability of the system by improving its fault tolerance. The capacity is increased simply by putting together a number of disk drives. The improvement of performances and of the fault tolerance is, however, a more complex affair. It is based on two basic techniques:

1. *Redundancy* is the mirroring or repeating of the same content on more than one disk. When a fault occurs on one drive, the same content will be available from another drive.
2. *Data striping* is the spreading of blocks of each file on several disks, thus improving considerably the performances of the system but without improving its fault tolerance.

RAID systems can use different combinations of these techniques. Depending on a given configuration, it is possible to identify several types or *levels* of RAID configurations:

- Level 0 is constituted by a disk array where only data striping is used—data written in sequence over more than two disks. As indicated previously, such a system has excellent performances but is vulnerable to faults since a failure of one disk may result in inaccessibility of all data stored in the array.
- Level 1 provides the mirroring of disks, that is, all data are recorded twice on two different disk drives. When a fault occurs on one drive, the other drive is automatically put in action and there will be no loss of data. This level offers excellent protection but is considered rather inefficient since it requires 100% redundancy of the stored data.
- Level 2 is very seldom used and is constituted by striping the data at byte level and generating an error-detection and error-correction symbol for each stripe. That error-correction data is recorded on a separate drive.
- Level 3 is based on byte-level striping over multiple drives with a dedicated parity disk. Level 3 RAID systems have a complex configuration and could be difficult to reconfigure after a drive fault.
- Level 4 stripes data at block level and also introduces a dedicated parity disk. If one drive in the system fails, the data from the parity disk are used to create a replacement. This configuration allows multiple access, but does not offer any advantage compared to Level 5 so it is very seldom used.
- Level 5 consists of a system where data are striped over multiple disks and the necessary parity information is also distributed over multiple disks and

not concentrated on a dedicated parity disk, thus offering a very efficient system with a minimum overhead.

- Level 6 is a kind of extension of Level 5 since data are striped over multiple disks and two sets of parity information are generated and distributed over all disks. Such a configuration offers an excellent fault tolerance but requires a rather complex configuration, which unavoidably influences its price.
- A number of other combinations have been developed recently. Some of them represent combinations of the levels described above (for example RAID 0 plus RAID 1) or some proprietary solutions of a given manufacturer.

The selection of a RAID level depends on the intended storage use and the respective needs of speed, efficiency, or reliability. In any case, RAID systems offer a considerably increased capacity, increased data safety, and a very fast random access to any bit of stored information, but they are still not the definitive, ideal, 100%-secure solution. Many factors can affect the security of the stored data on RAID systems, its capacity for the storage of high-quality video signals is still insufficient, and, finally, the price per stored bit is very high. As will be discussed in Chapter 12, for a number of years to come, acquisition, postproduction and archiving operations will be based on hybrid systems using both tape-based and tapeless solutions.

Video Editing

11

Editing is the essence of all storytelling. The ancient storyteller edited the story by selecting words, sentences, pauses, accents, images, and specific tricks of the trade, by deciding how to put them together to achieve the greatest impact. Writers and painters have been, in practice, doing the same thing—selecting elements and deciding on the ways they will be put together. However, in the twentieth century, with the emergence of a new form of artistic expression, with the birth of film, the assembling of basic storytelling items—individual shots in this case—became so important that it got a title and became one of the most important elements of the art of moviemaking. Editing—a "montage of attractions" as the famous Soviet film maker Sergei M. Eisenstein used to call it—was born practically at the same time as film. From day one it was necessary to arrange the assembled shots in a logical order and develop a coherent narrative structure out of that crude material. It took 15 years of research and experimentation to transform such a simple assembling of shots into a specific form of artistic expression. When television appeared in the mid-1930s, editing was already a highly developed form of expression, which the new medium, based also on moving images, had to adopt.

11.1 The Development of Video Editing

From a technical point of view, film editing is extremely simple. You select the desired last frame of a given shot, cut the film at that place, and glue that end to the beginning of another piece of film, which has been cut just before the selected initial frame of the next shot. That operation, called *splicing*, is quite simple to perform since film frames are easily identifiable and recognizable even to the naked eye. Equally easy is the detection of the space between two consecutive frames (*photograms*) where the cut must be placed.

The situation in television is more complex. First, it is possible to differentiate three sorts of editing, depending of the medium used:

1. **Film editing**. Film is used as the recording medium.
2. **Live editing**. Cuts are made between different picture sources and some special effects are added during live transmissions.
3. **Video editing**. The rough material is recorded on videotapes, hard disks, or any other supports that do not require chemical processing for the display of recorded images.

In terms of tools and approaches, film editing for television needs is identical to the editing used for movie film productions aimed at theatrical distribution.

To ensure a coherent continuous stream of pictures in film production, it is mandatory to edit film by cutting it precisely in the space that separates two adjacent frames. Similarly, in the case of video signals it is necessary to locate the cut in the space between two video frames—in the vertical blanking interval. Consequently, for live editing it is necessary to develop appropriate tools, called *program switchers*, *vision mixers*, or *production switchers* that will have the capacity to locate the vertical blanking interval and to time all cutting commands in such a way that the cut is always located in the vertical blanking interval (VBI).

In video editing the same requirement has to be scrupulously observed—the cut must be located inside the VBI. That means that while in live editing, there is a need to detect the moment of arrival of the first vertical blanking interval after the reception of the cut command and to execute the command at that moment; for the editing of recorded video signals, there is a need to detect the physical place on the recording medium where the VBI is recorded and to locate the cut there. The ways and means used to locate that particular place on the recorded medium, the approaches of marking and handling the frames that have to be edited together, the incorporation of special effects, and the enlargement of creative capabilities of editing equipment represent the essential landmarks of the history of the development of video editing.

The urgent need fulfilled by the first VTRs developed in 1956 was ensuring a time delay—recording a whole live television show and replaying it, without any intervention, at some later time. However, immediately after the introduction of the first VTRs it became obvious that they could be great production tools only if one could edit recordings. As mentioned earlier, editing required locating the place between frames on the tape where the VBI was recorded. Since in magnetic recording it was impossible to see the recorded picture with the naked eye, it was necessary to introduce an additional signal that could be read or detected and that would be collocated with the recording of the VBI so that its detection would automatically show the position of the vertical blanking interval. That signal, called the *frame pulse* or *edit pulse*, had a repetition rate of 30 Hz (25 Hz) corresponding to 30 fps (25 fps) of the 525/60 (625/50) television scanning standard and was superimposed on the control track. By permitting the detection of the VBI and the positioning of cuts within it, edit pulses made the editing of video recordings possible. However, that editing was extremely crude—it required the actual physical cutting of the magnetic tape, making the *editing resolution* (the minimum distance in time between two consecutive cuts) and the editing precision obviously very poor—but it was the introduction of that humble pulse that started a dynamic development of the video-editing technology that is still underway.

Cutting a magnetic tape was far from an ideal approach to video editing, and in 1961 the first electronic editor appeared on the market. The appearance of electronic editing was extremely important since its basic principles have been used in all linear editing systems from 1961 to our time. *Electronic editing* essentially consists of ensuring a controlled transition from play mode to record mode at a selected position in an existing recording and making sure that the right piece of new video material appears at that same moment at the input of the recorder. In order to perform such an "edit," special circuitry had to be developed.

Electronic editing enormously improved video postproduction. But it had a severe drawback—a serious lack of precision. The position of an edit had to be determined on the fly: during the playback of the existing recording, the operator had to locate the agreed position of the edit and at that point activate the start of the edit procedure by manually pressing the edit button. Such a procedure not only lacked precision but also made it virtually impossible to repeat the edit at the same position. If that needed to be done, the only method was to sacrifice several additional frames before the edit point and give the manual command a fraction of a second earlier than was done the previous time. To improve the precision and facilitate the repeatability of cuts at the same point, a new feature, the cue tone, was introduced in 1962: during the review of an existing recording, the desired position of the edit point was determined and at that place a short burst of audio, the *cue tone*, was recorded on the cue track. Once recorded, that cue tone would activate the editing circuitry and, as many times as it was necessary, would place the cut at the same location. In addition, it made possible the *edit rehearsal*. In the rehearsal, or *preview mode*, the cue tone would only switch audio and video monitors from the reproduced to the incoming signals, thus simulating an edit while leaving the original untouched. If the rehearsal was judged successful, the cue tone was used to trigger the real edit at that same viewed place. If not, it was possible to reposition the cue tone and select another position for the edit.

In 1970 the SMPTE and EBU introduced a digital code, called *time code*, as a means of precisely addressing each television picture on a tape. The time code was recorded on a longitudinal track and was readable at all tape speeds. Since it was recorded simultaneously with video and audio information, it had a solid relationship to all video information and offered a precise and unambiguous address for each recorded video frame expressed in terms of hours, minutes, and frame numbers. With the assistance of special reading devices, it was possible to control the tape-transport mechanism and find any desired frame. Time-code information could be stored in the control device and used to trigger the start of an edit operation. At the same time, the time-code information was used not only to determine the exact position of the first frame of the new piece of program material to be added at the edit point but also to control the transport of both the recording machine on which the edit session was performed and the playback one that reproduced the raw material. The time code offered the opportunity to program all details concerning the edit point—to have a simple audio and video cut, to have dissociated cuts of the audio and video tracks, to have a crossfade, or a sweep transition and so on. In short, the time-code information offered the most precise and flexible means for the control and execution of an editing operation.

The reading and decoding of the *longitudinal time code* (LTC) becomes difficult and erratic at very low speeds and during jog operations (when the tape is moved very slowly reproducing the recording almost frame-by-frame) and is impossible in freeze-frame modes. To overcome these problems, in 1982 the SMPTE and the EBU developed a *vertical interval time code* (VITC), an additional code addressing information related to the LTC and inserted in the vertical blanking interval of the video signal during recording. When the tape is stopped or runs at a very slow speed, the video head continues to rotate at its standard speed and reads the recorded frame normally, including its vertical blanking interval and the inserted VITC.

Time code opened the way to new editing techniques. Editing and postproduction on film had always been performed on a *work print*, a positive copy of the original negative, produced especially for the purpose of postproduction. All decisions, all changes, and all insertions of effects were performed on that work copy, keeping the precious negative safely stored. Once all decisions were made, the film negative was assembled in accordance with work print decisions, and prints were produced for release. In videotape recording, until the advent of time code, all postproduction was performed by using original materials. In addition, in linear editing all changes of original edit decisions meant either repeating the whole editing process or producing another generation, which in the time of analog recording was detrimental to the final quality. With the introduction of time code it was possible to duplicate in the videotape domain the working-print approach of the film technology. A copy of all original recordings was made and used for *offline postproduction* (as it was called). During such postproduction, all edit decisions were recorded on an *edit decision list* (EDL). Since both the original recording and the working copy had the same time-code information recorded on them, it was possible to use the EDL generated during the offline process to produce the final version from the original recordings. The production of this final version was called *conforming*. Originally, the EDL could have the form of a simple printed list in which all the selected time-code numerals were marked. However, very soon, electronic EDLs were developed. These EDLs could be directly supplied in their electronic form to the *edit controller* that controlled the machines handling original high-quality recordings. Throughout the years, essentially two types of electronic EDLs were developed and are still used—the CMX and the Sony code.

In the mid-1980s, different offline editing systems were developed. Some of them were based on the use of working copies made on consumer recording formats such as Betamax or VHS, but others tried to profit from the features offered by computers and their hard disks. Since these disks had a very limited capacity, high compression ratios were used, resulting in poor but sufficient picture quality for the needs of offline editing and the generation of EDLs. However, the use of computers and disks showed all the advantages that could be drawn from the features specific to that sort of technology. Online editing with a computer-based unit became very desirable. The increase of capacity of hard disks and the development of disk-based external computer memories and of efficient compression methods created the necessary critical mass for the development of new *nonlinear editing systems*. These systems were composed of high-end PCs using internal and external hard disks, special video cards based on Motion JPEG compression, and sophisticated editing software. Nonlinear editing systems appeared on the market by the end of the 1980s and the beginning of the 1990s. Ten years later they were the dominant approach to editing operations.

11.2 Linear Editing

The simplest linear editing system consists of two analog or digital VTRs and one edit controller that could be part of the recording machine or a standalone unit. One of the two VTRs, the *recording* or *master VTR*, must be equipped with electronic editing circuitry. Both machines must be controllable by time code. The playback machine is loaded with a tape carrying the original recordings. They are accessed linearly, that is, the tape has to be rewound all the way to the position of the desired clip. Once the first clip is found, it will be transferred (*dubbed*) to the other machine. A frame called an *out edit point* is selected at the end of that clip, and an edit is programmed by using the time-code information. The first frame of the next clip, called an *in edit point*, is also identified through its time-code address. The edit controller is loaded with these two time codes, and the edit command is given. From that moment on, the controller unit will control both tape transports and the electronic editing circuitry of the master machine.

A linear editing system or suite can be enlarged by the introduction of at least one additional playback machine, production and audio mixers, special-effects generators, and graphics units. With such a configuration, known as the *A/B roll system*, it is possible to perform different sorts of transitions at the edit point—fades, dissolves, wipes, effects, and so on.

Linear editing can be performed either in the assemble or the insert mode. In the *assemble mode* (see Figure 11.1) the master tape is a clean tape (unused or erased), and all clips are transferred one after the other and connected by edits. As mentioned earlier, these edits can be either simple cuts or complex transitions, executed with the help of external production switchers. In assemble mode all tracks—video, audio, and control—are gradually constructed piece by piece. The end result of the process is a recording in which all these tracks are continuous and uninterrupted.

In the *insert mode* (see Figure 11.1) the master tape has to be prepared—*black-striped* (or *preblacked*) before the editing session. The black-striping consists of continuously recording a video signal over the whole tape or at least over a length that corresponds to the expected duration of the edited program. Usually that

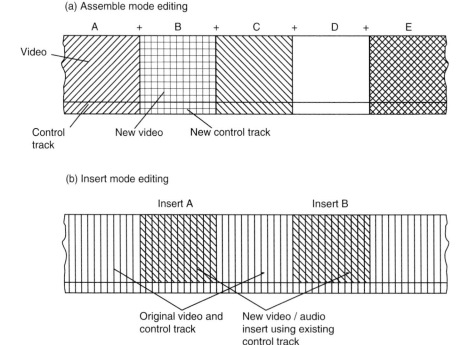

Figure 11.1   Assemble- and insert-mode editing.

video signal is the *black–and-burst signal* consisting of a continuous black level (video signal corresponding to the picture that is permanently and uniformly black) with standard synchronization signals, including the color burst. During the black-striping process, no signal is fed to the audio input. At the same time, the continuous recording of video ensures that an unbroken recording of the control track with its superimposed edit pulses and a continuous longitudinal time-code signal will also be recorded during that black-striping session. In insert-mode editing, both the time code and the control track are kept unchanged and only the video and audio content are changed by transference from the playback machine. For that purpose the in edit points (the selected first frame) and out edit points (the selected last frame) are defined on the video clip that has to be transferred, and so is the in edit point on the master tape (the selected last frame of the previously transferred clip). Such a marking is known as *three-point editing*. The edit controller will use these time codes to control all machines in the system and to ensure the execution of edits at selected points.

Linear editing is based on electronic editing, which, as mentioned earlier, is a controlled transition from the play mode to the record mode at a selected point of an existing recording (or the reverse—a controlled transition from record to play mode at the exit edit in the insert-mode editing). Such a controlled transition is necessary in order to ensure a visually seamless passage from one shot to another and a smooth continuity of all pictures of an assembled program. If a transition from play to record happens to be executed without the assistance of special control circuitry, the appearance of the point of transition will be totally unacceptable:

- The uncontrolled passage cannot ensure the positioning of the cut within the VBI.
- The control track shows a discontinuity at that place, and the combined effects of these two factors result in a serious picture instability.
- On all VTRs the sound track is recorded on a separate track or on a separate segment, and in spatial terms a piece of audio is not collocated with its corresponding video frame. For example, in component analog recording, the audio head is usually positioned after the drum containing video heads, and consequently an audio bit is recorded on tape ahead of the video frame corresponding to it. The spatial relationship between those two recordings is strictly defined by documents that describe the recording format in question (standards, recommended practices, or other recognized formal descriptions of recording formats). In the absence of special editing circuitry, the activation of the record command would switch on the erase head and start erasing both video and audio without taking into account their spatial relationships.

It is obvious that special circuitry is needed to ensure a smooth and seamless transition at the edit position between the old and the new pieces of recorded material. That special editing circuitry has the ability to detect the first frame pulse following the reception of the record command, and at that point it can activate the erasure of the previously recorded video and the recording of the new video from the machine input. The circuitry must also perform the same operation with the control track that will be erased and re-recorded from the position of the detected frame pulse (as mentioned earlier, in insert-mode editing the control and the time-code tracks are prerecorded and kept unchanged during the editing session when only the video and/or audio signals are replaced).

The editing circuitry also takes care of the spatial disparity between audio and corresponding video recordings and activates audio and video erase and recording heads in accordance with that spatial disparity. In order to achieve all these precisely timed erasing functions, VTRs have several erase heads. One of them, the *main stationary erase head*, has a gap length equal to the tape width and consequently will erase indiscriminately and simultaneously all signals recorded on tape. That head is used for a straightforward re-recording of a tape when no editing is planned. Component analog recorders have separate stationary erase heads to handle the erasure of the control track and of the two audio tracks during editing. Since video signals are recorded on slant tracks, the achievement of an edit requires that from one point onward, old video tracks are erased one by one and replaced by new ones having different contents. To ensure such a selective erasing, the edit video erase head (*flying erase head*) is installed as an additional rotational head in the head drum and precedes the record/reproduce head by one track.

In all digital videotape recording formats, audio channels are recorded as separate segments on the same slant track and by the same head that records the segments containing video signals. In the recording process the same head is simply switched between video and audio signals at the beginning and the end of the corresponding segments of the same slant track. Consequently the erasure in the editing process is performed by a flying erase head that precedes the record head by one track and is similarly switched on and off depending upon which segment has to be erased.

11.3 Time Code

As previously noted, all edit activities are controlled by a time code—a digital code recorded on tape that ensures an unequivocal address for each recorded video frame. It is a continuous stream of increasing, binary-coded numbers. The selected code is known as *Bi-phase mark* or *Manchester I code*. It is a self-clocking code that has very good noise immunity (operates very well with rather low signal-to-noise ratios) and can be decoded at diverse speeds, which is very important for the time-code application when it is expected that the code is decoded at tape shuttle speeds during the search of a selected frame. Each television frame is addressed using 80 bits. The address itself (expressed in hours, minutes, seconds, and frame numbers) uses 26 bits; 16 bits are reserved for synchronization and detection of the tape motion direction (forward or backward), 4 bits are used for flagging purposes, 2 bits are unassigned, and 32 bits are user bits (left for the storage of information, which would be needed and defined by any user). These 32 bits can be used to encode four alphabetical letters or eight numerical digits or any acceptable combination of letters and numerals. They can be used to indicate the cassette number, the date of recording, the code of the recording location, or any other similar information.

Although developed some 10 years after LTC, VITC is very similar although not fully identical. VITC includes additional bits so that each address is constituted by 90 bits. Since VITC is inserted in the vertical interval blanking period, it has to follow the field rate and not the frame rate that LTC follows. Consequently, one of the additional bits is used as a field mark, facilitating the differentiation of even and odd fields. Another difference is the decoding position: VITC is decoded at the start of a field, and LTC is decoded at the end of a frame.

VITC is recorded and reproduced by the video head. That means not only that a separate time-code head is not needed but also that such a configuration excludes any mechanical offset error. LTC is recorded and read by a separate stationary head that is positioned outside of the head drum. If, due to a manufacturing error, the position of the time-code head on the replay machine is different from the position of the head on the machine where the original recording was made, that mechanical offset error will translate into a misreading of the correct relationship of the recorded pictures and their addresses. By 1982, when VITC was introduced, the industry had gained a lot of experience with handling and even recording of digital signals. That experience led to the introduction of an error-protection strategy in the VITC concept. The first protection measure was the introduction of the *cyclic redundancy check* (CRC) code that permits the detection and correction of errors that may occur in the record/reproduce process. As a protection against burst errors caused mainly by unavoidable dropouts, VITC is recorded twice in two nonadjacent lines in the vertical blanking interval. Since VITC is a field-rate code, the same address of a single frame is recorded four times in four different places, which considerably reduces the danger of losing information due to the appearance of drop-outs.

Since VITC is inserted in the vertical blanking interval and then recorded on tape together with the video information, it is not possible, as is the case with LTC, to prerecord that timing and addressing information prior to an editing session. For that reason a special recording method had to be developed. The first clip to be transferred from the original tape to the master tape was transferred together with its original VITC. However, the record machine contained a special *slave time-code generator* that could use the VITC information from the first clip as a lead and replace the original VITC contained in the incoming video of subsequent clips by a new one whose count would be the exact and synchronous continuation of the count of the first segment. Since VITC is inserted in the vertical blanking interval and then recorded on tape together with the video information, it is not possible to prerecord that timing and addressing information prior to an editing session, as is the case with LTC. At the same time, in order to retrieve all desired frames normally, it is necessary to have a continuous, or at least ever-increasing continuation of the time-code information. In other words, it is necessary that each recorded frame has a time-code address that is posterior in time to the address of the previous frame.

The time-code information is essential today not only in video editing. It also represents a very important tool for all postproduction methods and techniques. It is used for the synchronization of different audio and video sources, it is used in the creation of electronic special effects for movie film production, and it is even used as timing information that runs the clocks in television facilities.

11.4 Nonlinear Editing (NLE)

Linear editing reached high levels of sophistication. Edit controllers were able to control a number of VTRs and several other pieces of production equipment. With offline generation of EDLs it was possible to reduce the wear of the original tape and produce better-quality recordings as well as to perform the time-consuming task of making edit decisions on low-cost consumer machines while reserving the professional-quality expensive ones for the final assembling of the master recording. However, linear editing (see Figure 11.2) was burdened by several shortcomings inherent to its basic nature:

- Accessing individual clips recorded on different cassettes was usually time consuming.
- Complex layering effects required a number of generations. In the analog world that was "lethal" for the final quality. Even in the digital domain very high postproduction demands could lead to some multigeneration problems.
- To change the appearance of edited clips (shortening or lengthening a clip that was already part of the edited scene) it was necessary either to re-edit whatever was already done after the clip in question or to dub the edited material, performing the desired changes during that process, thus producing another generation.

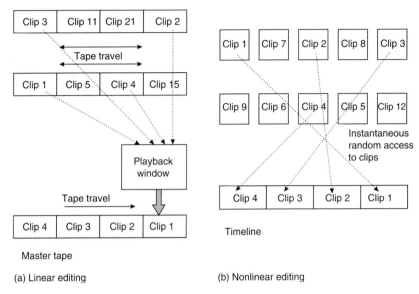

Figure 11.2 Linear and nonlinear editing principles.

Videotape editors considered that film editing, with its fully random access to all rushes, was the example to follow. In the later years of linear editing, some hybrid solutions appeared on the market. It was then possible to transfer a limited amount of material on disks and to shape the edit in an almost nonlinear way. The major obstacle to developing such hybrids into full-scale nonlinear editing units was the limited capacity of hard disks and the very high bit rate associated with uncompressed video signals.

The almost simultaneous development of efficient compression methods and of hard disks with high storage capacity facilitated the full development of a new approach to the editing of video signals—nonlinear editing (NLE). Essentially, an NLE system consists of the following:

- a computer platform possessing a sufficient amount of internal or external random access memory (internal hard disks and external RAID arrays, where the raw material can be stored in its digital form)
- software that controls access to and identification and memorization of the addresses of the desired start and end frames of selected series of clips as well as later facilitating the playout of all these clips in the selected order

Nonlinear editing starts with the "digitization" of the raw material. This term is no longer adequate for present-day operations when the signal that reaches the NLE is already a digital one, but it is a relic from past years when acquisition was essentially accomplished with analog recording formats. The new, more precise term for the transfer of the material recorded in the field to the memory of the NLE units is *capture*. The capturing process is very important as it sets the quality limit of the NLE unit. Namely, the quality of the capture card used to transfer analog video into the adequately compressed digital form of the NLE system or to transcode the digital signal received at the input into the compression profile of the editing unit, will determine the quality of the compressed video that will be stored on disk.

Depending on the system used for the capture process, capturing can be performed in real time or several times faster and the material can be stored on disk in its native form—in the same compression ratio and in accordance with the same compression method in which it was originally recorded or recompressed into another format. When the capturing is done in anticipation of using online editing, the material is kept in its native form or, if such are the requirements of the editing system, transcoded into another compression format but kept at the same compression ratio. However, if offline editing is planned, the material will most frequently be recompressed at a considerably higher compression ratio thus significantly reducing the storage requirements. It is very important to bear in mind that here we are faced with using a string of compression codecs, which is made even more critical by the fact that in the editing process, complex transitions and effects require decompression and consequent recompression of the video bitstream. As discussed in Chapter 6, compression and recompression many times over can have a detrimental effect on the overall quality of the sounds and pictures. Therefore, in the domain of nonlinear editing, as in any other television operation, it is important to keep the number of transcodings to a minimum. That can be achieved by careful planning of the whole chain, for example, by selecting digital recording methods for acquisition that permit use of less critical capturing methods or even by creating standard MXF files and using file transfer methods for the transport of program material (see Chapter 8). An additional beneficial approach would be to select an NLE system that uses the same compression method and the same compression ratio as the selected digital recording gear. Clearly the best possible concept would be to organize the whole acquisition-postproduction-storage-distribution system based on a single compression method and ratio and to use transcoding only when it is necessary to revert to the basic 601 bitstream for the sake of performing complex transitions or adding special effects.

Once the material has been stored in the memory device of the NLE editing station, the editing can begin. Nonlinear editing is arranged in a very visual manner, that is, the editing software offers a screen display that looks very logical and straightforward even to an untrained person (see Figure 11.3). A large window contains the selected frame or shot. The time line underneath is a very simple

Figure 11.3   View of the screen of an NLE system. (Courtesy Incite)

tool for assembling the selected clips in the desired order. The audio time line, usually included in the video time line, has the same function for audio, and there are usually several audio tracks allowing for more complex audio postproduction. On the other side (or on another screen) the editor can see the *poster* frames (frames belonging to each of the clips stored in the system and freely selected by the user) and can access them randomly.

The editor selects the desired clip and its precise frame (with a mouse, a light pen, a dedicated control panel, etc.) and with a corresponding command moves the clip on the time line. The editor can arrange clips in their final order or can put some clips on the time line, leaving blanks to be filled in later by some other program material. As in the case of linear editing, it is possible to edit simultaneously the video and audio content that are linked together, but it is also possible to dissociate the two and edit them separately. For example, it is possible to compose the final audio on its track and then edit video clips accordingly. However, it is important to underscore that video clips and audio bits are not moved or changed physically; rather their selection and transfer on the time line at selected in and out edit points generates adequate time-code pointers that are stored in the PC memory. Once the editor decides to play back an assembled part of the program, the clips will be played from their original position on the disk but from one pointer to another. All changes are still possible since they can be made by changing the pointers—additional material can be inserted between a selected out edit point of one clip and the corresponding in edit point of the next clip without the need to re-edit all subsequent material. All complex transitions and some other special effects can be created in the same way. However, it should be repeated that while cut edits can easily be performed in the compressed domain (especially if the compression is restricted to the removal of spatial redundancy— that is, intraframe compression), more elaborate transitions or special effects must be performed on full 601 signals. Consequently, for such effects the video signals used are decompressed back to the full bit rate. The desired effect is performed in the 601 domain and rendered, and then the result is converted back to the stored format. Powerful NLE systems have the ability to render almost all effects in real time, but the less powerful ones usually take the video content that has to be part of a special effect or complex transition separately and render it at slower than real time. Once rendered, that bit of video information is stored on disk as a new clip whose pointers are adequately linked with the pointers of the clips preceding and following it.

Nonlinear editing systems can answer the most demanding postproduction requirements. They offer the possibility of building complex effects, layer by layer, or easily making several versions of the same program. It is quite common in the case of big productions to transfer the result of an editing session to tape, organize the viewing of that version, and later return to the NLE station to introduce all the required changes and "trimmings" before releasing the final copy.

NLE stations can be *stand alone* (a PC with or without additional external hard disks) or *networked* (linked to a central storage system). The second solution is particularly attractive for news and sports operations where it is usual to have a number of different editors accessing the same material in order to prepare different edited versions for different programs or program segments. As can be seen in Chapter 12, such systems have a rather complex architecture that offers editors a mixture of actual and historical material, gives journalists the opportunity to browse the clips and even make a rough edit, permits the news editor to view all edited and unedited materials from the desktop and make appropriate decisions, and so on.

It could be concluded that the value of a given NLE station is defined by the type and power of its hardware, the computer platform used, the quality of the capture card, and the versatility of the employed software. Low-end NLE systems can be used on standard PC platforms, while for complex postproduction demands it is necessary to use computers with more memory and considerably higher processing power. For the most demanding applications, such as the execution of special effects for the film industry, it is necessary to use high-performance computers, such as those produced by Silicon Graphics (SGI). However, defining the optimum platform for a specific editing task depends very much on the moment when such an evaluation is made. The capacity of memory, processing speed, and power progresses at such a fast pace that present-day standard desktop machines offer practically the same performance as the highly specialized machines from several years ago.

The video capture card is responsible for digitizing the analog input signal and for transcoding the digital input signal when it does not correspond to the compression system implemented in the NLE unit, as well as for packing content on the disk drive. Consequently, it is positioned at the input of the editing system and unavoidably defines the maximum level of transparency the system can achieve. It is therefore understandable that there are various configurations of video capture cards on the market with wildly different price tags. Needless to say, for professional applications it is hard to avoid using the high-end, relatively expensive video cards. However, as mentioned earlier, the whole chain from acquisition to playout is today most frequently digital; transcoding instead of digitization could be needed at the input of an NLE system. As mentioned earlier, when the whole production/postproduction chain is based on the same compression scheme and features the same bit rate, there will be no need to use transcoding, recompression, or capture cards, which would not only simplify the whole system but would also improve the final video and audio quality.

Editing software is available in different configurations, from the simplest that can be easily added to any Windows-based PC, to the most sophisticated types used in high-end television or film productions that have to be installed on high-end workstations or specialized hardware. All these software solutions differ in the number and complexity of the facilities offered to the editor and, to a lesser degree, in their speed of operation. Although all offer more or less the same solutions for the execution of the operational workflow and for the presentation of the *graphic user interface* (GUI)—the appearance of the screen and the disposition of different windows and time lines on it—the high-end systems are usually more profuse in the number of functions and commands displayed on screen (or on two screens).

Being essentially software based, NLE systems are subject to the usual "upgrading" and "debugging" syndromes of operational software. Several months after a new software product appears on the market there will be announcements of updates, service packs, and patches that will improve the operational capabilities of the software in question, remove bottlenecks, or solve operational problems. After a number of such upgrades, a new version appears, but usually the old version can be upgraded up to the new one. All this leads to the introduction of the maintenance contract, which offers (in exchange for an annual flat fee) interim upgrades, debugging, and even the upgrade to a hypothetical new version that may appear in the foreseeable future. Each user has to consider such maintenance contracts very seriously and carefully analyze all the aspects of such an expenditure and its returns.

12

The Networked Production

Conventional analog production facilities were based on a system of interconnections carrying standard composite PAL or NTSC signals. With the advent of digital, the concept did not dramatically change. Practically all analog PAL or NTSC signals were replaced by a *serial digital interface signal*—SDI. In both cases, the production processes were sequential—that is, all operations were carried out one after the other. Every single process in the sequence had to wait to receive material produced in the previous step. The standardized file formats and the corresponding change of workflow led to the development of a new concept—the networked production facility. The conventional interconnection structure that conveys analog or digital signals in real time was replaced by a replica of a computer network. With such a system it was possible to abandon the strictly sequential production approach and to apply to a large extent a simultaneous approach where a number of production teams could use the same original material simultaneously for their respective applications. The networking approach also permitted a parallel accomplishment of different phases of the same production flow. For example, it offered the opportunity to edit a piece of material on an NLE station while the same material was being used simultaneously on other workstations for the creation of a special effect, for sound editing, or as input material for another NLE unit.

Replacing the conventional studio cabling concept with a network had an additional advantage. In addition to being better adapted to draw all the benefits from IT-based pieces of equipment, it was possible, for example, to almost seamlessly integrate elements located miles apart into one single system, to easily access from a local workstation program material kept in a mass storage facility located in a different part of the city or even in another town. The new concept of networked television production, or of a fully IT-based production, meant that in such a production environment, audio, video, and metadata signals would not be recorded on tape but would be stored in computer-type storage and transported as data files. It also meant that the whole production would rely heavily on the use of metadata, that the content would never be physically transported but would be transferred (*streamed*) by several users and in several quality levels, and that the whole system would be run and administered by fully integrated, IT-based systems.

Such a system already looks very attractive indeed, but its realization has to overcome a number of obstacles:

- It is difficult to squeeze all operating practices into one single concept or mold that will satisfy all users. Historically, different workflow and operating practices have developed in various production organizations, and it would be very hard today to standardize one single operational model.
- Television production applications are very demanding. They require very large bandwidths, and the majority of operations are to be performed in real time with huge bit rates.
- Television production operations have a variable level of complexity of operations. Some operations are extremely simple, but they are followed by very complex ones. Consequently, newly developed systems must be able to be equally well adapted and user friendly for both types of operations.
- Television operations require a high level of security and reliability, higher than that currently offered by present-day IT systems.
- The digital approach and the file-transfer system unavoidably generate serious latency problems (due to compression, wrapping, unwrapping, etc.) for which appropriate solutions must be found.
- Standardization and interoperability are still relatively new concepts for the IT world.
- The major part of the building blocks used to assemble IT-based television production systems are standard computer-network products. However, due to the specific needs of television production applications, the remaining elements of such systems, both in the hardware and software domains, have to undergo a very expensive customization.

Present-day television production simultaneously uses highly specialized audio and video products (cameras, production mixers, video and audio recorders, etc.), fairly standard IT hardware (workstations for NLE, playout, graphics, etc.), specially developed software for television applications, standard IT-based storage systems, complex dedicated graphic user interfaces (GUI), and standard network products as well as files that are purposefully developed for demanding television applications.

The attractiveness of the network concept led a number of research institutions and manufacturers to concentrate their efforts on finding appropriate solutions for all the aforementioned problems. Some of them joined forces with end users to develop a system (represented in Figure 12.1) , which should have the capacity

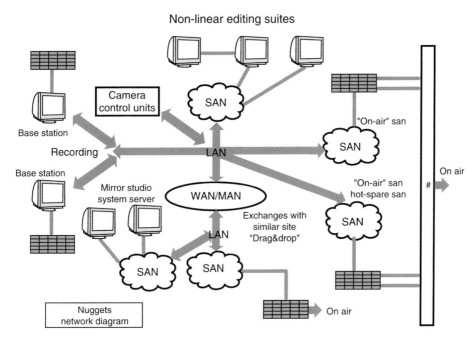

Non-linear editing suites

Figure 12.1 Fully networked production system (the Nuggets project).

to overcome the in-house and public-network constraints. It is expected that the new system will have the ability to integrate not only all IT-based production tools but also A/V broadcast equipment in a network environment. This system could also open the way to high-quality interchange of program materials (including low- and high-resolution essence and rich metadata) and control data over several storage-area and local-area networks, all connected through metropolitan- or wide-area networks. Such a system should permit integration of cameras, viewing, storage, and control and interface devices and should ensure a high quality of service and a fast responsiveness typical of broadcasting operations.

A fully networked production facility is clearly a concept for the future, but already today some important segments of television production and distribution systems are organized as specific networks located inside more conventional installations. Two most prominent examples of such systems are the integrated news desks and complex, media asset-management systems.

12.1 Basic Aspects of Networked Systems

A particular advantage of networked systems lies in the fact that in addition to conventional and specialized IT-based production tools, they also include many elements that are massively used in any type of computer network. Such a commoditization of structural elements has an undisputed beneficial influence on the overall price of such systems.

We can differentiate two basic types of networks:

- networks established inside one single facility and known as *local area networks* (LANs)
- external networks that span large geographical distances and are known as *wide area networks* (WANs) and a WAN subset, the somewhat smaller *metropolitan area networks* (MANs).

A LAN is established inside one production facility, and the devices that constitute it are usually connected by using Ethernet or Fibre Channel technologies.

Ethernet technology is widely used in establishing all sorts of LANs with different throughput capacities. However, in television applications a *Gigabit Ethernet* with a throughput of 700 Mbps is the most frequently used configuration.* That basic configuration is composed of a number of different devices connected to the same *bus* (i.e., a signal pathway that makes it possible for all bypassed points to input to or output from it). Such a configuration is straightforward to implement, but it can generate problems of traffic bottlenecks. To overcome that drawback, there are a number of solutions including the introduction of redundant links that can increase the traffic capacity of a given network. One advantage of Ethernet is that it is a network technology used for a number of applications from the most basic office networks to complex specialized configurations. Consequently, its building blocks are standard commodity products, and the cabling is done with relatively inexpensive *unshielded twisted pairs* (UTP)—that is, the equivalent of the simplest pair of isolated copper wires like those used in classical telephony. However, the maximum length of a simple Ethernet network is about 100 meters, and it is necessary to introduce some additional technical measures if the distances are larger than this limit. Content is moved over Ethernet networks as packets transmitted by using the standard *Internet protocol* (IP) developed for general-purpose IT communications. The content to be transmitted is packaged in *IP datagrams*—bit arrangements that encapsulate the content to be transmitted, the necessary IP origin and destination addresses, as well as IP headers, which contain information that is essential for the communication process.

---

*The nominal capacity of that network is indeed 1 Gbps. However, at least 30% of that capacity is used for housekeeping of data traffic, like reception acknowledgement, checking the completeness of the packets received, and so on. The remaining 70% is available for the transfer of desired information, that is, of the "payload."

Another organization of local area networks is Fibre Channel networking. The Fibre Channel (note the French and British spelling of the word "fibre" as opposed to the usual "fiber") is an integrated set of standards developed to answer the need for very fast transports of large amounts of data typical for multimedia and scientific imagery applications.

Two basic types of transport configuration coexist in the domain of data communications: the channel and the network. The *channel* is a direct or switched, point-to-point communication. It is a hardware-intensive, high-speed, and low-overhead type of data transport. For its part, a *network* is software intensive and constituted by a number of distributed nodes. It has its own protocol that regulates the interaction between the nodes. Generally speaking a network is slower than a channel. However, basing its functioning on the handling of any number of unanticipated connections, a network has the ability to perform a considerably larger number of different tasks than a channel.

Fibre Channel represents a combination of the best aspects of channel and network data communication. Its architecture is different from both the channel and network topologies since it has at its core an intelligent interconnection scheme called *fabric*. During the operation of a Fibre Channel configuration, the input/output (I/O) ports have only to ensure a point-to-point communication with the fabric, which then has the task of interconnecting the devices.

The Fibre Channel represents an efficient, cost-effective, and reliable transport system, developed in such a way as to be capable of supporting different data transfer speeds, offer a distance-insensitive high-bandwidth capability, and support both copper and optical-fiber media. It is based on standard components and is adaptable to different configurations that would correspond to various system complexity levels.

Wide Area Networks (WAN) are used to interconnect different production facilities or a production facility and its remote element (for example the storage with the processing equipment in the field). The dominant transport technologies over WANs are Internet protocol and *asynchronous transfer mode* (ATM). ATM is a particularly flexible communication technology developed over the years in the telecom domain with the goal of making possible the integration of voice, video, and data in one single network. Initially, various technologies were developed for different communication channels as well as for different types of traffic. The essential advantage of ATM is that it can be used on all types of communication channels (optical fibers, coaxial cables, and twisted pairs) and for all types of traffic (voice, video, and data) over a single network. ATM is designed in such a way that it can operate at a number of different speeds (from 1.5 Mbps to several Gbps) over the same communication channels. In the ATM mode, the content to be transported is encapsulated in ATM cells of 53 bytes each. Out of these 53 bytes, 48 represent the payload (the content), and the remaining 5 are reserved for the header that carries all information about the payload and the transport process.

12.2   Media Asset Management Systems

As explained in Chapter 8, in present-day IT-based technology, the audio and video parts of a given program are called *essence*. When metadata are attached, that combination of essence and metadata becomes *content*, and if information concerning the rights (intellectual property rights or, reverting to a somehow outdated terminology, copyright information) is added to the content, it becomes an *asset*. Assets are not a new category. They are as old as the concept of rights, and from the early days of the audiovisual industry the management of the assets was one of the major tasks of a business-conscious management. The audio and video in themselves do not represent an asset. Unaccompanied by the appropriate metadata, these could become unreachable. Depleted of rights information, they do not have a business value. Even worse, they can become a liability if used without the rights-holder's permission. For years and until recent times, *asset-management systems* were tape and film archives run through a cataloguing system that permitted journalists and researchers to find the desired piece of program material by investing a lot of perseverant efforts. That task was far from easy or straightforward, and it was always time consuming. The development of IT techniques and the merging of these techniques with television and communications resulted in, among other things, the development of modern *media asset management* (MAM) *systems*, also sometimes called *digital asset management* (DAM) *systems*, that opened completely new vistas in the domain of handling and managing program materials.

It is difficult to offer a simple, straightforward definition of a MAM system since it encompasses a wide selection of hardware and software units assembled in accordance with the needs and requirements of a particular user. An off-the-shelf MAM system does not exist. However, it is possible to list the basic functions each MAM system is expected to accomplish:

- controlling the ingestion of program material—its cataloguing and annotation
- ensuring adequate storage of the essence and metadata
- ensuring the means for content browsing and viewing from standard workstations, and even through Internet access, without the need to generate special dubs of the original material for that purpose
- ensuring the generation and storage of data concerning rights
- permitting the editing and enlarging of metadata through a comprehensive hierarchical model

- offering the possibility of keeping metadata both with the essence and in separate databases
- facilitating complex search procedures through metadata information
- offering the means to retrieve selected materials and to transfer them either to an edit station (where they will be trimmed, edited, and postproduced) or to any other destination
- being secure and reliable

MAM systems are powerful and flexible tools for creative handling of broadcaster's assets. They open the way to the introduction of dramatic changes in the domain of news making, program playout, and the handling of archived assets. The new integrated digital newsroom systems represent a radical change to the news-making workflow and offer the opportunity to streamline and speed up news operations, making them more efficient and cost effective. The introduction of MAM systems in the playout domain offers a completely new approach to the distribution and transmission operations, making them run much more smoothly and considerably more cost effectively. They transform the peaceful archives of the past into the booming profit centers of today.

However, broadcasters are not the only potential users of MAM systems. All institutions that use A/V media in their daily work, such as educational institutions, sports teams, and big production houses, can benefit from abandoning the manual cataloguing and searching process and introducing a digital MAM system.

A MAM system encompasses central storage and a number of servers that perform some specific applications as well as some types of broadcast equipment, all linked by a network (usually Gigabit Ethernet or Fibre Channel network). The size and type of the storage depends on the particular MAM application. All storage media can be evaluated in terms of speed of retrieval and cost per bit. As might be expected, in terms of today's technology, these two parameters are still in conflict: the cheapest storage medium, magnetic tape, has the longest retrieval time, and the fastest medium, RAM, is the most expensive. Consequently the storage of MAM systems appears in several forms:

- online storage constituted by a system of hard disks usually in a RAID configuration that has to ensure a sufficient level of redundancy, guaranteeing 100% availability of stored data
- near-online storage constituted by robotic tape or disk systems that offer the possibility of transferring the desired stored item on demand (and relatively quickly) to the online storage where it becomes generally and instantaneously available

- offline storage that is usually constituted by a traditional tape library, tape being used as the cheapest content support

Online storage is connected to the servers that run the management elements of the system but also serve as storage devices for some particular applications, such as the application database or the proxy server that stores the low-resolution browse-quality dubs of all the items stored in central storage. All these elements are usually connected in a special-purpose subnetwork called a *storage area network* (SAN) configuration.

Particular attention in a MAM system should be paid to the protection of assets. Usually all assets exist in the storage system in two quality levels—the full-quality original items and their low-resolution browse-quality proxies. The browsing is

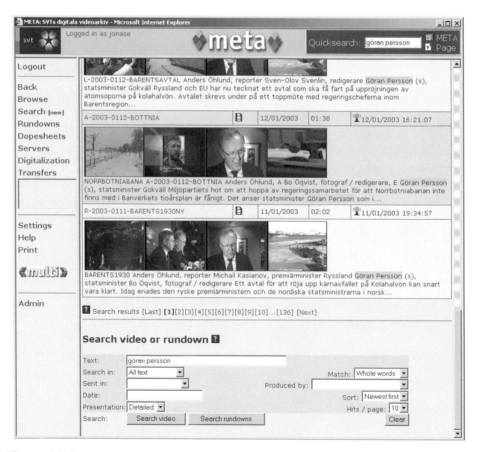

Figure 12.2 Searching tool for a MAM system. (Courtesy Ardendo)

permitted only on low-resolution-quality proxies, but that measure alone does not ensure sufficient protection. Consequently, a number of additional protective measures have been developed, from the insertion in the picture of the owner's logo to more sophisticated watermark systems. A *digital watermark* represents an inserted digital signature that is not visible in the decoded picture but can be detected by using special decoding engines and used as a proof of the ownership of that particular asset.

As indicated, MAM systems are a "made-to-measure" integration of a number of broadcast and IT, hardware and software engines and solutions. Such integrated systems must be designed with a full knowledge of present-day workflows, desired improvements, expected goals, anticipated developments in the future, environment in which they have to be integrated, and systems and databanks that already exist and will have to cohabitate with the new system. The introduction of MAM systems is not only an operational or technical decision but above all a business decision, and the investment costs have to be evaluated against the expected *return on investment* (ROI). Consequently, a move toward MAM systems must be very carefully studied and planned. The design and decision-making process must include not only engineers with knowledge of IT systems and those who have fully mastered broadcast technologies but also program and operational staff as well as financial experts. That preparatory planning work must concentrate sequentially on four essential tasks:

1. the systematic scanning and registering of all parts and details of the existing structure
2. the detailed analysis of all workflows and of all their parts, linked to the careful assessment of new requirements
3. the technical build-up and definition of the new system
4. the financial analysis of the estimated costs and expected savings

A number of roadblocks have to be removed before networking becomes the standard solution for all types of electronic media facilities. However, some very important and efficient networks with a MAM system at their core are already operational around the world. They represent "network islands in a cabled sea" much like the "digital islands in the analog sea" of some years ago. Typical and very popular examples of such systems are *integrated digital newsrooms*, known also as *electronic newsroom systems* or *server-based newsroom systems*.

12.3 Integrated Digital Newsroom Operations

News operations have always been a crucial part of television stations. It was always important to develop more efficient ways to handle the vast amounts of incoming information and, especially with visual information, to process it and prepare adequate *rundowns* (i.e. ordering of news clips for playout). Throughout the whole process from acquisition to the airing of newscasts, time was of the essence. That was the reasoning behind the introduction of ENG techniques, which replaced 16 mm film with electronic capturing and magnetic recording methods. However, back in the television station, the processing was traditional, relatively slow, and insufficiently flexible:

- Cassettes recorded in the field were physically transported to the station.
- If time allowed, the cassette was viewed, basic editing decisions were made, and the material was then linearly edited. Most frequently, however, the tape was transported directly to the edit suite and the material was edited according to the rudimentary indications given by the reporter and/or the cameraperson.
- Once edited, the material was dubbed on the *program tape* that contained all the finished stories planned for a given newscast. When the time between the end of editing and the beginning of the newscast was too brief, the tape containing the edited story was loaded on a separate player and reproduced during the program.
- Such a system was not particularly flexible as all changes in the running order of news clips were delicate and difficult to make. With the advent of cassette-based VTRs, that approach was replaced by another method: four cassette players were reserved for the newscast, and each news item was recorded on a separate cassette. That system offered the needed flexibility to the news editor but represented a rather delicate and complex operation for VTR operators.
- The development of multitransport cart machines somewhat changed this workflow as it solved the problem of the last-minute changes of the play-back order of news items: all cassettes containing one news item each were inserted in the *cart* (cartridge) machine, and their playback order was entered into the cart-control mechanism; if necessary, the playback order could be quickly and easily changed.

The news items recorded in the field by a station's own reporters and ENG crews were not the only source of information. A station usually received written news information from different news agencies as well as visual materials from agencies or on a reciprocal basis from other television stations. Reporters were sometimes far away from the base and had to send their stories by satellite, microwave links, or other telecommunication means. In short, crucial material was continuously flowing from different sources and arriving in the newsroom in parallel.

These multiple sources were carefully monitored, and materials were accepted, handled, processed, selected, arranged, and eventually transmitted within the framework of scheduled newscasts. Although all participants in the process felt comfortable with such procedures and apparently managed to effortlessly produce all the planned news programs, under careful scrutiny the workflow revealed much human and hardware inefficiency, excessive operational costs, and a number of potentially vulnerable points in the production chain.

The first attempt to improve the workflow by introducing IT-based techniques was the development of newsroom automation systems. These systems consisted of networking all the computers used by journalists and their editors and developing a software system that would allow access to all printed news materials from the journalist's desktop—to process these materials, write new commentaries, circulate these texts in the newsroom, send them to the dubbing room where they would be read by an announcer, or to convey them directly to the prompter PC from which they would be replayed during the newscast. Of course these newsroom systems had a number of other important features, but essentially they were designed to work with written materials and were not able to handle still or moving pictures, sounds, or graphics.

The conversion to digital and the ongoing merging of computer, television, and communications technologies opened the way to the development and implementation of the integrated digital or server-based newsrooms. They were designed to bring to news operations all the advantages of the merging of information and video/audio technologies. An integrated digital newsroom system is a LAN that ensures a seamless integration of the newsroom computer system, playout center, and media devices such as video or file servers, NLEs, proxy editors, or graphics devices. At the same time, the LAN is connected to external sources either through classical point-to-point communication links or through IT-networking systems. The smooth operation of the system is based on the use of various software solutions, which create a unified user-friendly system out of a plethora of different devices and subsystems. The conceptual framework of such systems mirrors the usual workflow of news operations. However, the usual workflow does not mean a standard workflow because in news production, as in any other television production operation for that matter, it is not possible to speak of "standard solutions." Each television organization has its own practices and consequently server-based news-production systems are custom made for each particular broadcaster. Nevertheless, as shown on Figure 12.3, it is possible to identify a number of standard processes that have to be part of any particular workflow (ingesting, logging, storing, retrieving, editing, archiving, etc.).

The precise details of these processes, interrelations, and hierarchical relationships will differ from station to station, thus leading to somewhat different

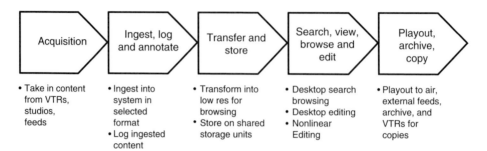

Figure 12.3 Basic workflow of news operations.

workflows and consequently to different digital newsroom systems, each optimized for a particular user.

The process starts with content acquisition. All content generated by ENG crews, studio recordings, or originating in some external entity has to be ingested into the system in an appropriate format and logged. Essentially there are two types of ingesting procedures—the manual one when a cassette brought from the field is inserted in a player and the content is ingested in the system (either through an *ingest server* or through any of the NLE stations) and the "scheduled" operation, which handles content coming through terrestrial and satellite feeds (news agencies or news exchanges) following some previously announced timetable. The ingest operator controls the ingest procedure and should detect any problem immediately. At the moment of ingest, the material is catalogued and indexed, which is crucial for later easy retrieval. In order to allow sensible browsing and material research and recovery, it is essential to develop a comprehensive system of keywords, annotations, and thumbnails, a system of metadata that will permit not only the retrieval of the needed material through the use of different search criteria but also will display on the search-result screen all relevant information concerning the retrieved essence (from content-related information to rights). When acquisition is performed with the latest tapeless camcorders, the essence could already be packed in files and the transfer from the camcorder support to the storage will not be a typical ingest procedure but just a file transfer. Once the material is ingested, it is transferred to shared storage. The shared storage stores the material in two quality levels:

1. *high-resolution* ("hi-res") level – the same compression level as used for acquisition (usually 25 Mbps for news productions), which will be used later for postproduction and airing
2. *low-resolution* ("low-res") level – also called the *browsing* level (usually MPEG-1 with a bit rate of 1–1.5 Mbps), which requires a modest storage

capacity; low-resolution browse-quality proxy clips are the product of a transcoding process performed automatically with all input materials at the moment of ingest.

The low-resolution material is accessible by journalists from their desktop workstations. They can browse it and generate edit decision lists (EDLs) but also perform rough-cut edits and add all information relevant to graphics and transitions. Journalists can add their voice-overs to the roughly assembled material. Since it is customary to keep a certain quantity of well-selected "current" archive material in shared storage, the journalist can browse it and, if needed, select pieces to be used as additional or background information (see Figure 12.4). In more elaborate and comprehensive installations, an online archive offering a large selection of archive materials to the journalist is connected to the system. A further extension of the archive system could be achieved by a near-online archive. That additional archive is usually a robotic *streamer* tape player, that is, a system that uses tape cartridges developed for the storage of data that can store large quantities of program material at a reasonable cost and which are installed in a multicartrige automatic playback machine. The access time to retrieve the content stored on streamer tapes is not immediate (as it is for the material stored in an archive server), but it is fast enough not to seriously impede the news operations. Once the EDL is generated, and possibly a live commentary added, that material is sent to an NLE station where, using information from the EDL and grabbing from the shared-storage high-resolution material, the editor assembles the final version of the story and sends the completed story back to the shared storage where it is again stored both in high and low resolution.

The stored high-resolution material is simultaneously accessible from all NLE units, which can start using it even before the completion of the ingest process or, more precisely, as soon as the first ingested frame reaches the shared storage. Thanks to such configurations, several NLE stations can use the same material at the same time to produce different versions of a given story.

Once the story is edited it can be immediately included in the playlist and transferred to the playout server. It is of course possible to prevent the story's inclusion in the playlist or transfer to the playout server until the story is viewed (at the browse-quality level) by the duty editor or producer who authorizes or does not authorize its inclusion in the playlist. The edited news item is protected, and although a number of workstations can access and view it, only the authorized one can change its content or its position on the playlist. The playlist can control and air the material directly from the shared storage, but most frequently additional playout servers are used for the storage of listed material and its playout during the newscast. As breaking news can occur at any time, it is usual to

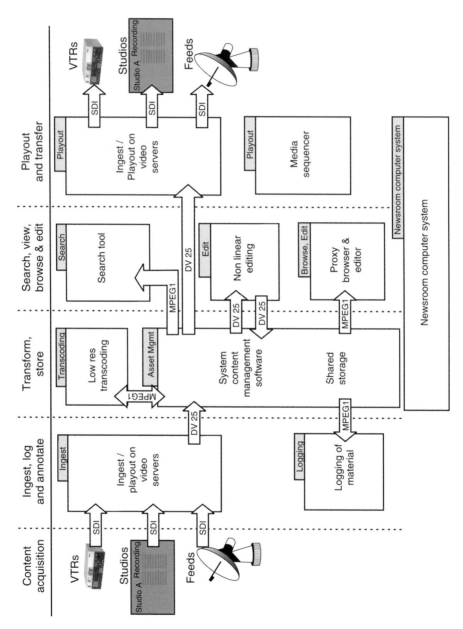

Figure 12.4   Overview of processes in an integrated digital newsroom. (Courtesy IBM)

implement solutions that will permit the airing of a story as soon as its first frame reaches the playout server so that last-minute events can be integrated without delay into the playlist. A number of integrated newsroom configurations feature two playout servers with mirrored content as an additional security measure. All that media movement is controlled by a number of software programs, which must be seamlessly integrated to allow smooth and user-friendly control of all operations. In fact, the software integration usually represents one of the most delicate problems in putting together an integrated digital newsroom system. Namely, software solutions for newsroom computer systems, NLEs, and playout or ingest frequently come from different sources. It also frequently happens that a news operation is already equipped with a newsroom computer system, already accepted by all its users. When such a station decides to implement a fully integrated digital, server-based system, it logically requires that the selected system and its software integrate seamlessly with the existing situation.

One of the important features of server-based newsroom systems is their ability to handle two-way communications with numerous bureaus and traveling crews. Television stations, and especially the 24-hour news channels, usually have a large number of bureaus and correspondents scattered in key places around the world and at the same time a fleet of roaming crews covering "hot spots" on the planet. Communicating with those outside units and integrating all their feeds in a continuous newscast is best handled by server-based systems. All reports from around the world will arrive by a number of satellite channels, by terrestrial links, as digital video recordings, as Internet downloads, and even as videophone reports. Once reports are at the base, they are all immediately annotated and stored in a central system that represents a single source to the journalists and editors in the newsroom for all available material. On the other hand, the reporter in the field can access the central archive via the Internet and download pieces of archive material in low resolution and insert them into an edited report. Once the editing is complete, the reporter can send the full report back, and when the report is received, an editor can easily replace the browse-quality material with high-resolution footage. These high-resolution pieces are easily retrieved since both the browse-proxy and the high-resolution versions are unequivocally defined with the same set of time-code and metadata information.

Server-based news systems are undoubtedly a tremendously valuable tool for any news operation. If the workflow is correctly set and the metadata generation and handling comprehensively designed and scrupulously implemented, such systems can immensely improve the cost-efficiency and quality of news operations. They could ensure an unimpeded flow of all relevant news materials, offering journalists access at their fingertips to the whole breadth of content, from the latest incoming footage to archived recent or historical recordings. These systems facilitate an easy integration of feeds from numerous sources and guarantee user-friendly and unambiguous tracking and retrieval of any piece of information that has entered the station.

As mentioned earlier, the server-based integrated newsroom operates as a network, but its contacts with the outside world, either with other parts of the same television station or with external entities, are most frequently made through conventional communication means, that is, through real-time streaming. However, it can be expected that with the generalization of network technologies and with the development of adequate solutions for all aforementioned problems, it will be possible to fully integrate this particular network into a generalized network environment and therefore draw all benefits that integrated IT and A/V technologies have to offer.

13

Television Graphics

Initially the term "television graphics" encompassed all text (information and credits) and all stills used to complete, enhance, or help explain the moving-image content of a television program. However, the development of digital techniques and the introduction of IT-based production tools enlarged considerably that initial definition, and "graphics" today encompasses all the previous items as well as all sorts of animation, compositing, virtual elements (such as sets), or advertisements), and, who knows, perhaps one day also virtual actors and presenters.

Although frequently overlooked graphics are extremely important for the overall impact of a given program and, by extension, of a given broadcasting organization. If the styling and design of graphics is adequate, they will help considerably in establishing the right atmosphere and viewer acceptance of a program. Graphics can set the mood, help carry the message, and identify the message originator.

13.1 Basic Technical Requirements

To be able to fulfill all the aforementioned tasks, television graphics have above all to be "readable." In other words, they must be appropriately matched to the technical requirements of a given television system. A number of parameters have to be set in such a way that the viewer is able to see everything the artists wished to put into the final product. To achieve that goal, at least several crucial parameters must be observed:

- Keep in mind the average size of the receiver screen and the usual viewing distance at home.
- Be conscious of possible repercussions of aspect-ratio differences.
- Observe the so-called safe area.

- Take into account the maximum resolution of the television system.
- Observe the limits of the television contrast ratio.
- Carefully select the colors.

The observance of the screen size and the viewing distance implies setting the size of text characters and other graphic elements so they are easily legible in all circumstances. It is common knowledge that all sizes of television screens exist in viewer households. At the same time, the usual viewing distance at home is at least six times the screen height. Therefore, in designing a graphic illustration, you have to make a strategic decision to ensure that all details will be visible and easy to interpret on a given screen size (that is, say, 17 inches in diagonal) observed from a distance of about 2 meters.

Until recently the aspect ratio of all television standards was fixed at 4:3. However, with the advent of advanced and high-definition television systems, a new aspect ratio of 16:9 was introduced. Since we are far from a complete transition to widescreen programming (and even further away from the point when the majority of receivers in the field will be equipped with wide screens), programs produced in 16:9 aspect ratio are viewed on 4:3 conventional screens in the letter-box format as shown in Figure 13.1 (a 16:9 picture is presented on the middle of a 4:3 screen framed with two unused black areas).

The visible picture surface on camera viewfinders, studio monitors, and even computer screens is usually larger than the surface seen by the viewer on the

Figure 13.1   The letterbox format.

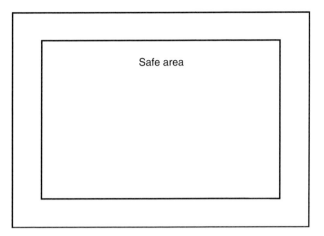

Figure 13.2   Screen format and the safe area.

screen of a home receiver. That is why it is recommended that graphics be composed over the whole visible surface of the workstation but that elements carrying information that the viewer must see be positioned inside the *safe area* (also known as the *protected zone*) (see Figure 13.2). The width and the height of that zone are 20% less than the same dimensions of the entire visible screen surface in the studio. Most present-day character generators and other graphics stations have an outline of the safe area displayed on the screen so that the artist can easily and correctly position all the elements of the composition.

Every television system has a definite resolution capability defined by the overall system bandwidth and the number of lines. However, not all of that resolution is always available at the viewer's home. The transmission path, especially in analog terms, has the tendency to reduce the bandwidth, thus reducing the resolution. The domestic receiver will also sometimes contribute to the bandwidth reduction, and as a result the viewer will quite frequently see a picture of a lesser resolution than the one seen in the studio. That effect has to be taken into account when designing a graphic, and, while avoiding extremely fine details, the end result should be assessed on a video monitor rather than on a computer screen.

Aesthetic value is a very important aspect of television graphics. In that respect, the use of color has certainly a dominant importance. Use of color also has technical importance. As explained earlier, each color is characterized by its hue, brightness, and saturation. From the technical point of view it is important to carefully select all aspects of the colors used. For example, some hues (like a saturated red) should be avoided for large surfaces because of visible impairments that frequently appear on such surfaces. Further, to ensure that characters are distinct against a background, their respective colors must not only be distinguishable by their different hues but it is also recommended that the respective brightness values of the characters and the background differ by at least two steps on the standard gray scale.

13.2   Computer Generated Imaging

For years television graphics were produced in the most traditional way with paper, pencils, paints, photographs, and so on. Once composed as a drawing or a collage, the graphic would be presented as an *opaque* (i.e. impenetrable to light, not translucent) in front of a camera, or a slide of the graphic would be inserted in a slide projector or a special slide scanner. However, for the past two decades, television graphics have been produced, practically exclusively, with the help of pieces of equipment that belong to the big family of computer-generated imaging.

The history of computer-generated imaging begins with a doctoral thesis presented by Ivan Sutherland in 1962 at the Massachusetts Institute of Technology. The thesis described "Sketchpad," a human-machine communication system that could enable operators to draw different shapes using light pens and some dedicated commands. In the years that followed the publication of the thesis, the work on improving computer-generated imaging was pursued at universities and in U.S. government institutions that saw its big potential for a number of important national projects. Over the years, a number of developments transformed the initial PhD thesis into a mature tool for graphics representation. It is interesting to note that the Sketchpad solution is still at the core of the large majority of graphics programs.

For some time, computer-generated imaging remained the province of big corporations and government institutions that used it for flight simulation or the design of future products, among other things. However, in 1979 another young PhD, Richard Shoup of Xerox, designed a system that NASA used to create television-news animations of their Pioneer missions. These animations were the first computer-generated imagery broadcast on television. Shoup left Xerox some time later and created Aurora, one of the first companies that produced digital paint systems.

Since then, many existing and new companies have joined the domain of computer-generated imaging, and that discipline has rapidly evolved from the exclusive domain of big institutions like NASA to being an everyday tool for television production and an indispensable tool for the generation of film special effects. Simultaneously, graphics systems migrated from mainframe computers through large workstations and custom-built PCs to reach the stage today where they can use standard off-the-shelf PCs equipped with appropriate video cards. The span of different electronic graphics tools is very large and goes from complex and powerful top-of-the-line systems used for generating special effects for the movie industry to the most basic software that runs on a standard PC thereby transforming it into a versatile character generator.

At the base of computer-generated imagery is the ability to individually manipulate each of the pixels that compose a digital television frame. That frame, in both scanning standards (625 and 525), has 720 pixels in each television line. Each of these pixels has its own address and, through bit mapping, is assigned a certain number of bits. The number of assigned bits, or the *bit depth*, determines the number of possible color combinations. The bit depth starts with 24 bits (8 bits for each of the red, green, and blue primaries), but systems with 30 or 36 bits are frequently encountered. A greater bit depth offers more colors, more space for details, and more delicate shadings—in short, a larger creative space for the graphics designer and the opportunity to more easily achieve a "realistic" look for the final product.

13.3 Character Generators

Character generators (CG) are important tools for television production and especially for news and sports broadcasts. They are also relatively uncomplicated members of the computer graphics family. Their essential task is to generate alphanumeric characters that will be keyed into a live or recorded television picture. Although they are used during postproduction to create written information or to generate credits, the main application of CGs is in live transmissions. Character generators are constituted by a memory in which all the required fonts are deposited. In the process of font generation, special *antialiasing* processes are used to avoid the jagged look of the letter's outline that appears whenever that outline crosses television scanning lines. The fonts are called out from memory through a conventional computer keyboard using special commands to position the letters on the screen and to define their size and color. Even simple character generators usually have the ability to rotate, spin, blink, and otherwise manipulate the generated characters. In addition, CGs are equipped with another memory whose capacity is several pages in which the text and graphics already composed by the operator can be saved and then called out one by one to be fed to the production mixer that will insert them into the program signal. In terms of computer-generated imagery, a page represents all graphic elements (such as alphanumeric signs, logos, illustrative details, drawings, etc.) that appear simultaneously on the screen and represent the electronic equivalent of a single piece of paper on which these same graphic elements would be drawn or printed. An alternative to the page-by-page display of generated inscriptions is to make these inscriptions crawl or roll.

Over the years, character generators enlarged the palette of their operational capabilities. With the growth of the capacity of disk drives and the increasing processing speed of computers, it became possible to include in the CG a number of graphics options, such as painting capabilities, a memory bank of different backgrounds, the ability to memorize still pictures that could then be manipulated and used as building blocks of new graphic representations, and the option to create templates for different applications and to customize them just prior to transmission. Today's CG uses standard techniques of two-dimensional (2D) picture generation with the addition of a number of predesigned elements, such as standard or custom-designed alphanumeric signs that are stored on disk. All these functions are part of a specific software package. The disk drive and the processor of the platform to be used have to correspond to the breadth of functions offered by a particular CG program. The simple generation of alphanumeric signs and their display onscreen with a limited amount of sign manipulations can be used on a typical off-the-shelf PC equipped with a normal broadcast-quality graphics card. However, to ensure all the features offered by top-of-the-line systems, which are more graphics workstations than CGs, it is necessary to use higher-performance PCs that can ensure a considerably larger memory and faster processors.

13.4 Graphics Workstations

Graphics workstations have a number of graphics applications. They can support painting, 3D modeling and animation, and compositing. These tasks are performed by a system composed of the following components:

- purpose-built or standard workstation that acts as the central processing unit and whose processing power depends on the demands of the graphics system of which it is a part
- specially developed software solution that allows the designer to create a number of different graphics
- memory in which all the raw visual materials and finished graphics are stored
- user interface in the form of a tablet with a light pen, mouse, and keyboard
- graphics monitor (a large high-resolution computer screen)
- video monitor on which all final results must be checked

Although some manufacturers still insist on using purpose-built platforms, more and more graphics software solutions are developed for standard Mac, PC, or SGI platforms. Graphics workstations can be specialized for just one sort of graphics creation but also can offer a whole palette of graphics possibilities. The span of graphics possibilities and the complexity of graphics interventions are determined by specialized software. The software can be limited to the creation of titles and inscriptions and to a reduced amount of coloring and manipulation of alphanumeric characters or it can offer an extremely large palette of graphics tools that can be used to create stunning stills or even animated sequences. Therefore, a graphics workstation can be programmed to perform only one class of visual effects, such as painting, and to offer at the same time options such as time-warping effects (artificially changing the speed of a shot) or morphing (creating a transition between two images by matching the morphology of the objects in these two images—for example the effect of a surreal transformation of a human face into a beast's face). Manufacturers can choose to put on the market a powerful and versatile graphics workstation that has in one single package a number of different imaging programs, like painting, 3D modeling and animation, compositing, and so on.

In the case of painting, the work can begin as in conventional painting with an empty screen as the equivalent to a blank canvas. The first step could be to select the background color, but it is also possible to input in the frame memory any still and treat it as the raw material for the composition of graphics. The work is usually performed with a tablet and a light pen. The *tablet* is a spatial sensor that corresponds to the digital television frame. Each point on the tablet has its corresponding pixel or group of pixels on the frame. When the tip of the *light pen* touches a point of the tablet, the processing circuits generate an adequate change of brightness on the corresponding point on the screen. Therefore, when the operator "draws" a line with the light pen on the tablet a corresponding line appears and remains on the screen because the digital signal corresponding to that line is automatically stored in the random access memory (RAM) and remains there until the reception of an erase command. The width, shape, and color of that line are determined by a set of separate commands that can be activated either by the light pen itself or by means of some other control device. All these commands will generate digital signals that determine the description of each pixel in the frame in terms of the three R, G, and B primaries.

Similarly, the light pen is used in conjunction with the installed software to transform, cut, or change any picture recorded in the frame memory. The correspondences between the actions of the light pen and of the activated commands and the generation of a new digital signal representing the drawn object are performed by the computer's processing circuitry under the control of the specialized graphics software. As mentioned, the processing power and speed have to be correlated with the complexity of graphics work performed by a given workstation.

Once a graphic illustration is composed, the light pen or keyboard is used to determine the name or the address of the composition and to store it under that name on disk. The capacity of the disk depends on the projected application. Usually it has to store a number of templates, many works in progress, and some finished items. The number of finished items to be kept depends on the overall system philosophy. If the same unit is used for both the creation and playout of graphics, it has to have a larger memory. But if the system is essentially used for the creation of graphics that once created are transferred to another storage location (archive or playout), then the memory can be designed to keep only a limited number of finished products. However, the price of memory has decreased dramatically over the past decades (from one dollar per bit to one dollar per million bits), and therefore the capacity of the memory attached to a graphics system is no longer an economic issue.

The term "3D modeling and animation" refers to objects on the 2D screen that, when moved, give the impression that they are 3D. That sort of modeling starts with the creation of *wireframe* objects composed of *vectors* (an element possessing both a magnitude and a direction), which enclose the *polygons* (surfaces enclosed by the vectors). The number of polygons and their complexity determine the complexity of the curved surfaces that will be represented. The designer selects the shapes to be represented, either by drawing them directly or by using predetermined shapes from the library that is part of the 3D-modeling software. It is, of course, possible to combine these two methods or to input 3D-models through special scanning devices. Once the wireframe model is created, the animation can begin. The animation is usually achieved by determining the key frames that characterize two given phases of a movement and letting the computer generate all the necessary frames that will have to be interpolated between the two key frames in order to create the effect of a continuous movement. Once the whole animated sequence is realized, the wireframe model is used as a framework onto which the selected texture is placed through a rendering process. If the surface of the animated object is complex, the rendering process can take a very long time. For that reason different approaches have been developed. One of them consists of interconnecting a number of workstations in a *rendering farm* that automates the rendering task so that it can be performed after hours. Another approach is to try to develop new software that will facilitate real-time animation of already rendered models.

Compositing is the combination of graphic elements with live-action images. This sort of graphic design technique is most often used in film production (for the creation of surreal situations in which real persons are confronted with some imaginary or extinct species) and in television commercials (for the creation of high-impact messages, like the combination of live shots of children combined with animated characters representing some brands of cereals).

Since nonlinear editing systems can use several time lines to assemble different elements of a composite image, a rather wide gamut of compositing possibilities are now included in some NLE packages so that the editor can create effects, correct colors, and produce composite images. As could be expected, the reverse is also true—some computer graphics workstations offer nonlinear editing capabilities. However, although such versatile systems could be very appropriate for small facilities where one or two persons perform all the painting, compositing, and editing using one workstation, larger facilities prefer to create dedicated workgroups composed of different specialists. Such a workgroup comprises a number of workstations, each equipped appropriately for a given function (animation, editing, paint, audio, etc.) and connected in a local area network (LAN) in such a way that all of them can access the original material, exchange clips they have already processed, and create the final product of their combined efforts. Such a configuration can ensure superior quality since it employs specialized operators for each of the production disciplines and each workgroup is equipped with appropriately configured and optimized workstations.

Workgroups are frequently specialized in a given area of graphic design and are part of the "networked production" concept. Namely they can be connected through a wide area network (WAN) to other specialized postproduction companies and to the producer of the program. In that way they can share original materials, do their tasks, and then transfer the semifinished product to somebody else who may perform another kind of processing, or to several postproduction houses who can take the same material, do their parts of the processing, and then send the result of their work to those who will put all of it together and deliver the final product. An alternative practice is for a production team to send the frames to its graphics artists to be modified on large disk drives, many over a terabyte in size. These drives are easily plugged into a workstation where each artist will modify the frames, place them back onto the disk, and then pass them along to the next artist in the production chain.

13.5 Virtual Sets

The advent of color television considerably enriched the program producer's tool kit by adding a new and powerful effect—the chroma key. The *chroma key effect* consists of positioning a foreground subject or object in front of a monochromatic background, usually blue or green, and then replacing that monochromatic background with a still or moving picture from another picture source. This effect is also called *blue screen* or *blue box* because a specific shade of blue is most frequently used as the background color (although a shade of green is also used in many instances). The selection of a monochromatic color for the background is dictated

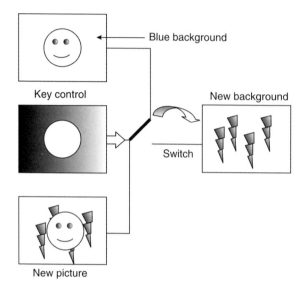

Figure 13.3   Chroma-key effect.

by the desire to select a hue that will be very distinct from the color of the human face, which is always the center of attention of every shot where human beings appear.

As shown on the simplified diagram in Figure 13.3, the video signal of the foreground figure positioned in front of a blue background is fed to special circuitry that detects in each line the blue and the nonblue content, switching between one and the other, thus creating a *key-control shape*. That key-control shape is a sort of stencil that will be used later to combine the selected part of the foreground and the new background. The key-control shape is then used to activate another switching device. By switching between the original image and the selected new background at the boundary of the "keyhole," this device replaces the blue content of the first shot with the selected background content. It is possible to select the content that will fill the keyhole. It can be, and most frequently is, the same content as was used to create the keyhole. In that case, the result obtained is that the figure or object that was originally in the foreground is "keyed" into the new background. However, it is also possible to fill the keyhole with other content and then create a composite picture where a figure that has the shape of the foreground figure but a different content will move across the new background.

The chroma-key effect is indeed a very good and versatile effect, and it is used in all sorts of programs. However, this effect has a very serious shortcoming. Namely, once the keying is made and the size and angle relationship between the foreground and the background established, it is not possible to change one or the other by zooming or panning since every such movement will change the established geometrical relationships. To explain that problem, let us imagine that a foreground figure is shot in a real environment—for example, a person standing in front of a building. If we zoom forward toward the person or pan across the scene, both the foreground figure and its background will change accordingly and will keep their natural relationship. However, if the person standing in the foreground is in fact chroma-keyed into the background picture of the building, when the camera shooting the foreground zooms or pans it will change the perspective of the figure but the background will remain unchanged and reveal the truth—that it is not a real shot but a special effect.

Long ago, attempts were made to overcome that problem by using two cameras, one shooting the foreground and the other a picture of the background. These two cameras had their zoom lenses and camera supports fitted with sensors and servo motors. The camera shooting the foreground was controlled by a cameraperson and the movements of the other camera were controlled by servo motors. When the first camera and/or its zoom lens were moved, these movements generated control voltages in the attached sensors. These signals were fed to a computer unit that processed them and generated command signals for servo motors installed on the second camera and through them controlled all its movements. The whole system, known as *Scene Sync* was rather cumbersome and the end result was far from perfect.

The problem of the foreground and background geometrical relationship remained unsolved until the development of *virtual sets*. A system ensuring the generation and use of virtual sets has several parts:

- the model of the set
- a powerful computer capable of real-time rendering
- a system that will detect the movements of a camera (or several cameras) and of a zoom lens that covers an actor (or a group of actors) on the set
- a chroma-key system

The model of the set is usually created by a computer graphics workstation. That model is then stored in a powerful computer capable of real-time rendering. As mentioned earlier, in order to achieve a realistic effect it is necessary to ensure the change of the appearance of the sets in the background synchronously with the change of the camera position or the optical zoom adjustment. That change will be ensured by the computer workstation that is fed with data representing the momentary camera position and optical zoom adjustment. Several methods can be used to generate that necessary data:

- using *motion sensors* – captors attached to the camera whose position is detected by special units installed near the studio ceiling

- with a *motion control head* – a device that is installed on the camera itself and detects all tilt and pan actions
- with a *pattern recognition system* – applying a special pattern of vertical and horizontal stripes of a paler blue on the chroma-key blue background and using special circuitry to detect that pattern and, on the basis of that pattern's momentary appearance, compute the camera position and the zoom adjustment

Data detected in that manner are fed to the computer, and it will then recompute the stored model, making it appear as it would look if it were a real set seen from the detected camera and zoom position. With a chroma-key system, the actor is then keyed into the new appearance of the set model. Since the set appearance is recomputed whenever the framing is changed, the resulting final picture will remain quite realistic, that is, it will give the illusion that the actor is moving in the middle of real and solid sets. With the virtual-set system it is also possible to include in the combined picture a number of different "objects" created as computer graphics. With some amount of rehearsal, actors or presenters can move among virtual objects placed inside the virtual set, thus creating quite a convincing impression.

It is worth noting that a very similar technique is used for the insertion of virtual advertisements during sport broadcasts. It is possible to replace broadcast images of real advertising billboards at the stadium with virtual ones, to replace the image that is really visible on the stadium's large display with another one that will be seen only by television viewers, or even to place the image of a sponsor's logo "on" the playing field and at the same time preserve the full visibility of the players and of the game.

Although they first appeared in the mid-1990s, virtual sets are still a developing technology. They remain relatively expensive and have not gained general acceptance.

13.6   Selecting a Computer Graphics System

Computer graphics systems continue to evolve. New software developers appear on the market every day and offer either completely new products or, even more frequently, additions (*plug-ins*) for the well-established ones. At the same time, thanks to the continued validity of Moore's law (a prediction made in 1965 by Gordon Moore, the cofounder of Intel, that the number of *transistors* per square inch on *integrated circuits*, and therefore the power of such chips, would double every eighteen months), the hardware becomes more powerful and more affordable. The new outlets for the entertainment industry, such as DVDs, HDTV broadcasts, the D-Cinema, and others, offer new challenges and new opportunities for computer-generated imaging. That situation is certainly invigorating but also worrying for all those who have to purchase computer graphics systems. There is a definite fear that even the short time that elapses between the acquisition and the start of operation of a graphics system is sufficient to make that system obsolete.

The situation is probably not so dramatic, but it is undoubtedly necessary to be very careful when purchasing a graphics device. The future user must first evaluate with great precision the real needs of the facility. Is it really necessary to purchase the most versatile software operating on the most powerful platform, or will it be sufficient in view of the planned production to acquire a middle-range character generator? It is also important to make a selection between systems advertised as *open platform*, meaning that they operate on any PC or workstation of adequate performance, and those called *dedicated*, meaning that they are developed to operate on a customized computer. Another element to be taken into consideration is the speed of operation needed. The same complex graphics can be created at a considerably lower price if the user is ready to accept a slower operation (which is most usually connected with the rendering capacity of the system). Finally the future owner of a graphics system is always confronted with the dilemma of whether to take a well-proven system that, in spite of all the advertised upgrades, is perhaps getting a little bit old but that is also thoroughly debugged or to select a new product on the market, which encompasses all the latest technological breakthroughs and offers the prospect of a relatively long life but has almost certainly a respectable number of still-undiscovered bugs that may make initial operation rather troublesome. Whatever the final decision, remember that computer-generated imaging is certainly a marvelous and powerful production tool but nevertheless just a tool; as with all other program production tools, the quality and attractiveness of the result does not depend on the tool but on the one who handles it.

HDTV

14

In the domain of audiovisual production and distribution, the past 20 years have been punctuated by a recurrent statement that high-definition television (HDTV) was just around the corner, that it represented the imminent future of television. For the last 10 years, that statement has been most frequently opposed by negative assertions that HD will never take off or that "high definition is not high enough." Now suddenly HDTV has again become the "talk of the town," and, what is much more important, the object of serious consideration as a technology everyone pays attention to. It is not anymore an object of laboratory research or theoretical debates, but a real-life production and transmission format used in a number of regular programs on different channels around the world.

14.1   Development of the HDTV Concept and Technology

"What do you expect us to do with signals like those?" grumbled Cecil Browne back in 1932 when he was shown the first crude attempts of an EMI team to build a television camera (*RTS Journal* 1975). Four years later, that same EMI team furnished all the necessary tools for the beginning of the first regular television service. That service and its technical performance were announced at the time as "high definition." From today's perspective, to give such a name to a system that featured 405 lines was a little bit overstated.

Developed for the needs of the small display screens of black-and-white receivers, television was restricted by the state of electronics development in 1936 and in 1945, when television services were resumed after the interruption caused by the World War II. Limited by the transmission spectrum availability television signals, their supports and displays, reached a maximum definition of 625 lines, pitifully lagging behind the performance of 35 mm film. Television resolution was considerably lower, its contrast ratio much narrower, and its line structure visible even on medium-sized display screens. However, in the post–World War II period, the electronics industry showed its most spectacular development.

Some empirical estimations made in the mid-1980s showed that between 1945 and 1985, electronics featured a 400% development rate, while, for the sake of comparison, precision mechanics for that same period of time showed an advance of only 25%. That tremendous achievement in the field of electronics boosted the development of television technology, and by the end of the 1960s, NHK Labs in Japan started working on a new project then called "television for the next century." The goal of that new television system, which was later nicknamed HDTV or High Definition Television, was to offer a certain number of very visible quality advantages when compared with the television that we are still watching today, which, according to a number of specialists, has reached its limits of development.

According to the *NHK Monograph on High Definition Television*, the NHK engineers started with the assumption that current conventional television systems fail to attain the level at which the functions of the human visual system can be effectively utilized. Therefore they started their research project with a series of investigations of the psychophysical reception of moving images. Early in the process they realized that the closer the viewers sit to the screen, the more the image fills their viewing field and, as a result, the more involved they are with the displayed content. In the case of cinema, the large screen and the dark environment in movie theaters are the prerequisites for such an involvement. In the domestic environment, it is necessary to sit closer to the television screen to ensure a similar effect, but such closeness can quickly make you feel dizzy. To avoid the dizziness, it is therefore necessary to sit farther away from the television screen, but then the image seems remote and the involvement is considerably reduced. The Japanese researchers tried to find the optimum distance by conducting subjective assessments involving a number of volunteers. They finally came to the conclusion that it would be ideal to watch the screen from a distance of three to four times the screen height. However, with conventional television systems (525 and 625) at such a distance, the line structure is unpleasantly visible and the resolution shortcomings are apparent. Consequently, to achieve a system that would allow a closer viewing of the screen and facilitate a greater involvement of the viewer, it was necessary to increase its resolution and number of lines. It had to be a resolution that could be watched on a very big screen at a very short distance (three times the picture height, as had been determined) and offer subjectively excellent quality under those circumstances.

These psychophysical experiments led also to the conclusion that the 4:3 aspect ratio was far from satisfactory and that a wider screen would be better adapted to the panoramic character of the human vision system. It should be noted that the movie industry had reached that same conclusion many years before, but television, blocked by the immense number of 4:3 television sets in the field, was not able to follow that path. NHK Labs began to study the possibilities of developing a new television system. At the same time they put in front of the International Telecommunication Union (ITU) a proposal to initiate studies of a new system that would meet the requirements of entertainment and education in the twenty-first century, a system with the following basic parameters:

- approximately twice the vertical and horizontal resolution offered by present-day 625 and 525 systems
- wide-screen picture with an aspect ratio between 5:3 and 2:1
- wider color gamut
- considerably better sound performance

By the beginning of the 1980s, Japanese broadcasters and manufacturers agreed on a single system that had these basic parameters:

- 1125 lines
- 60 fields
- 16:9 aspect ratio

Although the number of lines was carefully selected to be somewhere between twice the standards of 525 and 625, and the aspect ratio was intended to satisfy nearly all wide-screen movie systems, the proposal was not accepted as a "compromise," but was sharply felt to be a new threat for the European and U.S. electronics industries. The reaction came immediately in the form of a counter proposal from the European side:

- 1250 lines
- 50 fields
- 16:9 aspect ratio

Following that showdown, there was a stalemate on the HDTV front. The Japanese continued to promote their system, the Europeans were feverishly developing their standard trying to catch up with the well-advanced Japanese, and the ITU was trying to find a way out of that deadlock. Although the question of how to broadcast HDTV signals with their huge bandwidth in the overcrowded spectrum further complicated the situation, the major stumbling block appeared to be the frame rate. The proponents of 60 Hz claimed that such a rate ensured a considerably better movement rendition since it offered a higher temporal sampling of the movement, while the supporters of 50 Hz objected that the difference in movement rendition was practically unnoticeable but that a 60 Hz system could have serious problems when operating in a 50 Hz environment. Furthermore, neither side was ready to discuss proposals that advocated some compromise solutions based on adopting the rates that were already common in the computer industry, such as, for example, 75 Hz.

The maturing of digital television and the development of digital compression methods (that, as mentioned in Chapter 6, owed a lot to the research conducted by General Instruments in the United States and aimed at developing a transmission system for HDTV) changed the original deadlock between the two competing systems by establishing a *common image format*, that is, a digital representation of an HDTV picture that would be common for both 50 and 60 Hz standards. The agreed-upon common image format had the following essential characteristics:

- 16:9 aspect ratio
- 1920 active samples per line
- 1080 active lines
- square sample distribution (the disposition of samples is orthogonal, that is, all samples are disposed on perpendicular lines, and the luminance and color difference samples are co-sited)

Unfortunately, acceptance of the common image format did not put an end to the disputes. One of the major causes of contention was the question of the type of scan. As described in Chapter 3, the interlaced scan was introduced as a means of ensuring a sufficient refreshment rate of the screen, reducing flicker to an acceptable level, and keeping the overall bandwidth unchanged. That was a very clever solution, but it had a price tag attached. The most important problem with a direct bearing on the picture quality and its processability was that two adjacent lines on the screen were in fact separated not by 64 μs, that is, a standard duration of one television line, but by 1/50 of a second (the duration of one television field in the 625/50 system). Namely, as explained in Chapter 3, the scanning beam scans first all odd and then, in the next field, or 1/50 of a second later, all even lines. Consequently in all interlaced systems two adjacent lines on the screen belong in fact to two different television fields. That problem became acute when complex special effects and image manipulations became feasible because the lengthy time gap between two adjacent lines created processing problems. In addition, a number of subjective assessments showed that when comparing two pictures that have the same number of lines and frames, where one was progressively scanned and the other generated with an interlaced scan, the progressively scanned picture was regularly judged as clearly superior in overall picture quality. Unfortunately, just like the progressively scanned standard-definition television in the mid-1930s, the progressively scanned high-definition television in the mid-1990s had bandwidths and bit rates that required equipment and transmission channels beyond what could be cost-effectively manufactured. For that reason, the ITU recommendation that stipulated all parameters of the agreed-upon common image format noted that the progressively scanned format was the real goal but that for the time being, the interlaced scan would be accepted for practical reasons.

Very soon after the adoption of that recommendation, another concept started gaining more and more supporters. Its proponents argued that if it was difficult to achieve a cost-effective working system based on 1080 progressively scanned active lines, and if it was generally accepted that progressively scanned pictures looked considerably better than the corresponding interlaced ones and offered superior processing capabilities, why not select the progressive scan and reduce the number of lines to the point at which it would allow the construction of a rational system? As a possible standard they proposed a system with 1280 samples per active line and 720 active progressively scanned lines, claiming that pictures scanned in that way looked at least equal to if not better than the ones composed of 1080 interlaced lines. Although the table of "standard" values from the Advanced Television Systems Committee (ATSC)—the body empowered to research, evaluate, and propose a high-definition standard for the United States—had a plethora of figures and possible combinations, two major contenders emerged eventually: the 1080 lines interlaced and the 720 lines progressive. The same two possible formats were also envisaged for HD transmission in other parts of the world. The discussion between the 1080 and 720 camps is still (in the year 2005) very ideological, and the divide separates not only users but also manufacturers. However, as the HD concept progresses, it can be expected that manufacturers will return to their usually neutral position relatively soon and start manufacturing and selling any type of equipment the market is prepared to buy.

14.2 HDTV Production Equipment

As mentioned, both scanning models have their proponents and opponents, and consequently it is possible to find equipment on the market based on both progressive and interlaced scanning. In addition, these two groups are subdivided into two categories each, depending on the frame rate used (50 or 60 Hz), which makes four possible variants for each piece of equipment. However, the overall bit rate for 720 progressive is not drastically different from the bit rate corresponding to 1080 interlaced, so equipment for one or the other standard have quite similar levels of complexity. In addition, the same compression methods can be used and the resulting bit rates would again be very similar. All these factors lead to very similar price tags.

A close scrutiny of HDTV production equipment easily reveals that the overall bit rate to be handled represents the major difference between standard- and high-definition television. All basic production tools that are developed for high-definition television, such as cameras, recorders (tape-based or tapeless), graphics engines, and so on, are based on the same concepts and operate in the same manner as the corresponding units manufactured for 525 or 625 standards. The only difference is the difficulty in developing practical and cost-effective pieces of equipment that would be able to handle considerably higher bit rates at comparable speeds. For example, it is challenging to develop CCD chips with twice the number of pixels, but those chips operate in the same manner as the chips described in Chapter 9. A lot of research is needed to put together graphics and special effects units that would be able to process (under the same time constraints) the bit rates on the order of 1 Gbps, but the architecture of these units does not differ substantially from those used in standard-definition television. Some pieces of equipment, such as production mixers, are available today as universal units that can accept and handle both standard-definition (SD) and high-definition (HD) signals in the same way. In the domain of magnetic videotape recording, the market offers several recording formats that operate in the same manner as the formats described in Chapter 10. In the domain of magnetic tape recording, the first HDTV machines were in fact transformed and adapted "conventional" recorders: a modified format C or four interlocked digital D1 recorders that split between them the huge bit rate to be recorded. Such a configuration even received a nice historical name "Quadriga," like the Roman chariots drawn by four horses. The most frequently used recorders today are, in a sense, extensions of standard-definition recorders—variations able to handle higher bit rates. For example, the DVCPRO 100 format is just an extension of the DVCPRO family, and the HDCAM is based on solutions developed for the Betacam and DVCAM series of equipment with the addition of solutions needed to handle considerably higher bit rates. It is true, however, that HD camcorders developed for the D-Cinema market feature a number of cinematic gadgets, such as a special viewfinder and zoom controls of the type that are preferred by filmmakers, but all these attachments do not change anything in the operating principles of the camera. Finally, numerous IT-based pieces of equipment are definition agnostic. They handle HD and SD signals in the same manner, the only difference being the storage capacity when expressed in terms of time. For example, one can find paint units on the market that exist in SD and HD versions, the only difference being the bit rate each of them is able to handle and store. All the rest, from the tablet and keyboard to the graphical user interface, are practically identical.

However, from the early days of HDTV development, this new technology and its developers looked toward the film industry, making sporadic offers and trying to persuade it to abandon film in favor of magnetic tape, or, as Lasse Svanberg, a professor at the Swedish Film Institute put it, "to replace silver with rust "(L. Svanberg, Report to the IBC Council 2000). And once the intrinsic quality of HD and of digital HD equipment made it possible to generate high-quality special effects and to successfully perform delicate correction tasks, electronic equipment drew the attention of the film community.

14.3 HDTV and D-Cinema

When presented to the film industry in the mid-1980s, HDTV was, with very few exceptions, snubbed. Nevertheless, it would be wrong to say that the film industry ignored the world of electronics completely. Even before the emergence of HDTV, the advantages offered by video were recognized, especially in the area of film special effects. A number of very complex schemes were developed for the video-to-film transfer of short electronically processed sequences for the sake of their later inclusion in a film that was otherwise produced in a standard way by using 35 mm film stock. On the other hand, some filmmakers were so attracted by the potential of video that they embarked upon audacious adventures, like Michelangelo Antonioni, who in 1981 made his *Il Mistero di Oberwald* completely on videotape, transferring the final, edited, and postproduced version to film. Unfortunately that courageous attempt had two fatal flaws. First, the movie was not a success with audiences. Second, Antonioni's experiment was conducted in the pre–HDTV and predigital era. Therefore the film suffered both from the very limited resolution of the standard 625/50 scanning system and from a loss of a good part of the initial quality in the process of analog postproduction. This example did nothing to prompt other moviemakers to try to investigate other means of integrating the video and film industries. On the contrary, it provided a massively convincing argument for all the film diehards against integration.

But the ever-growing program hunger of the television industry and the opening of the worldwide program market introduced a kind of combined film and video production method. That hybrid formula was based on 35 mm acquisition, which was followed by video offline postproduction, thus leading to a 525/60 NTSC end product. Unfortunately, the inadequate standard conversion process of that time resulted in marginal quality of the converted 625/50 PAL copies. The solution was either to return to the end-to-end 35 mm film production and postproduction (which was too costly for the bulk of the standard low-budget–low-price sitcom/cops and robbers/melodrama types of series) or to start with a 35 mm acquisition and then, with a clever frame-recounting system, use the same edit decision list to create two edited masters in 525 and 625 respectively.

This was all very good for a product aimed at the television market, which was still at that time considered a second-class market compared to the movie theater (like a cheap department store compared to a classy boutique). But nobody was prepared to even think about using video for the production of theatrical films. It is true that some in Hollywood were more receptive to the challenge of video and tried to use it as an auxiliary tool for moviemaking, as, for example did Francis Ford Coppola who made a video storyboard for his *One from the Heart*.

By that time, HDTV technology had reached a sufficient level of maturity to allow experimental productions by a number of producers. Coppola, Barry Rebo, and David Niles in the United States, Kohei Ando in Japan, and major public broadcasters in Italy, France, the United Kingdom, and Germany produced a number of shorts aimed at demonstrating HDTV's production capabilities. The Italian public broadcaster RAI went so far as to produce a feature-length movie *Julia and Julia* using exclusively HDTV technology. Nevertheless, further and larger application of this new tool was stalled. One of the main reasons being the analog technology combined with the diversity of analog HDTV standards (1125/60 and 1250/50) and their uneasy relationship with the film frame rate. Namely the 1125-line standard developed by Japan and supported, at that time, by the United States and Canada had 30 frames per second, while the European 1250-line standard had 25 frames per second. Neither standard was directly convertible to the 24 fps of film, although the conversion of 25 to 24 fps was somewhat less difficult than that from 30 fps.

The development of digital technologies and their applications in the field of HDTV finally offered the opportunity for a breakthrough and for the creation of sophisticated high-performance production tools. With its rich experience in developing HDTV tools and systems, Sony spearheaded the new movement and established a new department in its base in Hollywood that specialized in film-to-tape and tape-to-film transfer and digital-image processing. That unit was not only intended for the creation of special effects but also for all sorts of correction of pictures shot on 35 mm film (reframing, erasing of unwanted details, changing the overall lighting appearance of the scene, and correcting the colors). To perform all these operations, they developed and built a series of unique pieces of processing equipment that otherwise were not available on the market and could be used only at Sony's facility. With such an approach they reinstated the decades-old philosophy of the Image Transform Company, another Hollywood company that had had a similar approach in the late 1960s and early 1970s of offering tape-to-film transfer on unique, specially developed and built equipment that could not be purchased.

The success of the Sony facility started a wave of developments, and very soon a number of HDTV-processing devices were available on the market and postproduction houses around the world enlarged the gamut of their offerings by including HDTV-processing equipment and HD computer-generated imaging to create all the stunning effects that "overburden" a good part of today's movie production.

However, the movie community remained skeptical. They argued that electronic systems were very good for special effects but that their usefulness in the moviemaking domain did not extend outside the borders of such niche applications. Their arguments were centered on several factors. They claimed in general that the overall picture resolution of the 35 mm film was still superior to the one offered by any of the proposed HDTV standards and that an electronic system intended for moviemaking applications should have at least 2000–4000 pixels per active line. Beyond the question of intrinsic picture quality, there is another argument permanently put forward by the "celluloid" community—the "film look." What is the film look? What is that magical or mystical attribute, which seems to be unique? Although it is difficult to describe it precisely, it could be said to be a combination of several objective characteristics and a number of indescribable sensations, which film aficionados claim to feel when they watch a 35 mm product projected on a big screen.

It is clear that the objective characteristics are the only ones that can be analyzed. Among them the most frequently mentioned are the depth of field, the contrast ratio, the overall picture balance, the color-correction capabilities, and the frame rate of 24 fps. With the latest advances in lens technology, special features developed by several manufacturers, and adequate lighting of the stage, it is possible to achieve today with an electronic camera a depth of field that fully satisfies the goals set by filmmakers. Owing to the latest camera circuitry, one can balance the camera in such a way as to imitate the look of a selected film stock. However, the contrast ratio of electronic pick-up chips still remains basically different, or, to be more precise, more modest than the one offered by 35 mm film. On the other hand, the range and precision of color correction and balance adjustments are considerably improved with the introduction of a new type of high-definition camera that delivers R, G, and B signals at its output. These signals are not matrixed (see Chapter 4) to create Y, R-Y and B-Y components, but directly digitized as R, G and B signals and memorized as such on an IT-based storage unit. Having in store the original R, G and B digital signals offers an excellent opportunity to improve the final picture quality by performing all color adjustments and corrections directly on primaries and not any more on color difference signals.

Another and very important innovation brought the film industry much closer to the adoption of electronic production tools. At first sight, the innovation was not spectacular—it consisted of a slight change of the HDTV standard, replacing the 50 or 60 interlaced scanning by a 24 progressive one, commonly called *24p*. This apparently simple modification offered the film industry a high-performance tool that allowed adequate repurposing of the same product for different markets: movie theaters, high-definition and standard-definition television broadcasts, and DVD and video markets. This new standard, called *1080/24p* or *1080/24ps* ("s" for "segmented") was based on 1080 active lines and 24 progressively scanned frames. Such a system could have several important advantages for electronic cinematography as it avoided the artifacts of interlaced pictures and was fully compliant with film's 24 fps rate. However, pictures scanned at 1080/24p had to be processed in technically mixed environments and had to be delivered in different configurations in order to satisfy different standards of the distribution media:

- 24 progressive for theatrical projection
- 1080/60 interlaced for HDTV transmission
- 625/50 (or 525/59.94) interlaced for conventional television

To ensure such flexibility it was necessary to introduce the concept of 24 *segmented frames*. At the scanning level, 48 interlaced fields were produced out of 24 progressively scanned frames (24p). In fact, each of the 24p frames was divided into two segments each having odd and even lines (as in traditional interlaced scanning standards). The segment containing odd lines was sent along the output line, and the segment with even lines was delayed by a 1/48 of a second and then sent along. The result of that operation was a stream of sequential "odd" and "even" segments. However, these fields or segments should not be considered conventional interlaced fields because the temporal relationship that existed between two consecutive fields in a traditional interlaced scan was not present here. In the case of the 24ps standard, adjacent lines had the correct temporal and spatial relationship of a progressively scanned picture. A simple picture memory could perfectly reconstruct a real 24p format. In fact one could consider that the 24 segmented format is a kind of video data multiplex.

In the modus operandi of a CCD sensor built for interlaced scanning, the vertical sampling and the temporal sampling are linked by a tight relationship, which is in fact the cause of all the problems attributed to that scanning scheme. In the case of the newly proposed 24 segmented frames, such a relationship does not exist since the picture is in fact progressively scanned. The creation of two segments out of each scanned picture is part of the digital processing of generated signals. In fact a progressively scanned 24p video signal is transported via a sequence consisting of 48 segments per second, where one segment carries all odd and the other all even lines. However, these odd and even lines are not generated sequentially, as in the case of traditional interlaced signals; they are the result of a separation accomplished after the completion of a progressive scanning process. Therefore, once the whole frame is reconstructed two adjacent lines will be separated by the time span of one television line (i.e. scanned one after the other) and not by 1/50 of a second (i.e. scanned in two separated fields).

Therefore, from the temporal-vertical perspective that sequence of segments is a multiplex and not an interlaced signal.

The 24p scheme is based on the assumption that acquisition could be made either on 35 mm film or with 1920/1080/24p electronic cameras. If acquisition is made completely or partially on film, the telecine transfer will be done in 24 progressive frames and the whole subsequent postproduction will be based on the same 1920/1080/24p standard. Once the final version of the program is completed, the 1920/1080/24p master recording can be relatively easily converted to different distribution formats—either by transferring it to 35 mm film, or by converting it electronically to the desired scanning standards of high or standard definition.

Therefore, putting aside the "indescribable feelings," since it is impossible to argue with them, it seems that the electronic pick-up has developed all the necessary means to ensure that its final result will have a "film look." It is necessary to add to that list of new features, the development of graphics and special-effects systems with a considerably higher bit depth that makes it possible to achieve extremely realistic-looking final results. The appearance of very high-resolution CCD sensors also helps explain why electronic production and postproduction systems and methods have finally seduced a large number of Hollywood filmmakers.

The steady, although slow, acceptance of electronic production and post-production methods by the film community very soon became just a part of a much wider project—the introduction of digital or *D-Cinema*. This new expression covers the idea of a whole electronic or digital chain from acquisition through postproduction to distribution and screening. D-Cinema supporters claim that everyone involved would draw serious benefits if movies intended for theatrical distribution were produced and stored in digital form to be distributed later over telecom networks or satellites, ingested at the movie theater in a disk-based storage system, and screened later using video projectors that would replace mechanical film projectors. Their opponents claim that since a good part of electronic movie postproduction and the totality of its distribution is based on compressed digital signals, such a chain would unavoidably and seriously affect the quality seen by the viewer in the movie theater. On a theoretical level, this argument is difficult to contradict. But on a practical level it is necessary to take into account a number of additional factors.

One of them is the fact that distributing a movie in an electronic form is certainly more economical than producing a large number of release copies. In addition, if the electronic master is distributed via satellite or other broadband telecom networks, serious savings could be achieved on shipping and transportation costs, especially in large countries like the United States, China, or Russia.

Furthermore, the all-electronic distribution should help to overcome the unsolvable problem of the deterioration of film copies. After a number of projections in movie theaters, the film copy becomes scratched, occasionally breaks, and is subsequently simply shortened by a number of frames and then spliced together. That splice usually provokes a projection irregularity. In addition, a number of projectors demonstrate a gate judder, which is not only objectionable as such, but also reduces the perceived resolution. This list would not be complete if we did not mention all the imperfections due to clumsy or negligent operators, such as bad focus or imperfect roll-switching, although it should be said that they could burden any projection, film or video. All in all, the quality of projections is too frequently seriously degraded by the accumulated defects of the copies and the shortcomings of mechanical projectors. The electronic playout from digital disk-based storage is, by definition, considerably more robust and more immune to those kinds of degradations. Highly efficient error correction and concealment circuits allow an infinitely larger number of "projections" or, to be more precise, playouts before the correction/concealment system becomes overloaded and visible degradations appear.

Another advantage results from the move toward electronic projection, and it should not be neglected—the question of piracy and copyright protection. As is well known, one of the serious problems content producers have to face is the illegal copying of their latest releases and the appearance of video cassettes or DVDs on the video black market. The sources of such copies are numerous, but one of them is certainly the unauthorized use of movie theater copies for the production of a digital master. In the case of electronic distribution, a number of protective measures could be introduced. For example, the movie could be encrypted and then stored on a server. The use of a password would be needed for each playout of the stored material and each playout would be automatically registered. In addition, the stored material could have digital "watermarks" as an additional protection.

Of course, D-Cinema is not yet here. A number of technical and economic problems have to be solved, with one of the very important ones being standardization. With the merging of the video world and the domain of computers, which has an extremely fluid and loose understanding of standards and of backward compatibility, standards begin to resemble dragonflies—their lives are colorful but rather short. So what will the future bring? Will the rust overcome the silver? Are we witnessing the last years of the 35 mm standard, set, as the legend goes, by Mr. Edison and Mr. Eastman during one peaceful afternoon over a cup of tea? Or, on the contrary, are we living in the beginning of another century of celluloid moviemaking?

Acronyms and Selected Abbreviations

A

AAC Advanced audio coding; recently developed audio compression method featuring a higher compression efficiency than previous compression methods

AAF Advanced authoring format; a file exchange format developed specifically for network interchange of materials in the postproduction process and compatible with **MXF**

AAF Association Industry association formed for the purpose of developing the **AAF** file exchange format and promoting its wide introduction

A/B roll system Linear videotape-editing method that makes use of one recording machine and at least two playback machines, thus permitting cross-fades and other complex transitions between edited clips

AC 3 Audio compression method developed by Dolby Laboratories and used in **DVD**s, 5.1 surround-sound systems, **ATSC** digital transmission standard, and so on

A/D Analog-to-digital (conversion)

AES Audio Engineering Society; international engineering society whose goal is the advancement and betterment of audio techniques as well as the development of necessary audio standards

AM Amplitude modulation

AMPEX Anatoliy Mikhailovitch Poniatoff Excellent; name of a manufacturing company that is no longer active in the broadcasting business but that played a key role in the introduction of audiotape recording and the development of videotape recording techniques

ASPEC Adaptive Spectral Perceptual Entropy Coding; audio compression method developed by **AT&T** Bell Labs, the German Fraunhofer Society, the manufacturer Thomson, and the research institute **CNET** from France

ATM   Asynchronous transfer mode; flexible communication technology developed over years in the telecom domain with the goal of making possible the integration of voice, video, and data over a single network

AT&T   American Telephone and Telegraph Company; a telecommunication giant in the United States

ATSC   Advanced Television Systems Committee; a body created in the United States with the goal of investigating all approaches to advanced and high-definition systems and of making an official consensual proposal to the **FCC** for the standard to be adopted in the United States

B

BBC   British Broadcasting Corporation; the public broadcaster in the United Kingdom with a long and distinguished history as the initiator of the first regular television service in 1936

B-frames   Bidirectionally predicted frames (taking information from both the preceding and the following frames) in the **MPEG** system of rejection of temporal redundancy during the digital compression process

C

CBS   Columbia Broadcasting System; a broadcasting network in the United States

CCD   Charge-coupled device; solid-state opto-electric sensor used in present-day television cameras

CCETT   Centre Commun des Etudes en Télédiffusion et Télécommunications (Joint Center for Broadcasting and Telecommunication Studies); a research institution founded jointly by French Telecom and French public broadcasters

CCIR   Comité Consultatif International en Radiocommunications (International Radio Consultative Committee); former body of the **ITU** responsible for studies in radio communications (including broadcasting) and for issuing recommendations for that domain; corresponding body under the current organization of the **ITU** is the ITU-R Sector.

CCITT   Comité Consultatif International en Téléphonie et Télégraphie; body of **ITU** responsible for studies in wire communication systems and for issuing standards in that domain; the corresponding body under the current organization of the **ITU** is ITU-S Sector.

CCU   Camera control unit; electronic circuitry mounted in a frame that is separated from the camera head and that is used to control all photographic parameters of the generated picture

CD   Compact disc; laser disc designed for the recording of music. Current variants on the market include CD-R rewritable discs, CD-ROM read-only memory discs for computer applications, and so on.

CG Character generator; digital engine designed to produce alphanumeric signs as well as a gamut of graphics solutions

CNET Centre National d'Etudes des Télécommunications (National Center for Telecommunication Studies); French state-funded research institute, now the research and development arm of France Telecom

CRC Cyclic redundancy check code; digital code used to detect and correct errors that may occur in the digital recording/reproducing process

CRT Cathode-ray tube; the conventional device used for television and computer screens

D

D1 First full broadcast-quality digital videotape recording standard developed for the recording of uncompressed 601 digital component signals

D/A Digital-to-analog (conversion)

DAB Digital Audio Broadcasting; standard for digital broadcasting of radio programs, developed in Europe by a consortium of manufacturers, research institutions, and broadcasters

DAM Digital asset management; see **MAM**

dB Decibel or "deci Bel"; one tenth of a Bel, where the *Bel* is a unit used to measure the relative logarithmic rapport between two values

D-Cinema Digital cinema; unofficial term coined to cover a new approach to the cinematographic industry, in which the whole chain (from acquisition through postproduction, distribution, and theater screening) would be performed by using digital electronic signals and equipment instead of classical film materials and mechanical cameras and projectors

DCT Discrete cosine transform; a mathematical process used to facilitate the removal of spatial redundancy from television pictures

DICE Digital intercontinental conversion equipment; the first all-digital television standards converter

DMS-1 Descriptive metadata scheme 1; defined by selecting the number of descriptions usually accompanying magnetic tapes and cassettes and adopting that list as a standard that should cover most of the requirements of content production, distribution, and archiving

DPX Digital picture exchange; a file exchange format developed for electronic postproduction (electronic intermediate) in the movie industry; the acquisition is done on film, the recorded film picture is transferred to digital electronic signals, postproduced in that form and then reversed back to film

DRM Digital Radio Mondiale; standard for digital broadcasting of radio programs in former **AM** bands (medium and short waves), developed in Europe by a consortium of manufacturers, research institutions, and broadcasters

DSP Digital signal processing; system of control and signal processing in present-day electronic cameras

DV see **DVC**

DVB Digital Video Broadcasting; a set of standards for digital broadcasting of television programs over satellite, terrestrial, cable, and cellular distribution networks; developed by a large international consortium of manufacturers, research institutes, and broadcasters

DVC Digital video cassette; a compression method developed by a consortium of mainly Japanese companies for application in consumer products, later renamed **DV**. With some slight adaptations, this method is widely used in broadcast recording under the brand names of **DVCAM** and **DVCPRO.**

DVCAM Digital video recording format developed by Sony and based on the use of 1/4-inch tapes and on the slightly adapted DV-compression method

DVCPRO Digital video recording format developed by Matsushita (Panasonic) based on the use of 1/4-inch tapes and of the slightly adapted DV-compression method

DVD Digital video disc or digital versatile disc; optical disk with high packing density developed for the consumer market; records compressed video and audio signals

E

EBU European Broadcasting Union; association of European public-service broadcasting organizations, encompassing non-European broadcasters as associate members also. In the technical domain, it very actively participates in the development and standardization of new systems and sets recommended practices for its members.

EDL Edit decision list; list of all edits, which includes information needed to locate the right shots and to perform the desired transitions. In its simplest form an EDL is just a list of time-code information written on a sheet of paper, but it can also be in an electronic form, which, when fed to an appropriate system, can run the editing of raw material automatically.

EEPROM Electrically erasable programmable read-only memory; solid-state nonvolatile memory chips that do not require an uninterrupted electrical supply to keep written information memorized; used in flash memory cards

EMI Electrical Music Industries; a British company that played a crucial role in the development of the first all-electronic television system. Although it remained for a number of decades a very important broadcast equipment manufacturer, EMI has returned today to the vocation indicated in its name to the production and distribution of music recordings.

ENG Electronic news gathering; the gathering or collection of news stories intended for broadcast during different television newscasts, with the help of camcorders, which combine electronic color cameras and recorders in one single unit

F

FCC   Federal Communication Commission; regulatory body of the U.S. Government

FIT   Frame interline transfer; a type of **CCD** sensor that combines two charge-transfer methods in order to overcome the limitations of each of them

FM   Frequency modulation

f-number   A number obtained by dividing the focal length of a lens by its effective diameter. The f-number, also known as the f-stop, defines the amount of light that reaches the sensor.

FT   Frame transfer; a type of **CCD** sensor

G

Gbps   Gigabits per second; a bit rate of one billion bits per second, indicated also as Gbit/s

GOP   Group of pictures; a segment of an **MPEG** video bitstream. A group of pictures is formed by two spatially or intraframe-compressed pictures and all uni- or bidirectionally predicted pictures that are between them.

GUI   Graphic user interface; graphics display on the screen that shows all options and commands for a given PC-based operating system

GXF   General exchange format; file format developed by the **SMPTE** as a general-purpose standardized format

H

H.264 AVC   Advanced video coding; highly efficient video compression method

HAD   Hole-accumulated diode; a type of **CCD** sensor; its more advanced form is known as Hyper-HAD

HAS   Human auditory system; the ear-brain combination that permits us to detect and interpret vibrations of air particles as audible sounds

HDCAM   High-definition videotape recording format

HDTV   High-definition television

Hz   Hertz; frequency measurement unit representing the oscillation of one full cycle in one second

I

IBA   Independent Broadcasting Authority; previously the regulatory body for commercial television in Great Britain

IEC   International Electrotechnical Commission (part of **ISO**); international organization concerned mainly with hardware standardization

I-frames intraframes. In the **MPEG** bitstream, I-frames are compressed by the rejection of spatial redundancy only and used for the generation of **P-frames** (predicted frames).

ING IT news gathering; term coined by Panasonic for the purpose of promoting the concept of its tapeless recording based on the use of **SD memory cards** as recording supports

IP Internet protocol; method by which data is sent from one computer to another on the Internet

IRT Institut für Rundfunktechnik; research and development institution founded and financed by public-service broadcasting organizations from Germany, Switzerland, and Austria

ISDB Integrated Services Digital Broadcasting; a standard developed in Japan for broadcasting digital television signals and other services over terrestrial and satellite transmitters and for distribution over cable systems

ISDN Integrated Services Digital Network; a communication standard for sending voice, video, and other data over digital telephone lines

ISO International Standardization Organization

IT Information technologies; term used to encompass all computer-based techniques and technologies

IT Interline transfer; a type of **CCD** sensor

ITU International Telecommunication Union; a body of the United Nations concerned with all aspects of communications. It develops international standards and recommendations and regulates the frequency spectrum.

J

JPEG Joint Photographic Experts Group; body created by **ISO**, that developed a compression method for still pictures, which bears the same name. A variant of that method, known as **Motion JPEG**, or M-JPEG is used sometimes for video compression in PC-based editing stations.

K

KHz Kilohertz; a frequency measurement unit representing one thousand Hertz

kbps kilobits per second; a bit rate of one thousand bits per second, indicated also as kbit/s

KLV Key, length, value; coding method for coding elements inside an **MXF** file

L

LAN   Local area network; a group of computers and associated devices that share a common communications line or wireless link and the resources of a single processor or server within a restricted area (for example, within an office building). See also **MAN** and **WAN**

LTC   Longitudinal time code; information recorded on one of the longitudinal tracks on the videotape and used to determine the exact address of each frame recorded on that tape; see also **VITC**

M

MAM   Media asset management, also called digital asset management (**DAM**); a set of coordinated technologies and procedures that allow the efficient storage, retrieval, and reuse of content in its digital form

MAN   Metropolitan area network; a network that interconnects users with computer resources in a geographic area or region larger than that covered by a large local area network (**LAN**) but smaller than the area covered by a wide area network (**WAN**). The term is applied to the interconnection of networks within a city into a single larger network.

Mbps   Megabits per second; a bit rate of one million bits per second, indicated also as Mbit/s

MHz   Megahertz; a frequency of one million oscillations per second

MOD   Minimum object distance; the shortest distance between the first (front) glass element of the lens to the object being photographed

Motion JPEG or **MJPEG**, video compression method based on **JPEG** techniques and used in early PC-based editing stations.

MP3   **MPEG** Layer 3; an audio compression technique that achieves high compression ratios while maintaining an acceptable sound quality; particularly popular for Internet download and exchange of music

MPEG   Motion Picture Experts Group; an international group of experts created by ISO/IEC with the task of developing an internationally agreed-upon method of compression for different applications

MPEG-2   Compression method or, rather, a compression tool kit consisting of several profiles and levels that correspond to different compression ratios and are aimed at different broadcasting applications

MPEG-4   "Object-based" compression method that offers a higher compression efficiency that its predecessor, **MPEG-2**

MTF   Modulation transfer function; describes the total performance of a lens in transmitting fine details over the whole range defined by the system bandwidth

MUSICAM   Masking pattern-adapted universal subband integrated coding and multiplexing; audio compression method developed jointly by the French research laboratory **CCETT,** German research institute **IRT,** and the Dutch manufacturer Philips

MXF   Material exchange format; a streamable file format that wraps video, audio, and other bitstreams ("essences"), optimized for the interchange or archiving by the content-creation industries, and intended for implementation in devices ranging from cameras and videotape recorders to computer systems

N

NASA   National Aeronautics and Space Administration

NBC   National Broadcasting Corporation; one of the big U.S. broadcasting networks

NHK   Nippon Hoso Kyokai; the Japanese public-service broadcaster

NLE   Nonlinear editing; PC-based editing system in which all the rushes (clips recorded in the studio or in the field) are kept on a hard disk and the editor can freely and randomly access any clip

NTSC   National Television System Committee; a body that set the color television standard in the United States; also the color standard defined by that body and used in the United States and other countries in the Americas and Asia

O

OB   Outside broadcast; television operations in the field usually accomplished with *OB vans* (mobile production units containing a number of cameras and corresponding video and audio control rooms)

P

PAL   Phase alternation line; color television system developed in Germany and widely used in many parts of the world

PC   Personal computer

PCM   Pulse code modulation; a sampling technique for digitizing analog signals, especially audio signals

PCMCIA   Personal Computer Memory Card International Association; an organization consisting of some 500 companies that has developed a standard for small, credit card–sized memory devices, called *PC Cards*, originally designed for adding memory to portable computers

PDC   Program delivery control; a set of data that identifies every program in a station's schedule and enable the viewer's home **VCR** to correctly record the desired program even if the actual start time differs from the announced one

P-frames Predicted frames; part of an **MPEG-2** bitstream. These are frames whose content is predicted on the basis of the previous frame, which can be either an **I-frame** or another P-frame.

R

RAI Radio Televisione Italiana; Italian public-service broadcaster

RAID Redundant array of inexpensive disks; a category of disk drives that employs two or more drives in combination in order to ensure higher reliability and performance. Such drives are used frequently on servers.

RAM Random access memory

RCA Radio Corporation of America; one of the leading electronic companies whose laboratories were responsible for a number of very important technological breakthroughs. Today the company does not exist any more, but the name survives as a brand of receivers owned by the French company Thomson.

ROI Return on investment; one of several approaches to building a financial business case. It evaluates investment potential by comparing the magnitude and timing of expected gains to the investment costs; simple ROI = (gains − investment costs)/investment costs.

S

SAN Storage area network; a high-speed subnetwork of shared storage devices

SDI Serial digital interface; a method to transfer uncompressed digital audio and video signals between digital devices in broadcast and postproduction facilities

SD memory cards A form of **EEPROM**; nonvolatile devices that store information on silicon chips in a way that does not require power to maintain the information in the chip. They offer fast read-access times and solid-state shock resistance, which makes them popular for applications such as storage on battery-powered devices (digital cameras, cell phones, or **MP3** players).

SDTI Serial data transport interface. Built on the **SDI** base, it provides a mechanism for exchanging digital audio and video signals in their native compressed formats. SDTI is designed to be simple and inexpensive to implement.

SECAM Séquantiel couleur à mémoire (sequential color with a memory); analog color television system developed by Henri de France and used in France and some countries in Europe and Africa

SGI Silicon Graphics Inc.; a computer manufacturing company specializing in high-performance computing platforms, visualisation, and storage

SMPTE Society of Motion Picture and Television Engineers; an engineering association established in the United States but having a large international representation in its ranks. It is very active in the studies and standardization processes in the domain of video and film technologies.

S/N ratio   Signal-to-noise ratio; a qualitative parameter used to assess the performance of a piece of equipment or of a system. It shows in a logarithmic manner the comparison between the peak value of the signal and the mean value of the noise. In principle, the higher the S/N ratio, the better the picture.

T

TC   Time code; a digital code that provides a precise address for each television picture on tape. The time code is recorded on a longitudinal track on the videotape and is readable when the tape is in motion. See also **LTC** and **VITC**.

U

U-matic   Analog videotape recording format developed for nonprofessional (industrial and consumer) applications but nevertheless used during the development phase of the **ENG** techniques.

UMID   Unique material identifier; marking system developed in order to ensure a correct linkage and, in general, an unambiguous identification of all materials

UPID   Unique program identifiers; simple labels generated through a registration process

UTP   Unshielded twisted pairs; a pair of isolated copper wires without any shielding protection, used as the simplest means for the constitution of a computer network

V

VBI   Vertical blanking interval; vertical retrace period during which the electron beam, after having scanned the first field, returns to the start of the first line of the next field

VCR   Video cassette recorder; usually applies to domestic recorders

VITC   Vertical interval time code; additional addressing information concerning pictures recorded on tape; The VITC is co-related with the **LTC** and is inserted in the vertical blanking interval (**VBI**) of the video signal during videotape recording

VPS   Video program system; a system developed and used in Germany offering the same features as the **PDC**

VTR   Videotape recorder

W

WAN   Wide area network; a computer network that spans a relatively large geographical area. Computers connected to a wide-area network are often connected through public networks, such as the telephone system. They can also be connected through leased lines or satellites. The largest WAN in existence is the Internet. See also **LAN** and **MAN**

Index